Professor J. E. (Teddy) Thomas was born and brought up in Haverfordwest, Pembrokeshire. He is a graduate of the Universities of Oxford, London, York, and Nottingham (D.Litt). During his time at the University of Nottingham he has been the Robert Peers Professor of Adult Education (now Emeritus in the Name), Dean of Education, and Senior Pro Vice-Chancellor. He has written twelve books and many articles on a variety of historical topics. These include histories of penal systems, of Adult Education, of Japan, of Australia, and of Wales.

SOCIAL DISORDER IN BRITAIN 1750–1850

The Power of the Gentry, Radicalism and Religion in Wales

J. E. Thomas

I.B. TAURIS

LONDON · NEW YORK

Published in 2011 by Tauris Academic Studies
An imprint of I.B.Tauris & Co Ltd
6 Salem Road, London W2 4BU
175 Fifth Avenue, New York NY 10010
www.ibtauris.com

Distributed in the United States and Canada
Exclusively by Palgrave Macmillan
175 Fifth Avenue, New York NY 10010

International Library of Historical Studies 71

ISBN 978 1 84885 503 8

A full CIP record for this book is available from the British Library
A full CIP record for this book is available from the Library of Congress

Library of Congress catalog card: available

Printed and bound in the UK by CPI Antony Rowe, Chippenham and Eastbourne
Camera-ready copy edited and supplied by the author

For Olwen
I loved you, so I drew these tides of men into my hands
And wrote my will across the sky in stars
To earn you Freedom, the seven pillared worthy house,
That your eyes might be shining for me
(TE Lawrence)

CONTENTS

ACKNOWLEDGEMENTS

I must express my thanks to Doctor Alaine Lowe for her help at the beginning of this research. I must thank the Reverend Professor John Heywood Thomas, and Professor W John Morgan, for reading the manuscript, and pointing out some foolish mistakes.

Anyone writing about Welsh history has to express thanks to the custodians of our antique documents. To the staff of Pembrokeshire County Archives in Haverfordwest Castle, to the staff of the Carmarthenshire Archives, and those of Cardiganshire Archives, to the staff of the Regimental Museums of the South Wales Borderers in Brecon, The Royal Welch Fusiliers in Caernarfon Castle, and The Welch Regiment in Cardiff Castle I owe a huge debt. It is a truism to say that they are all model professionals. They are courteous, generous and helpful, and I want to bear witness to that. I know that they rejoice in their anonymity, but I want to write an especial thank you to three members of staff at that most excellent institution, The National Library of Wales, Aberystwyth. They are Lona Jones, Charles Parry and Carol M Edwards. They might not remember me, but I do remember them. Ms. Jones drew my attention to papers concerning Thomas Evans, and Samuel Griffiths. Ms. Edwards and Mr. Parry searched for a work by Volney and this made a huge difference to my understanding of the mystery of why Welsh people were so energised by the idea of change.

This book is a collaboration by three people. Of course I am entirely responsible for its contents: and accept that all opinions, and mistakes, are mine. But I have to thank Olwen Thomas for many hours checking the manuscript, not the most interesting of jobs. I cannot thank Hazel Mills enough for her encouragement, and her constant, indeed persistent help with technical matters to do with the production of this book. She worked many, many hours, only because she wanted to. It is absolutely the case that its production would have been impossible without her.

INTRODUCTION

This is an account of the social unrest which was such a prominent feature of life in Britain in the eighteenth and early nineteenth centuries, and the means by which this unrest was contained. Some emphasis will be placed on Dyfed,[1] which provides such excellent examples of every aspect of the phenomena being discussed. The disturbances in Wales in the late eighteenth and early nineteenth centuries were on a smaller scale than they were in industrial England. Neither can be found the violence which attended such events in Ireland, nor the plethora of organisations to undermine authority with which Ireland abounded. But the passions were as strong, and the privations were as bad as any.

To understand the subject it is necessary in this Introduction to set out a few details of the social and historical context of the events which are the substance of this book. It is especially important to understand the fundamental changes which were consequent upon the Tudor usurpation, since this was to affect many aspects of Welsh life, including attitudes to the Crown and authority in the following centuries.

We begin with a note of the numbers of people who lived in Wales in the period we shall be discussing. One estimate of the population size of Wales in 1750 is 489,000.[2] At the beginning of the nineteenth century it had risen to 'nearly 600,000'. At that time only thirteen towns had a population of over 3000, while seven only had 5000.[3] Although from time to time there has been modest amounts of industrial activity, for example in coal mining in Pembrokeshire, or lead mining in Cardiganshire, Dyfed, like most of Wales has always been predominantly rural, and furthermore sparsely populated, as may be seen from these Census figures:

	1801	1831	1851
Cardiganshire	42,956	64,780	70,796
Carmarthenshire	67,317	100,740	110,632
Pembrokeshire	56,280	81,425	94,140

It is an area too which historically has, by common consent, been one of the poorest in Britain, and as we shall go on to see, observers have often looked to Ireland as an analogue, with conditions in the latter sometimes being pronounced superior. Although there were differences in the style of life, the methods of agriculture and so on in the three counties, these were slight, and it may fairly said that the overall social pattern was coherent. There is one notable exception, and this has to do with language.

This arises from the fact that south Pembrokeshire was settled by Normans, and famously Flemings, in the years after the Conquest. The result was, and is, that Pembrokeshire came to be divided linguistically by a demarcation called the Landsker. North of this line, which roughly cuts the county in half from Solva to Tenby, Welsh is the first language, while to the south only English is spoken. This phenomenon has always fascinated the visitor, and many diaries as well as official reports discuss it, sometimes in slightly, but only slightly, exaggerated terms. In 1804 Malkin wrote of Pembrokeshire:

> So different were the manners, arts, and agriculture, of the two peoples, that they have scarcely made an advance towards assimilation, in the space of nearly seven hundred years. So estranged are they from each other, that although they are only separated in some instances by a path in the same village, the common people do not intermarry; and it has singularly happened, on more than one occasion, that men from the same parish have been on a jury together, without a common language, in which to confer on the matters submitted to their decision.[4]

In the Reports of the Commissioners into the State of Education in Wales some forty years later, one noted that 'I found in the purely Welsh parishes about St. David's that a Roos or Castlemartin man was spoken of in much the same manner as we do of a Yorkshireman'.[5] In 1866 Mr. Culley also writes of Pembrokeshire:

> As an instance of how completely apart the English and Welsh races have kept themselves, I may mention that I have visited two cottages within about 100 yards of each other, in one of which I was not understood because I could only speak English, while in the other I should have been as little understood if I had spoken Welsh.[6]

It is a commonplace of Welsh history that there had been gradual erosion of the autonomy of Wales beginning with the Conqueror's encroachment in south Pembrokeshire. Then came the attacks on Wales by Edward I and his Statute of 1284 in which Wales was annexed to the English crown, and the penal legislation enacted by Henry IV after the defeat of Owain Glyndwr. Between 1400 and 1402 fourteen such Acts were passed. These, variously, forbade Welshmen to buy land in the Marches or in England, to own or carry arms or armour, or to hold office as justice or sheriff. Further, no Englishman could be convicted at the suit of a Welshman unless the justices were English, the *cwmwrth*, a tax levied for the support of bards was suppressed, and it was enacted that any Englishman who married a Welsh woman could not hold office in Wales or the Marches. But the greatest political changes, accompanied by massive 'cultural imperialism' came with the seizure of the throne by the Tudors. The consequent nature of Welsh society forms a continuing backdrop to the events dealt with in this book.

Henry VII was born in Pembroke castle and lived there for the first fourteen years of his life. According to Gwyn A Williams he spoke Welsh, and when he spoke English, he did so with a Welsh accent.[7] This claim, which is not attributed, may be fairly regarded as fanciful. but it is commonly made. Coupland, in pointing out that Henry had spent the first 14 years of his life in Wales, added that he was 'tended by a devoted Welsh nurse from Carmarthen, learning from her to speak Welsh as much as English'.[8] Nor does Coupland name a source for this claim. Chrimes in the standard work on King Henry VII gives a more impartial view:

> The Welshness of Henry Tudor can easily be, and often is, exaggerated… There is no evidence one way or the other that he ever spoke or understood Welsh even though it is true that he was brought up for the first fourteen years of his life in Wales… his father was only one third Welsh, and his mother was English. Owen Tudor, his grandfather was Welsh, but his grandmother Catherine was French and Bavarian.[9]

He might have added that Pembroke is right in the heart of the area which had for several hundred years been settled by those non Welsh speakers, whose lack of knowledge of Welsh has already been noted above. Chrimes also points out that Henry Tudor would have been unwise, at least in the early stages of his rebellion, to underline any relationship with Owain Glyndwr, since the latter had engaged 'in a prolonged and disastrous rebellion

against the first of the Lancastrian kings'. It would have been impolitic for
Henry to stress such a relationship when his claim was that he was the right-
ful heir of the House of Lancaster.[10] In point of fact 'Henry's VII's regality
was not altogether unimpeachable and therefore the imagery and symbol-
ism of his public shows aimed at emphasising his claims to the throne' but
'this official Lancastrian descent was unsound and was, accordingly, reinforced by another genealogical argument tracing the Tudor descent, through
the Welsh princes, back to the primitive British kings'.[11]

His birthplace was the key to the development of a culture which centred
upon the return of what Henken calls the 'National Redeemer'. Once again
it should be noted that the Welsh poets, since Glyndwr, had been prophesy-
ing, and from time to time identifying, a Welsh redeemer. Edward IV was
regarded as a 'royal Welshman' by Lewis Glyn Cothi, who claimed that he
was a descendant of Llewellyn the Great. So 'too much should not be made
of the eulogies of Henry as the example of a new cult; rather they were
part of a long tradition'.[12] But he was regarded as a reincarnation, and the
bards soon rallied round with exhortation to come as the new mab darogan
(predicted son): 'Tear of Cadwaladr, come and take the hand of your grandfather. Take your kinsmen's portion, make us free from our severe bondage'.
And again: 'Cadwaladr will come home… Jasper will raise for us a dragon,
blood of Brutus, happy is he'.[13] '" The Welsh"' said the Venetian ambassador
'"may now be said to have recovered their former independence for the most
wise and fortunate Henry VII is a Welshman"'.[14] The same enthusiasm was
on display upon the restoration of Charles II: he 'arrived by divine interven-
tion: "God of Heaven by his power has brought the bones of Cadwaladr
home"'.[15] Immediately after Bosworth in 1485, the Welsh no doubt felt that
Wales had recaptured London. Cadwalader's red dragon flew, although the
'weight of evidence is against a Cadwalader dragon'.[16] And after the birth
of Henry's first son, significantly called Arthur, poets engaged in a 'burst
of enthusiasm'. '"A new age of peace is at hand and the great King Arthur,
buried for so many centuries, now returns as prophesied."'[17]

But whatever the Welsh people expected by way of reward for their enthusiasm and loyalty they were due for another kind of reawakening, since
the reign of the 'Redeemer's' son, Henry VIII, saw a studied attempt to
end any Welsh ambitions once and for all. Henry VII never went back to
Wales, and 'Henry VIII seems to have been less concerned than his father
to proclaim his British descent'.[18] Nor did any of the Tudor monarchs visit.
This made them unique, because they 'were the only dynasty of English sov-
ereigns since the Norman Conquest not to set foot in Wales.'[19] It should be
remembered as some kind of a consolation that it was in the reign of another

Tudor, Elizabeth, that the bible and other religious books were translated into Welsh including that by William Morgan in 1588 which was to be so important, not only as saviour of the language, but in establishing a whole tradition of Welsh writing. Morgan's bible:

> rescued (Welsh) from vulgarisms and anglicisms, from dispersal into local dialects, from a general decay. It made it uniform, classic, permanent. And already in the earlier years of the seventeenth century more Welshmen were writing Welsh and it was better Welsh.[20]

Henry VIII passed two Acts in 1536 and 1543, which are commonly called Acts of Union. Under these all legal and commercial barriers between the two countries were to be removed. The counties of Wales, which survived until 1974 were created, and the Great Sessions were established which was a system of higher courts. And then the Act of 1536 turned its attention to the language. The Welsh, it was announced:

> have and do daily use a speche like ne consonaunt to the naturall mother tongue used within this Relme, some rude and ignorant people have made distinccion and div'sitie between the Kinges Subjects of this Realme and hys Subjectes of the said Dominion and Principalitie of Wales, wherby greate discorde variance debate division murmur and sedicion hath grown betwene his said subjectes.

And so the point was made that all courts shall be kept:

> in the Engliss Tongue – and also that – no psonne or psonnes that use the Welsshe speche or language shal have or enjoy any man (sic) office or fees within the Realme Englond Wales or other the Kings Dominions, upon peyn of forfaiting the same offices or fees, onles he or they use and exccise the speche or langage of Englisshe[21]

There are two incompatible assessments of the reasons why this legislation was passed, and the effect it had. The first is that the Acts were the proof of the generosity of the king towards Wales. This perception is that he was conferring the same benefits on Wales which were enjoyed by English people, and that there was an end to the anarchy with which Wales had been afflicted. Rhys Meurig of Cottrel was certain of it:

Now, since Wales was thus, by gracious Henry VIII, enabled with the laws of England, and thereby united to the same, and so brought to a monarchy, which is the most sure, stable and best regiment, they are exempted from the dangers before remembered; for life and death, lands and goods rest in this monarchy, and not in the pleasure of the subject... The discord between England and Wales, then, procured slaughters, invasions, enmities, burnings, poverty and such like fruits of war. This unity engendered friendship, amity, love, alliance... assistance, wealth and quietness. God preserve and increase it.[22]

The Pembrokeshire historian George Owen was another who detected great benefit from the embrace:

But sithence the time of Henry VII and Henry VIII that we were emancipated as it were and made free to trade and traffic through England, the gentlemen and people in Wales have greatly increased in learning and civility... no country in England so flourished in one hundred years as Wales has done sithence the government of Henry VII to this time.[23]

To progressive landlords, entrepreneurs, merchants, and religious reformers, belief in the merits of political assimilation with England was a sine qua non. In their eyes the Union of 1536-43 was a "remarkable deliverance". One believed that: The Lord had planned the marriage between England and Wales just as he had watched over Israel in the days of Ahasverus and Esther.[24] Lewis Morris spoke of 'the happy union with the valorous English' and Richard Morris thought that 'there should be no distinction between an Englishman and a Welshman in our day'.[25]

There are modern writers who appear to hold similar views, Coupland being an example:

To that must be added the greatest service the Tudors rendered to Wales. Taken as a whole and including as one essential factor in it the Welsh allegiance to the House of Tudor, it was the settlement of 1536 that saved Wales from the fate of Ireland – from taking, as the Celtic Irish took, the losing side in the two historic conflicts which rent and shook the British Isles in the course of the next hundred and fifty years and suffering the inevitable consequences.[26]

Lloyd too points out a desirable effect: 'The Act of Union gave Welshmen, now that they were emancipated, their first real parliamentary opportunity'.[27]

By the 1590s, when Owen was writing, there had been a considerable exodus of the more educated and the affluent in Wales to England, especially London, many to the Court. They revelled in their new status, and of course gained considerable material benefits. Welsh poets of the time 'did not disapprove of the acquisition of lands and offices by their patrons'.[28]

The alternative perception of the Union is that this was a final effort to destroy the Welsh people. How else, the argument is made, can be explained the studied banning of the Welsh language? The furore (and no other word will do) over the Welsh language has raged ever since, and in a later chapter some of the relevant arguments will be rehearsed. Certainly the banning of Welsh was an instinctive recognition that to destroy the integrity of a people the first target must be their language. Indeed it is the first stage in the process of what has come to be called 'cultural imperialism', and examples of studied attack upon the bastion of language are plentiful. One is the behaviour of the Prussians in 1864 after their conquest of Denmark. In what had been Danish territory German became the official language, and the teaching of Danish was forbidden.[29]

Another important view of the significance of the Acts is that they are called Acts of Union in error. This view is that the real engine of unification lies in Edward I's statute of Rhuddlan or Wales of 1284. Following the 'irresistible' conclusion of Goronwy Edwards', Chrimes states that the words of 1284 are 'perfectly plain on the point'. Wales was annexed to England. What the act of 1536 did was 'to unify Wales politically within itself'.[30] And yet the Welsh people, or more correctly the new Welsh oligarchy, continued to support the monarchy, and apart from the strange case of the Cycle of the White Rose, and the Sea Serjeants, which will be discussed, and where in any case they supported a different monarchy, evinced sympathy and affection for it.

The Welsh paper Seren Gomer for example published a number of englynion (an ancient form of Welsh poetry) in praise of William IV 'and acclaimed him as "the best representative of the Hanover family to have occupied the British throne"'.[31] The persistence of this support for royalty is the more remarkable because successive monarchs, even as princes of Wales, showed no interest at all in Wales or its people. James I, and James II visited briefly, and Charles I had his headquarters in Raglan for a few weeks, obviously for strategic reasons. There were no royal visits in the eighteenth century. George IV visited Holyhead, and Pembrokeshire, on his way to and from Ireland, and on one occasion he planted a tree in Montgomeryshire. Victoria 'spent a total of seven years in Scotland, seven weeks in Ireland, and seven nights in Wales'. Looking at these figures it is difficult not to agree with David Williams when he writes 'Her Majesty was always disdainful where the Principality was concerned'.[32]

John Davies reviews royal contacts with Wales, including the excess of fawning articles about Victoria. There are a very few honourable exceptions as when Thomas Gee declared '(praising her) would make us contemptible lapdogs, ready to kiss every scourge-and the scourger too'.[33] Her son, as Prince, made a few short visits to Wales, including one to the National Eisteddfod at Bangor in 1894. On this occasion a poet wrote an ode which noted that 'after six hundred years, the Prince of Wales comes home'.[34] Indeed one of the more inexplicable, and distasteful phenomena of the relationship between the Welsh elite, and the intelligentsia, especially in London, is the persisting, almost relentless determination to curry favour with the monarch and the Court. This curious relationship between some of the people of Wales and the monarchy has been dwelt upon here because it remained a cardinal cause of their conservative stance, in the face of any threat to social stability.

The explanation for this is that there were, in post Tudor times, not the simplistic majority of Nonconformists ranged against the Anglican landowners, but as we shall go on to see, several societies. If the dynamics of Welsh society in the eighteenth and nineteenth centuries are to be understood, then the central role of a theocratic elite has to be examined. This theocracy somehow managed to use Welsh history so that it has appeared as its hero against tyranny. In fact it never championed the cause of the poor, and quite the reverse, opposed it, but by the subtlest of means: for example by championing the cause of language, and above all the nurturing of a hatred against the church of England. And so they were able to deflect interest away from the concerns of the wretched of Wales.

The book begins with a discussion of Welsh society in the eighteenth and nineteenth centuries, concentrating on the contrast between the opulence of the landowners, and the pitiful situation of the peasantry. I go on to give an account of the considerable social unrest in the area, and from time to time, in other parts of Britain. I then examine how 'political' this was, arguing that despite the wretchedness of the ordinary people, they were well aware of what was going on in the world at a time of momentous upheaval: a matter upon which historians differ. But discontent was curbed. The means used ranged from the manifest use of force to more subtle and complex phenomena which will be explained and analysed. Naked force included the use of the militia, who were never quite reliable, except in the case of units from Carmarthenshire, and the deployment of the newly formed Yeomanry, the first in Britain being established in Pembrokeshire in 1794.

But there were other less visible ways in which control was exerted. These included the exodus, through migration, of arguably the people of best quality, with a consequent diminution of the vitality of resistance to oppression. Then a mature account has to be given of the question as to whether the inability to speak or read English was a factor in the impeding of challenging ideas. Yet another discussion will be about the abject failure of powerful Welshmen, especially in London to support the protests of their poorer countrymen. And finally one of the most important questions in this regard is the role played by religious bodies, especially Nonconformists, and how their considerable power was deployed in Wales, and how, over the course of time they became a theocracy albeit a highly factional one. The book concludes with an epilogue, describing how the events of the later nineteenth century led to little improvement, and finally asking whether the twentieth century changed the orientation of power in Wales.

1

THE WELSH SQUIREARCHY

'This whole country is governed by fear'.[35]

After the ascent of the Tudors society in Wales began to change, until it consolidated in all important respects into that structure which remained fossilised for some three hundred years. The essence of the process developed until by the eighteenth century the country had settled into the four hierarchical divisions described by Jenkins. These were, firstly, the *uchelwyr*, a group and a term which is usually translated as 'gentry' in textbooks, but in south Pembrokeshire were called, in living memory, 'gentlemen'. Then came the yeomen, who were the more prosperous of the farmers: next the ordinary farmers, and finally the labourers. There were also, especially in the towns professional men such as lawyers, and tradesmen such as tailors and saddlers. There was also, of course, as in any society an underclass of paupers.[36] Perhaps a measure of the particular poverty of Dyfed is the fact that in 1776 of the 19 workhouses in Wales, 11 were in Pembrokeshire.[37] These were the people who, famously, were hounded from parish to parish, and like the old and disabled woman in Tintern Abbey had nothing 'except her cell of misery'.[38] Even this brief recital is enough to support Philip Jenkins' summary that 'early modern Wales was far from being the simple peasant land of legend'.[39]

Like all social divisions these were not rigid, there being especial blurring between some of the ordinary farmers, at some times and in some places, and the labourers. The descent by the small farmers into the ranks of the paupers was also a normal occurrence. This tendency was noted at the time of the Rebecca riots by one of the most perceptive of commentators, Thomas Campbell Foster, *The Times* correspondent, who wrote in the issue of 1 September 1843 about 'The poor farmer, who is in reality nothing more than a farm labourer, having no money to purchase food, much less to procure manure and in sufficient quantity'.[40] The divisions between the gentry and the yeomen were more subtle and indeed fluid, since they were they were, like the lower orders still susceptible to good or ill fortune, the gentry being in that situation summed up by Tawney as being somewhat 'ragged at the edges'.[41] Yet there was a torpor in this social structure in Wales which would not be seriously be disturbed until the nineteenth century, and well into that century in the case of Dyfed. Peter Thomas sums up perhaps the main cause of this quietitude, especially in the eighteenth century as 'the absence of a resident aristocracy (which) was matched by the lack as yet of any middle class to pose a political challenge'.[42] This was compounded by the fact that:

> by the middle of the eighteenth century many Welsh estates had fallen into the hands of absentee English or Scottish landowners who seldom visited their patrimonies, had no great liking for the Welsh people, and little sense of obligation towards their tenants[43]

The physical, but not monetary movement of well established aristocracy to more profitable fields had happened much earlier. The family of the Earls of Pembroke, for example, had moved to Wilton by Tudor times, although they retained property in Pembrokeshire. Since the advent of the Tudors, with the consequent destruction of the remnants of the independence of the country, there had been little resident aristocracy, especially after the Stuarts, when several Welsh noblemen, or at least men with manifest Welsh connections, were penalised because they had supported losing causes. In Tudor times there had been the remnant of a resident or semi-resident aristocratic interest, such as that of the Devereux family, whose leader was the Earl of Essex. The second earl spent a lot of time in Pembrokeshire from his birth in 1567, and his building of a network of support in the region involved careful manipulation of the gentry whom he patronised, and the accumulation of considerable land. This occurred because of the turbulence of the times, including the fall of the Dynevor family, and the execution in 1531 of Sir Rhys ap Gruffydd. His estate went to Walter Devereux, who was amongst his many posts, Chief Justice of South Wales. This was the family which were to become the Earls of Essex.[44] The estate soon became substantial, through the acquisition of properties such as the episcopal seat at Lamphey in Pembrokeshire, 'one of the diocese's richest possessions'.[45] This not to say that there was no aristocratic influence in Wales. As late as the eighteenth century some of the leaders of the Tories had 'their chief interests in Wales', especially in east Wales, even though they did not live there. These were people like the Dukes of Beaufort, the Earls of Oxford, and Lord Windsor.[46]

In the process of social resettlement after the coming of the Tudors, one of the curiosities of the culture of the Welsh squirearchy was their assertion of relationship and descent from the medieval Welsh princes and aristocracy. This important cornerstone of status was encouraged by the bardic tradition, in which the praises of nobles were sung by poets and musicians, in return for patronage. There is no doubt of the reality of this important facet of Welsh mediaeval life. In the west Sir Thomas Philipps was the patron of one of the greatest of the bards, Lewis Glyn Cothi, at the end of the fifteenth and early sixteenth centuries. Indeed its remnants survived certainly until the mid seventeenth century: Sir Richard Pryse of Gogerddan who died in 1661 has been described as the last bardic patron.[47] But the demise of the bards effectively coincided with decline of a recognisable Welsh aristocracy and the emergence of a new, increasingly alien gentry which was anxious to claim descent from it.

Except occasionally, there were two factors which made such claims very dubious. The first is the paucity, not just of any reliable records, but of any records at all; and the second is the transformation of the Welsh naming system in and after the Reformation. Francis Jones, a considerable expert on Welsh genealogy, who is generally sympathetic to claims of lineage, has to agree that in respect of the Owens of Orielton in Pembrokeshire, 'no contemporary evidence exists to verify the statements.',[48] and more generally that 'there are no means of checking the accuracy of ambitious genealogists' who would trace the Owen lineage back to AD c450.[49] A John Owen of Manorowen in Pembrokeshire traced his pedigree back to fictional roots: 'I could go farther – placing one end of the chain in Pembrokeshire, and fastening the other to Mount Ararat'.[50]

Even the professional expert of recent times, armed with every kind of resource, is unable to state with certainty family details of well known figures. Some of a galaxy of examples are the doubt as when the notable Gelly Meyrick was born, and whether Sir Carbery Pryse was unmarried or not: one source says 'probably unmarried',[51] another 'unmarried', and incidentally that he died 'about' the year 1695.[52] In the Philipps family of Picton it is recorded that one of the Sir Johns was 'born about 1701'[53] and later, in the same family in the same century, a modern historian was quite unable to discover the date of birth of the first Lord Milford. This despite the fact that this at least locally eminent man died as recently as 1823, and five thousand people attended his funeral in St. Mary's Haverfordwest.[54]

The Welsh were not alone in this. The English kings were anxious to assert their pedigree, and links with Trojan and British kings; 'during the fifteenth century there was a proliferation of elaborate genealogical rolls which sought to trace the kings of England back to their remote forebears'.[55] The absurdity of much of this can be seen from the example of William Waldorf Astor, who in his attempt to gain acceptance 'published an elaborate genealogy which purported to trace his descent from French and Spanish nobility'.[56]

With regard to surnames, the problem arises from the changes in the period concomitant with, and consequent upon, the commonly called Act of Union of 1536. One of those was the insistence that the traditional systems of naming had to be changed. The classic form was to follow a given name with the word 'ap', meaning son of, and then the father's name. An example would be Rhys ap Owen. Now the pressure was on to develop surnames which could be passed on intact, in the English style. Often the ap would become part of the second name, the 'a' would be dropped, and the surname would become, in this case, Bowen. An adjective appended to a name might become stabilised as the surname. Llwyd, meaning grey, would be fixed as Lloyd.

There was also resort to biblical names, and so names like Absalom, or Isaac, were adopted. The relevance of this is that with such a massive change, not only in global, but in personal identity, especially from a traditional form which in itself was hardly a help to genealogists, makes accurate family history difficult.[57] To help in this, a whole industry of genealogy was in place after the Tudors. Because of the claims of racial purity, and the spurious nature of many, if not most of them, there was evidence of the snobbery which has always attended such claims. Jenkins notes how a Jacobean genealogist, John Jones, looks askance at the pretensions of what a later generation would call 'johnny come latelies'. He states that the Gwr Bonheddic cannot be created by law, but has to be 'paternally descendeth from the kings and princes of this land of Britain'. Jones goes on to observe that 'wealth, offices, or behaviour' do not qualify, since 'bonhedd consisteth in no transitory thing but in a permanent'.[58]

But this is not to say that there were no individuals, families or groups, who exercised complete control over the lives of the common people, since effective local power soon accrued to the gentry whose estates were either expanded in the sixteenth century or were created at that time. In this group should be included, as examples, and only as examples, the Wogans who held various estates, Owens of Orielton, and Philipps of Picton, all of Pembrokeshire; the Vaughans of Golden Grove, and the Mansels or Mansells of Carmarthenshire, and the Cardiganshire families of Pryse of Gogerddan, and Vaughan of Trawsgoed, often referred to as Crosswood. To such families since the accession of the Tudors, land was sold, accolades bestowed, baronetcies handed out, and at the social peak, at the end of the eighteenth and during the nineteenth centuries especially, there was the occasional ennoblement.

Especially after 1660 the 'eighteenth century became the golden age of the country squire'.[59] The prosperity of those who were already rich increased substantially after the Restoration, although many smaller landowners suffered grievously because of fining in the civil war. 'The economic climate favoured the prosperous, and property passed, almost inexorably, into the hands of the mighty'.[60] Some of these were the most powerful, as well as the oldest in their districts. The Wogans can be traced to the fourteenth century, and were at their central seat, Wiston in Pembrokeshire, by 1581.[61] The Owens, who are recorded in positions of power in Anglesey in the twelfth century, seem to have been established at their principal seat, Orielton, in Pembrokeshire in the reign of Elizabeth. This was achieved in a common enough fashion, which was the marriage of Hugh Owen to the heiress of a considerable estate, in 1571.[62] For three hundred years after this, the family were to be notable as members of Parliament, High Sheriffs, mayors, and one Sir Hugh, made a baronet in 1641, was a prominent supporter of Parliament in the Civil War.

The Philipps of Picton similarly were a family of ancient lineage, and they too occupied key posts in the county, and served as members of Parliament. One John Philipps was the victim 'of the prodigality of the early Stuarts in the distribution of honours'. Many gentlemen who were nominated 'protested that they had far from sufficient wealth' to take the honours. But in the early 1620s Philipps and four other members of putative powerful houses, in south west Wales were to be created baronets. These were John Stepney of Prendergast, Pembrokeshire, and Frances Mansell, Richard Rudd of Aberglasney, and Sackville Crowe of Laugharne, all of Carmarthenshire.[63] The Vaughans of Golden Grove were in most respects superior to their kindred in the three counties. Their ancestry apparently can be traced back to the eleventh century, and the influence they wielded is demonstrated by Jones in his account of the family. Five of the family were knighted, they served in the royal household, and were members of Parliament – in one case representing an uncontested seat for forty-two years.[64] Although Queen Elizabeth annulled the knighthood bestowed upon Walter Vaughan by Essex, he was knighted in 1617, created Baron Vaughan of Mullinger in the Irish peerage in 1621, Earl of Carbery in the same peerage in 1628, and

Baron Emlyn in the English peerage in 1643. He was a royalist general in the Welsh theatre of war albeit not very successful.[65]

The originating member of the Mansell family of west Wales was Francis, who was created baronet (of Muddlescombe in Carmarthenshire) in 1621. He seems to have moved from Glamorganshire at the end of the sixteenth century, again through the process of wisely appointed marriage. In that county the family had prospered; his grandfather Sir Rice had been in an official involved in the dissolution of the monasteries, and had established an estate from the monastic holdings in Margam.[66] Although the power base of the family remained at Margam, the Carmarthenshire section of the family was very powerful indeed. It was the Mansell family which was to produce 'the outstanding personality' of the period (mid seventeenth century) in the development of Jesus College Oxford.[67] The Pryse family of Gogerddan in Cardiganshire were considerable landowners in Cardiganshire and Merionethshire from the sixteenth century – the land-owning of such families were by no means confined to the county where they spent most of their time. Their power too was manifest. Lloyd records, for example, that members of the family sat as members of Parliament for Cardiganshire 13 times between 1553 and 1621.[68] By 1622 the head of the family was a knight, and in 1641 was created a baronet. In 1690 Sir Carbery Pryse discovered mines 'of such immense value, as to get the designation of "the Welch Potosi"'.[69] After prolonged legal disputes he, and other wealthy investors won the right to operate the mines.

As has already been pointed out, all such families reinforced their integrity, in the strict sense of the term, by judicious intermarriage. The examples are legion. At Trawsgoed in 1741 'Wilmot Vaughan inherited an estate on the verge of bankruptcy, but he managed to retrieve the situation by thriftily husbanding the resources of his patrimony, and above all by marrying well'.[70] One of the founders of the Stepney dynasty in the early seventeenth century, Alban married twice. The first time to Margaret Catharn the co-heir of the Prendergast estate near Haverfordwest, and secondly to the co-heir and daughter of William Philipps of Picton, a process which led to him leaving 'a very plentiful estate by his two matrimonial alliances'.[71] His daughter, and sister of the first Sir John Stepney of Prendergast married Sir Francis Mansell of Muddlescombe in Carmarthenshire whose first wife Catharine (sic) was the daughter and co-heir of Henry Morgan of Muddlescombe. The key member in the establishment of the Campbell estate in Stackpole Court in Pembrokeshire, Sir Alexander, whose family home was in Nairn, and to where his descendants returned in, (for them), the moderately ruinous twentieth century. He effected this in 1689 by marrying the Lort family heir to that estate.[72] His son married into the Pryse family of Gogerddan. There was much intermarrying too in the ranks of the Owens of Orielton, the Philipps of Picton, and the several branches of the Wogan family.

With regard to the difficult, yet sociologically critical and interesting matter of wealth in trying to determine status, before the eighteenth century the squirearchy of Wales seem not to have been especially rich:

> An income of £1000 marked a family as belonging to the landed elite on English standards... Cardiganshire in 1660 had only one gentle-man credited with £1000 a year, Edward Vaughan of Crosswood (Trawsgoed).[73]

But by 1695, John Vaughan, having served as Member for Cardiganshire in several parliaments, was powerful enough to be made a Viscount in the Irish peerage. Lloyd summarises the situation in his account of the possessions of the *uchelwyr* in the late sixteenth and early seventeenth centuries: 'in a poor society the gentry were themselves poor, and their standard of living modest'.[74]

Yet by the eighteenth and especially the nineteenth centuries these people were wealthy by any standard. There was a steady bettering of their condition, which was achieved through the steady accumulation of land, whether by leasing or purchase, or, as has been pointed out, by judicious marriage. Some families began this process very soon after the Act of Union. Lloyd describes how Richard ap Moris (sic) Vaughan gave Trawsgoed in Cardiganshire to his son Moris in 1547, when the latter married. From the nucleus of his inheritance, and the land brought by his wife, he and his descendants eventually accumulated a vast estate.[75] Over the next three hundred years so would others, so that at the peak of the power of the Welsh squirearchy in the last quarter of the nineteenth century 89 per cent of land was held by landowners, and only 10.2 per cent of land was owned by the people who worked it.[76]

Remarkably though, the lands purloined by the crown at the time of the Reformation were not as important a source of expansion as might reasonably be supposed. One reason may have been that they were simply not a good investment, or that they were too expensive. Even the Earl of Essex, although he took what was on offer in monastic lands, 'did not consider that these contributed greatly to his economic well-being', although this fact was a measure of their enormous wealth rather than the slight value of monastic holdings.[77] One notable exception to the lack of exploitation of monastic lands was the Barlow family. This family seems to have been from Lancashire in recorded time, and the first to be associated with Pembrokeshire was Roger. He had been involved in the discovery of Peru under Charles V, and returned to England at the command of Henry VIII with a promise of advancement. He would have gone on an expedition to search for the legendary north west passage, had the king not died. Unlike many Dyfed landlords, he took advantage of access to monastic lands, and in this he was especially fortunate because his kinsman William was appointed Bishop of St. David's in 1536.

The generally accepted picture of this bishop, even by the degenerate standards of the church at the time, is that he was a fanatical Protestant who was involved in bitter theological and personal disputes with the people of the diocese, and worse. Because, for example, of his supposed stripping of the lead off the roof of the Bishop's Palace, and his attempt to remove the ancient see to Carmarthen he has been described as 'a great spoliator of the Church'.[78] The value and state of the monastic institutions in Pembrokeshire were not great, and no doubt typical of Welsh religious houses which at the beginning of the sixteenth century added 'up to a picture of decay'. Of the seven houses in the county, the one which was of the greatest value was Slebech, formerly a house of the Knights of St. John, and the 'largest and wealthiest religious House in the county.'

In 1546 Roger Barlow and his brother John bought Slebech, and three other religious estates, and several rectories. Further buying from this base led to the development of a considerable estate, which by the early seventeenth century 'had earned them the enmity of several of their fellow landlords'.[79] The family's support of the king in the Civil War, led to the confiscation of their estates, with the notable burning by the iconoclastic parliamentary Colonel Horton of the valuable Slebech library. John Barlow was created a baronet in 1677, and his son continued the expansion, buying, for example, the nearby estate of Colby from the Owen family, descendants of the historian, and giving it to his brother John.[80]

Another means of expansion was by the familiar practice of enclosures. This had been common since Tudor times, and there were plenty of examples, as we shall see. In Wales generally the position was complicated by confusion over boundaries, and changing systems of land tenure and inheritance, although there were straightforward, if controversial cases.[81] But as Lloyd points out there are problems of definition in trying to determine the damage done to the peasantry compared with other practices. An often quoted case is that of Thomas Lloyd of Cilciffeth in Pembrokeshire who bought freehold land 'turning them into sheep-walks and dairies "to the utter decay" of the said freeholders and depopulation of the land so annexed.' But as Lloyd again points out, this was a practice not confined to the gentry but was 'engaged in during this period (1540–1640) by men from all levels of society'.[82]

At the lower end of the scale Jenkins notes another means of acquiring land which should perhaps be laid alongside the complaints of people like Ellis Wynn who observed that there is 'hardly one estate not founded by some oppressor or murderer or arrant thief'. This was *tŷ unnos*, a practice whereby 'cottagers established rights to common land by building a dwelling and lighting a fire in the span of a single night: and the practice remained common into Victorian times'.[83] But later many landlords took advantage of the opportunity to add to their holdings through enclosures. In praising his management of the land at the end of the eighteenth century, Hassall observed with approval the fact that Mr. Campbell (later Lord Cawdor) of Stackpole obtained an act of Parliament to drain and enclose 'several hundred acres' to add to his estate of 16,000 acres of the best land in Pembrokeshire.[84]

When it comes to politics, the general assessment of historians is that with a few notable exceptions 'the activities of the members for south west Wales proved rather more of a nuisance than an advantage to the House during the first thirty years of their regular appearance in the Commons chamber'.[85] This was an assessment of the political activities of the politicians of the area which was to continue until the twentieth century. One outstanding exception was Sir John Perrot, of Pembrokeshire and his son Sir James. The Perrots were powerful and wealthy, a wealth which, again, was rooted in skilful marriage arrangements from the early fourteenth century.[86] Sir Thomas married a member of the Devereux family in 1583 'thus uniting the two families of greatest influence in south west Wales'.[87]

The second half of the sixteenth century in south west Wales was a turbulent time when the locus of authority could be shifted by naked force. The Perrots were typical, in that to maintain their position they had both to occupy high office and engage in corruption and violence. Sir John, who was generally believed to be an illegitimate son of Henry VIII held several such high offices. Between 1562 and 1584 he was, at different times, Vice Admiral of coastal south Wales, member of parliament for Pembrokeshire, President of Munster, chief commissioner for suppressing piracy in Pembrokeshire, Lord Deputy of Ireland, and a member of the Council of Wales and the Marches. And he was one of only two local residents who were members for the southwest who 'played – any significant part in the parliaments of the sixteenth century'.[88] But he has also been described as the 'mainspring' of 'a strong and effective organisation for trafficking with pirates'.[89] There was nothing exceptional in that. Lloyd recounts how, in the sixteenth century, the gentry, admittedly with the active participation of the ordinary people, were commonly involved in piracy.[90] In 1556 Sir John Wogan, at that time Vice Admiral sold the goods on a Breton ship which had been seized. To this can be added smuggling and refusal to pay duties, often by the excise officers themselves.[91]

Typical too of Sir John's behaviour, and the mood of the times, was an incident in 1569, when the high sheriff of Pembrokeshire, having tried to arrest one of his followers, found himself at the receiving end of violence, legal machination, and accusations of corruption.[92] Finally however, his many enemies caused him to be convicted of treason, and sentenced to death, but he died in the Tower in 1592 before the sentence could be carried out. Nevertheless, his family remained powerful. Another (illegitimate) son, James, was very active in the Elizabethan and Stuart parliaments, especially in the cause of anti Catholicism. But once again the remarkable lack of interest of the other members meant that he was 'left to represent south west Wales, with little support from his colleagues – the 'quiescence of the others is almost distressing'.[93]

Another rare prominent political figure in the latter half of the sixteenth century was Gelly Meyrick, born in Pembrokeshire in about 1556. Called Gelly after Gelliswick the family estate of his mother, who had married Roland Meyrick the Bishop of Bangor, he was brought up with the Devereux family at Lamphey Court in Pembrokeshire, and devoted his life to the service of the second Earl of Essex. Although he was a member of parliament for Carmarthen borough in 1588, and for Radnor in 1597, his power and influence went much further than that position brought. Because of his relentless attempts to support the second Earl, the latter knighted him in 1596, and in the events leading to the rebellion of 1601, Meyrick tried to recruit supporters. But in the south west he found only two beside himself, and these rescinded their support. Meyrick, unrepentant, was executed in 1601.

There was one aspect of the political behaviour of the Welsh squirearchy which has been the subject of much interest and this was the arrival of William of Orange, which was accepted by some, but not all in Wales. James Owen, a supporter, wrote that:

> We were on the brink of ruin and knew it not – this island might have been swimming in a deluge of innocent blood and become the sad monument of French and popish cruelties.[94]

But for about a hundred years after the end of the reign of James II, there were several societies in Wales which allegedly, or in fact, opposed the Hanoverian dynasty, and supported the restoration of the 'true' line of Stuarts. One of the best known was a Jacobite society in north east Wales, founded in 1710, as the Cycle of the White Rose. The membership list contains the names of squires from Denbighshire, Flintshire, and further afield. This was reformed in 1724, and appeared again in 1886, as the Order of the White Rose, when a pamphlet was sent to prominent people asking them to join.[95] This club was especially active during the mid eighteenth century, during the domination of north Wales by a member of one of the most powerful families, the first Watkin Williams Wynn.[96]

The Jacobite cause rested on what they saw as the marginal support given to the accession of William III, and the subsequent Hanoverian succession. It may be that the outrage which caused such an expression of support for the Stuarts in Wales was based upon a shared perception of the fundamental illegality of the legislation so vehemently set out by the Marquis of Ruvigny and Raineval. Or it may be that the critical factor was the chronic division which followed, which gave the Whigs long term control, thereby politically dispossessing Welsh Tories. Whatever the reasons may have been, it is agreed that the Stuarts regarded Wales, as they regarded Scotland and Lancashire, as parts of Britain sympathetic to their cause. The particular manifestation of sympathy to that cause in Dyfed and also in Glamorgan, was the curiously named Society of Sea Serjeants. This organisation was in existence in 1726, although the view has been expressed that it was founded three or four years earlier and survived until 1762.[97] The first President was Sir William Barlow of Slebech, Pembrokeshire, who had been described in 1693 as 'a known enemy of their Majesties and Government'[98] Jones lists 92 members of the Society 'and with a few exceptions, all were members of landed families, largely related by marriage'.[99]

There are, broadly two views about the intentions and activities of the Serjeants. The first is represented by the considered opinion of Jones which is that: 'they were Tories who were against the government because it was in the hands of Whigs, and not – because it was Hanoverian.[100] This is a view with which Thomas seems to agree:

The main Welsh legacy from the seventeenth century was loyalty to the crown, manifested at one level by Parliamentary Toryism and at another in the long persistence of Jacobite sentiment.[101]

Indeed Peter DG Thomas goes further when he concludes that the Society was: 'neither secret nor seditious, and must be removed from any list of Jacobite organisations'.[102]

No less a figure than a President, Sir John Philipps of Picton, defended the innocence of the Society. He was contesting Bristol for a seat in Parliament and in answer to the charge that he was disloyal because of his position admitted that he was 'chief', but that they were 'well affected subjects', and went on to explain:

> The intent, indeed, of our annual meeting (which is always at some sea-port town, whence we are called sea-serjeants) is to spend a week together in innocent mirth and recreation, as other gentlemen in England do at a horse race, and for no disloyal purpose whatsoever that I know of, and I defy any person to charge us with any thing of that nature.[103]

There are two observations to be made about this defence. The first is that it had to be made. Obviously, he could not agree with the accusation. The second is that he made this statement in 1754, by which time any serious threat to the crown would have been unrealistic. And so one picture of the activities of the Sea Serjeants is that the annual meeting 'was spent in gaiety-dinners, teas, balls and boating trips'.[104] Its function as a kind of social club would seem to be confirmed by the fact that in 1760 the Freedom of Haverfordwest was bestowed on named members of the Society 'particularly for that they have been so good as frequently to hold their annual meeting within this town'.[105]

But it is arguable that there is enough evidence to support the alternative view, which is that far from being variously harmless or loyal, this was an organisation which was disloyal at best, and dangerous at worst. Some of the Presidents seem to have been very reluctant to accord loyalty to William III or the Hanoverians. Sir William Barlow, a Catholic who was elected for Pembrokeshire in 1685 has been mentioned, while Sir John Philipps of Picton, was described by his eminent cousin Horace Walpole as 'a distinguished Jacobite', and 'rankly Jacobite'. Furthermore, in a letter in 1746 on the subject of The Young Pretender's escape to France he wrote that 'he is a particular friend of my cousin Sir John Philipps'.[106] The famous Pembrokeshire Tudor historian Fenton, an important source of information about the Society, lists questions which were put to initiates. One of these was 'Will you, upon the honour of a gentleman, keep the secrets of the Society, and the form of your admission to it?'.[107]

This hardly supports the view that it was not a secret society, nor the assessment that 'there is nothing sinister about these questions'.[108] There were reports of 'rash utterances',[109] and the drinking of the health of King James. There was a famous incident in 1709 or 1710 when a group 'drank to the Pretender's health and return on their knees'.[110] Amongst those who did were William Barlow and Lewis Pryse of Gogerddan. This man, from a family which dominated Cardiganshire, was expelled from the House of Commons in 1716, because he was absent when the oaths were taken. After the 1696 Fenwick plot to assassinate the king, Thomas Mansel, together with seven other Welsh MPs, refused to sign the 'Association for the Defence of William III.[111] And allegations about Jacobite support were commonplace amongst the squires. Whig John Campbell of Stackpole wrote 'numerous letters' warning his son Pryse to be wary of the young man's uncle James Philipps of Pentyparc. One of these, in January 1744, advised him:

> When you are with Tories or Ja------, I take the ffamily of Foes, who I believe are now with you to be, it is better to hear their thoughts upon the state of affairs than to let them know yours.[112]

In fairness though it should be pointed out that Campbell regarded Philipps as an implacable danger to his personal political position.

When the Pretender was defeated in 1715, a loyalist meeting in Pembrokeshire was attacked by Jacobites wielding clubs[113] an event which certainly could not have happened without the direction, support, or connivance of the local gentry. Again, in 1717 the Earl of Mar, the Pretender's Secretary of State, wrote that in that year that there was to be an invasion. There would be a landing in Milford, on the Pembrokeshire coast. This letter was sent to Lewis Pryse 'and other loyal men'.[114]

And so the question remains. Were they dangerous? Or were they Tories – they were to a man – who merely banded together against a Whig oligarchy? Was this together with the claim that 'Welsh elections were primarily family contests for primacy in the county and the power of patronage'[115] why they banded together so often to canvass for Tories who were sometimes Sea Serjeants? They did so, for example in 1727, when one of their number stood for Carmarthenshire. The letter was signed, amongst others, by two Barlows, a Wogan, and a Philipps.[116]

Perhaps a cardinal pointer is the fact that none of them turned out in

1715 or 1745. Indeed, as Thomas points out, when the possibility of invasion arrived, many of them joined loyalist organisations. The most active response 'was yet another toast'. Charles Edward, contemplating the failure of Wales to come up with the support he had been encouraged to expect is alleged to have said 'I will do as much for my Welsh friends as they have done for me: I will drink their health'.[117]

There was one exception, from Glamorgan. David Morgan, a barrister, joined the Jacobite army in Preston, and tried to persuade the army to go to Wales. In the event he was executed in 1746.[118] The failure of the Pretender's supporters in Wales to turn out could have been due to a number of factors. It may have been that the Sea Serjeants were, indeed an innocent club, although their actions would hardly support that. It could have been cowardice. After all, in many of the remote Welsh counties, the reality of fighting must have seemed a long way away, and a rather dangerous thing to do. The area had a well established reputation for keeping away from trouble, even if before such trouble the gentry had supposedly been ready for action. The possibility of a landing in Pembrokeshire in 1599, and the Essex rebellion of 1601 are just two examples. The failure of the gentlemen of the south west to support Essex, when some might have been expected to do so, was probably not from motives of 'loyalty to the Tudors or to the hurried and precipitate events of the revolt' but more likely 'the self centred apathy to external affairs that was the hallmark of this region throughout this period and beyond'.[119] This was to be the case too when the French invaded Pembrokeshire in 1797. We shall see how Lords Cawdor and Milford complained that the gentry were very reluctant to fight. Finally, the explanation may have been in those qualities of lethargy, apathy, and that 'general lassitude' which distinguished the gentlemen of south west Wales.[120]

Membership of such a Society, whether convivial in form or dangerous in intent, does not account for the wealth of the gentlemen of Wales who were, at the end of the nineteenth century, at their wealthiest, and their most powerful. Any review of their position from the sixteenth century onwards must note a steady progression in the wealth and concomitant power of the gentry, even if the caveat about their fraud and tax evasion described by Lloyd is taken into account.[121] If we take just three examples, those of the Vaughans of Golden Grove (Carmarthenshire), the Owens of Orielton (Pembrokeshire), and the Pryses of Gogerddan (Cardiganshire), it can be seen that the evidence is strong that they and their kin accumulated enormous wealth, which came to a peak in the early to mid nineteenth century. In 1737 the Golden Grove income was worth £3200, which by 1790 was worth almost £8000:[122]

The family occupied a dozen country houses. At the height of its influence the parent estate, that of Golden Grove comprised over 50,000 acres, 25 extensive lordships, and six castles, and when these are added to the possessions of the many branches it may be truly said that nearly half of Carmarthenshire owned a Vaughan for a landlord.[123]

Hassall in his account of Carmarthenshire in the 1790s refers to the Vaughans in his day as those 'whose lordships are of extraordinary extent'.[124] Orielton, a close neighbour of Stackpole in Pembrokeshire, had an income of £93,000 in 1793.[125] Shortly afterwards, when Sir Hugh Owen of Orielton married, the rent roll for 1799–1800:

shows that he owned properties in fifteen Anglesey parishes, in eight Caernarvonshire parishes – in seven Carmarthenshire parishes, and in thirty-eight Pembrokeshire parishes – the total annual rental amounting to £8392.[126]

With respect to Gogerddan, at the end of the eighteenth century this estate consisted of some 30,000 acres in Cardiganshire, in addition to holdings in Pembrokeshire, Merioneth and Brecon.[127] Some of this wealth came from industry. 19 per cent of the total income of the Cawdor west Wales estate in 1798 came from collieries and lead mines.[128] It should be stressed that these are only examples, and similar families and estates, equally wealthy, could be found throughout Wales. Some of these were the Morgans of Tredegar Park in Monmouthshire, the Bulkeleys of Baron Hill in Anglesey, and the Wynns of Wynnstay in Denbighshire.

There were exceptions, of course, to the generally held view, already noted, that the gentry of Wales were politically uninvolved, and socially remote. Some of the members of the family of the Vaughans of Golden Grove were more active than most. The second Earl of Carbery, in 1676 persuaded Charles II to appoint a 'King's Printer for the British Language'.[129] Other west Wales gentry supported this including John Barlow and William Wogan.[130] The Vaughans were notable patrons, and 'fostered the genius of Dryden, Aubrey' and others. Their library was renowned, and the family produced writers 'in Latin and in the vulgar tongue'.[131]

Altogether exceptional was the Sir John Philipps of Picton who was born about 1666, and died in 1737. As well as being an MP for several constituencies in the district, he was a founder of the Society for the Promotion of Christian Knowledge, and founder and supporter of its charity schools in the region. He was, famously, the patron of a Welsh folk hero, Griffith Jones of Llanddowror the pioneer of the Circulating Schools which made such an impact on Welsh education. This interest in education was far from general, although another Vaughan, Sir John, gave an enclosed area for the establishment of a Grammar School in Carmarthen before 1609. And Thomas Lloyd of Cilciffeth, the same man who was castigated for his enclosure policy, gave property so that a school could be endowed in Haverfordwest. There had been a Grammar School in that town since 1488. These were noteworthy though because they were rare:

> the achievement of the region in this connection is not impressive in an era of exceptional growth in educational foundations in England by laymen catering for the needs of laymen.[132]

In 'The Blue Books' it is reported that several witnesses in Pembrokeshire and Carmarthenshire claimed that the largely absentee landlords did nothing to advance education.[133] Although one witness made exceptions of Lords Cawdor and Dynevor.[134] Some too had an impressive record of contributions to the Church. In his charge of 1866 Bishop Thirwall of St. David's 'mentioned Earl Cawdor, who had been responsible for the building of seven churches'.[135]

Amongst other virtues claimed for the squires include the supposed good treatment of tenants. Howell is one who draws attention to this, and exemplifies this with the case of William Wogan of Wiston who left £30 to people in the parish who had been 'reduced by misfortunes to a low estate'. After stating that tenants who met hard times 'were usually treated with kindness by their landlords', Howell concludes that 'it is fair to state that the landowners in these years were benevolent patriarchs of their immediate community'.[136] This is a bold claim, and it has to be said needs more precise evidence than has so far been adduced. Writing of a later time when landowners were selling off, John Davies, having stated that 'many landowners were prepared to sell off to tenants at prices lower than those which could be obtained on the open market', goes on to give just one sole example.[137] Moore-Colyer defends Welsh landowners even more strongly than Howell when he writes, using the example of Johnes of Hafod: 'the generalised criticism of the Welsh landowning class of the eighteenth and nineteenth centuries levelled by twentieth-century historians no longer stands up to close examination.'[138] However the article goes on to show that Johnes was, in fact, a very unusual example of a landowner 'however profound the intellectual torpor into which the majority of his Welsh contemporaries had descended'. And again he is exceptional in allowing access to his library: 'not for him the selfish attitude of Sir Watkin Williams Wynn, to whose great library at Wynnstay even bona fide visitors were denied access.[139]

Another consolation to be set against the evidence of squirearchical ego-centricity is the occasional claim that relationships between high and low were good. Malkin seems to have some kind of first hand experience of this, although he does not explain what he means when he wrote in 1804: 'In Cardiganshire there appears a remarkable fellow feeling; if I may so express it, a speaking acquaintance, between the higher and lower ranks of society.'[140] In writing of 'greater homogeneity' between Welsh squires and inferiors than is found in England, Francis Jones, the writer quoted by Jenkins, attributes this 'to the survival of the ancient royal and noble families of Wales'.[141] This highly speculative notion seems to be based on the observation that in the eighteenth century some *uchelwyr* lived in houses and held property 'essentially indistinguishable from their yeoman neighbours'. Saunders Lewis, predictably because of his yearning for a strange, almost mystical Welsh past, disagreed and explains the rejection of the gentry because of the latter's failure to cleave to 'matters which were traditional, older, more aristocratic, than anything else in Wales – The gentry betrayed their birthright, behaved like rich bourgeois, and denied their whole philosophy and betrayed the civilisation which they boasted they were cherishing'.[142] Morgan too rejects the "kinship of outlook between landlord, farmer and villager", which 'was much less evident in Wales'.[143]

But the overall picture of the gentry from the seventeenth to the nineteenth centuries shows them as much less concerned than isolated examples might imply. Sir William Owen, who was a Member from 1722 to 1774, never held office nor spoke in the House. Nor did yet another Pembrokeshire member, John Symmons who sat from 1746 until 1761.[144] The performance of William Edwardes, MP for Haverfordwest in 1747–84, 'gives the impression of creeping sclerosis: he never spoke in the House, never begged for any favour or office and never voted against a single government after 1760.[145] He did though apply for a peerage in 1779, arguing that he had never asked for anything for himself.[146] He got it, but was 'indignant' when Lord Milford supported Sir Hugh Owen, and Edwardes (Kensington) was defeated in 1784.[147] This absence of interest was not peculiar to Dyfed, since as Peter Thomas points out, 'the great majority' of Welsh MPs never spoke at all, and that:

No Welsh MP sat in the cabinet between 1711, when Robert Harley quit his seat for the Lords, and 1822, when Sir Charles Watkin Williams Wynn attained that status.[148]

In short, with a few exceptions, when it came to politics, in a memorable summary Geraint Jenkins notes that 'Welsh members of Parliament – have few claims upon the curiosity of posterity'.[149]

The overwhelming evidence is that they were much more likely to spend their time and money on having a good time. The richer people would spend time in London during the Season, or, together with their somewhat poorer neighbours, in towns, some of which were substantial by the standards of the time, such as Haverfordwest. To accommodate their social needs, they sometimes owned town houses. Wherever they were, they engaged in an interminable round of gambling, balls, drinking of coffee and alcohol, watching the fighting of cocks, dogs and people, plays, and above all hunting.

Their gambling was sometimes legendary. One of the Vaughans of Golden Grove was 'rumoured to have lost from £20,000 to £30,000',[150] while Sir Herbert Lloyd of Peterwell killed himself in London after losing heavily.[151] In respect of hunting, their passion for it seems to have been insensate. Often tenants were obliged to keep dogs for the purpose.[152] Some of the fathers, in their many recorded pleas for better financial management by their children included less hunting. One of the Pryse family of Gogerddan who was 'an inveterate hunter', suffered an unusual revenge since he was bitten by a fox, and died.[153] And there is much else to deny this somewhat rosy picture. In the seventeenth century, a powerful family such as that of Golden Grove used its grip on the administration of justice, not to enforce it, but to corrupt it in its own interests. And so there was a plethora of 'hostile justices, with false charges tried before thoroughly partisan juries and biassed judges'.[154] The third Earl of Carbery when he was appointed governor of Jamaica in 1674 'acquired considerable wealth by selling his own servants as slaves'. Another Cardiganshire landowner, Thomas Powell of Nanteos: 'thought nothing in 1721 of gathering a posse of servants and tenants together, arming them with guns, blunderbusses, swords, pistols, and staves, and using them to intimidate alleged trespassers'.[155]

The common denominator between such men and their descendants was a contempt for the law, and contempt for other people. In Cardiganshire, a Cromwellian Major General opined that 'the county was "pitiful poor": the squires were "a shocking prospect of poverty and idleness, neglect and ignorance"'.[156] In about 1720 the English buyer of the great Erthig estate in Denbighshire observed: 'This whole country is governed by fear and the lesser gentry are as much awed by those of better estate as the poor people are'.[157] Later, at the time of the Rebecca riots, Foster of The Times reported that the magistrates were tyrannical, ignorant and unjust. The people told him they were treated like 'beasts'. Lloyd Hall was another who commented that they treated people brought before the bench 'like dogs'. The Sun newspaper described the magistrates as 'ignorant, conceited, proud – accustomed from infancy to perfect submission'.[158] And when literacy, and the Enlightenment took hold, the verdict was the same:

> Besides being useless and immoral, spending money on horses and harlots, they are merciless tyrants. They cruelly oppress those who work hard to keep them – The land has been usurped through fraud, craftiness and oppression, by a handful of unprincipled people – and spent on frivolous and sinful pleasures, and the country is thus greatly impoverished.[159]

One of the noteworthy elements in this extract is the significant intrusion of the word 'sinful'. This had already become part of the armoury of the Nonconformists, and although it is used here to attack social privilege, it was used more generally to deflect attention from the matter, and into that desiderata which saw salvation, not in the abolition of social inequality, but in the perfection of self, and the abolition of privilege in the Established Church.

But the power, and indeed the very existence of the gentry in Wales, as elsewhere, was not immutable. Vilfredo Pareto wrote 'that history is a cemetery of aristocracies' because of 'the accumulation of inferiors in the upper class or superiors in the lower'.[160] While the people who ruled Wales from the sixteenth century to the eighteenth, with the odd exception, were certainly not aristocrats in the sense of being of noble lineage, Pareto's dictum applies in the sense that during that time families lost their estates, direct lines through the males died out, although the habit of changing names conceals the fact from the casual observer, and titles became extinct. Strange provisions in wills left people with their titles and little else, or with estates and no titles. And there were always newcomers to replace those consigned to Pareto's cemetery.

The basic cause of this consignment was the infertility which was a feature of the male members of gentry families, what Geraint Jenkins calls 'the extraordinary failure of the male line'. 'Of eighty three resident or semi resident families who owned estates in Glamorgan in the 1660s, at least forty five had vanished as a result of the failure of the male line a century later.[161] Philip Jenkins sets out the arresting case of the Morgan family of Tredegar. At the death of Thomas Morgan in 1769 there were four sons, two daughters, and two nephews. But none of the six males produced children. In 1792 the estate passed to a daughter, who married a man called Gould, and their son took the name of Morgan.

In a long discussion of causes and effects, Jenkins suggests a number of reasons. These include not marrying, or marrying late, and a high rate of infant mortality, which affected all classes: 'The squires born in the early eighteenth century were between a third and a half as likely to have surviving sons as were their counterparts a century earlier.[162] He considers as possibilities too homosexuality, or more refined contraception. However, even kings who were homosexual produced heirs, and controlling the number of children through contraception has always been practised when needed. Another possible explanation is the degree of interbreeding in these families, which is accepted as likely to have adverse effects of all kinds, including fertility.

Yet some of the oldest families died out completely, at least in terms of wealth and/or title. In 1794 The last Wogan sisters sold out to Cawdor of Stackpole, including their principal seat, the manor of Wiston in Pembrokeshire. The last baronet of the Stepney line died in 1825, the Prendergast estate having been bought by the Owen family in 1772.[163] One of the more mysterious wills was that of John Vaughan of Golden Grove who died in 1804. Although he had no children he had 'hordes' of relations, but he left the enormous estate to his friend Lord Cawdor.[164] The Owen family provide an example of a will which separated title from wealth, and incidentally a change of name. In 1809 Sir Hugh Owen of Orielton died without an heir and the title went to his father's first cousin. But Hugh left the huge estate which included £135,000 in gilt-edged securities to his second cousin John Lord, and the latter changed his name to Owen and was made a baronet in 1813. In 1810 he became a member of Parliament, and so began the process which led to him leaving only £450 pounds at his death in 1861. This was in part because of extravagance and in part because of the considerable expense incurred through fixing elections, especially in this case the Haverfordwest election of 1831.[165] By 1856 their huge estate had gone. At the same time the last of the Owen baronets of the original 1641 creation died, and with him, of course, the title.[166]

Two other examples of name changing are those of Meyrick and Philipps. There was a descendant of the famous Sir Gelly, Thomas Meyrick, whose only daughter in 1820 married a man called Charlton. In 1858 the latter changed his name to Meyrick and was created a baronet in 1880. The name of the Philipps family of Picton too would have come close to extinction, had it not been for the changing of names. Similarly several of their titles only continued, and continue to exist because they were recreated. In 1776 Sir Richard Philipps was created Baron Milford in the Irish peerage. This was a 'solatium for having been refused permission to make a carriage road up to the front door of his house'.[167] This was just one example of a often capricious reward system much employed by Pitt, with an 'unprecedentedly large lists of nominations' having to be reluctantly accepted by George III.[168] Milford died in 1823 and the title passed to a distant cousin, but the estate passed to a man called Grant, who was a kinsman at some remove. He died in 1857, having been created Baron Milford of Picton Castle, without children, and the estate went to his half brother the Reverend Gwyther. He died in 1875, had no son, and so his daughter inherited, and her husband, like all the previous non Philipps, took the name of Philipps. He was created a baronet in 1887. There was another creation of baronetcy in 1919 – Laurence Richard – and he was the subject of yet a third creation of Baron Milford, this time of the United Kingdom, in 1939. In very recent times the second Baron Milford-Wogan Philipps (1902–93) was deprived of the Picton estate, which went to his brother. This was another example of dividing the title and the estate, and was no doubt because the first baron disapproved of his son's political persuasion, which included being a communist, and fighting in the International Brigade in the Spanish Civil War.

With regard to the once powerful Barlows, created baronets in 1677, the last was Sir George who died in 1775. His only daughter Anne married a John Symmons of Llanstinan in 1773. There was no issue, so the estate was sold to Nathaniel Philipps, who because of extravagance was forced to sell to William Knox, a controversial figure and the same man who founded a local Agricultural Society. The Earldom of Carbery was to become extinct with the third earl who died in 1712–13. Although the Vaughans remained powerful, the title died with him. When Sir Carbery Pryse of Gogerddan died about 1695, the title died with him. Another ennoblement was that of another Vaughan, Wilmot, a viscount in the Irish peerage, who was made earl in 1776 in the same peerage.

Thus it can be seen that peerages and elevations in Wales flew thick and fast from about the 1770s, usually, as we have seen for weird, or even hilarious reasons. Some survived, although the twentieth century was to see them in reduced circumstances.

We have seen examples of the accidents of birth, or non birth, which were the hallmark of the gentry. But undoubtedly the most important factor in the demise of these estates before the first half of the twentieth century was the incompetence, profligacy, and general degeneracy of the people who owned them. Especially at the end of the eighteenth century, perhaps inspired by their London experience, and the concomitant increase in their wealth, there was a rash of building and rebuilding. This was often dangerous or even fatal. Sir William Hamilton was warned in 1768 that his programme at Colby in Pembrokeshire would be very costly, whilst Symmons, in 1776 the owner of Slebech, engaged in such ambitious projects that by 1783 he had to sell it to William Knox.[169]

There were more careful owners and from those there were constant appeals to their sons to be more prudent. In 1683 Sir Erasmus Philipps of Picton wrote to his son John, later to be dubbed the 'good Sir John', about his extravagance, and hoped for 'no more foolish frolics'.[170] And Sir Pryse Pryse, who tried to arrest the decline at the end of the nineteenth century wrote angrily to his heir Edward after his incessant appeals for money that 'inevitable bankruptcy would be the only consequence of his rash expenditure of foxhounds and entertaining'. The case of this estate of Gogerddan is typical. In 1779 Lewis Pryse was succeeded by his daughter who was married to a man called Edward Lovedon of Berkshire. Another example it may be noted of the end of a direct family name. Their son eventually changed his name to Pryse, having inherited in 1784. Although he was a Whig MP 'he did not enjoy an especially illustrious parliamentary career'. He was depressed, inherited considerable debts from his father, and borrowed heavily. From his time the land was sold off, and although a descendant Pryse Pryse from about 1895 helped it to recover somewhat, his children were spendthrift and feckless. Sir Lewes (sic) succeeded in 1918, and presided over the final dismantling of the estate. In 1950 the mansion was sold to the University College. Their neighbours and kinsmen in Carmarthenshire went the same way.[171] During the nineteenth century the exemplar mentioned earlier, Golden Grove, lost 59,000 acres.

Earlier in this chapter ED Evans' summary was used as a quintessential statement about the eighteenth century being 'the golden age of the country squire'. This was even more so for most of the nineteenth century. But the twentieth century saw the final demise of many of the estates which have been discussed here, and with them was swept away the many of the privileges and much of the wealth which they had enjoyed for so long at the expense of the peasantry.

We will now examine the very different lives of the peasants. JV Becket[172] urges caution in the use of the term 'peasant' in part because there is little agreement about its meaning, and in part because it is widely regarded as a term of abuse. I use it deliberately for two reasons which answer these two principal concerns. The first is that in Wales, the bulk of the population were landless labourers, or at least had such small amounts of land that they could certainly not be described as farmers, much less yeomen, which is generally, but not invariably understood to mean farmers of substance. Furthermore, in many parts of Wales in the period under discussion, most miners were also labourers on other people's agricultural holdings, and although the miner it could be argued was not a peasant, we will go on to see that his connection with the land excuses his being put into the same category. Finally, I take the view that in the context in which this book is set, the term 'peasant' far from being an opprobrious designation, is one denoting great dignity, patience, and of quintessential social worth.

2

THE PEASANTRY OF WALES

'The inhabitants of Pembrokeshire shall be found to be in
the greatest distress'.[173]

The lives of the Welsh eighteenth- and nineteenth-century squires were roundly comfortable. At Hafod in Cardiganshire, Thomas Johnes had 'enriched his residence with paintings and sculptures by the best masters',[174] while Malkin on a visit to Hafod lists some of the painters: Caravaggio, Rembrandt, and Van Dyke.[175] The Duke of Rutland, on his visit to Pembrokeshire in 1798 and while at Stackpole Court, the home of Lord Cawdor, examined 'the kitchen garden, which is extensive, and has a great length of hot houses well stored with fruit'.[176] And when he visited Picton castle, he approved of the 'extensive and variegated grounds' and the 'music from an organ placed in a gallery above the great hall'.[177]

Even modest estates displayed evidence of wealth. Castle Maelgwyn in north Pembrokeshire, for example, was characterised by the 'romantic walks...constructed through the wild dingle of Morganau – than which, more secluded and delightful walks could not be found in any part of the country'.[178] And Walter Davies in 1814 was equally impressed. Writing of south Wales in general he reports:

> Of course the houses of the opulent are, in magnificence and taste, equal to those of any other country... commanding a compound scenery of the grand, the beautiful, and the sublime.[179]

But as one would expect from Davies he has a cautionary tale to tell of a gentleman 'noted for his liberality to his tenants' who spent more than £20,000 improving their farms. His successor 'tried what doubling of rents would do'. This greatly improved the estate more 'than all the benevolence and forbearance of his predecessor. The tenants were now compelled to do themselves, what another did before them'.[180] This is consonant with all his views, for example in respect of the Poor Laws which 'have very materially contributed to multiply the number of paupers', since they adversely affect 'the industry, parsimony, and moral precaution of the labouring class'.[181]

Davies need not have worried. The life of the west Welsh peasantry, as was the case throughout Wales, was much different from that of their masters: even Davies was surprised at the feudal relationship between master and servant, and the low rates of pay and absence of 'victuals', which were usual. But in his relentless attempt to be fair to the wealthy, he points out that they are given:

> a house, garden, and keep of a cow, at a low rent; the setting of a quantity of potatoes in a fallow, and bread corn at a fixed rate per bushel all the year round, which in general is considerably below the market: but these perquisites are far from being general.[182]

He also draws attention to the cases of people like Sir John Morris of Clasemont near Swansea who was the 'most extensive individual builder of comfortable habitations for the labouring class'.[183] But in Dyfed he did not find a counterpart, apart from 'a cluster' near Llanelly.[184] However, referring to Hassall's comments on the state of housing and farm buildings Davies claims that 'many instances of the causes of complaints when *then* (his italics) are now removed'. [185] This, and many other reports, as we shall go on to see, shows that the life of the Welsh peasant was far from the romantic idyll which was sometimes claimed.

It was a country where 80 per cent of the people lived in rural areas, and this meant that it was included in some surveys of agriculture in the late eighteenth and early nineteenth century, although Wales, and especially the south west was often not included in others. As well as the official accounts, a rich source lies in what Thomas in his study of the Napoleonic period calls 'literary evidence'.[186] There is a good deal of this. There were more than a hundred books of 'tours' in Wales in the second half of the eighteenth and the first half of the nineteenth centuries.[187]

West Wales was an area which seems to have been visited a good deal by travellers from England, especially at the end of the eighteenth century, and many of these left accounts of what they saw. But then, as now, there were protests at the flying visit followed by the authoritative book. One such is in the *Cambrian Register* of 1796. Here, the writer 'Cymro' complains that 'most of those who have honoured Wales with a visit' suffer from a 'lamentable deficiency', which is that they cannot speak the language or have 'too transient an acquaintance'. 'Gleaners' is the word the writer uses to describe them, and they covered so much ground that 'the man in the seven league boots was a snail to him'. He also complains about their spelling, which is somewhat unfair since the spelling of Welsh place names, even by residents, varied considerably at the time, (and for that matter still does). Yet, having attacked Morgan's *Tour to Milford Haven*, and Warner for his spelling mistakes, of the accounts of Haverfordwest and its district he writes: 'I again subscribe with pleasure to their general correctness.[188] The value for this study lies in the fact that the visitors together describe a remarkably similar picture of the lives of common people.

One such 'gleaner' was the teenage Duke of Rutland, who visited west Wales immediately after the French invasion, in 1798. In his view the major towns seem to have been almost universally disagreeable. The exception was Tenby – 'the first sight of it is delightful'; the town 'hangs prettily on the declivity of a hill, on one side of a most charming bay'.[189] He writes of Carmarthen on the other hand that 'there are not any good houses in it, and most of them are whitewashed which gives it a glaring appearance'.[190] Haverfordwest was worse, being 'very inconvenient and unpleasant' with the walk known as the Parade being 'the only promenade belonging to this wretchedly dirty town',[191] a view shared by another visitor who reported that the 'the streets are narrow and dirty, and so steep as to be seriously dangerous'.[192] But another visitor thought Haverfordwest was a place of 'opulence and comfort… more apparent here than in most of the towns in the principality'.[193]

Rutland thought Pembroke was 'small and miserable'. Later several miles of 'bad road' led to the 'small and pitiful town of Newport',[194] and when his party arrived in Cardigan, there was not much to cheer them up there. 'I cannot', he observes, 'say much respecting the goodness of the inn and the whole appearance of it was shabby and dirty'.[195] His impressions may have been shaped, at least in part by the fact that his visit was attended by that atrocious rain, which operates to the considerable benefit of the cultivator, but is often the despair of the visitor. On one occasion, for example, the party, in the process of travelling to Picton castle near Haverfordwest, found themselves up to their knees in mud.[196]

His adverse comments were subscribed to by others. Over a signature Gwinfardd Dyfed, someone writing in 1795 claims that Fishguard 'in the aggregate looks well, and conveys to you the idea of a large flourishing place'

but goes on to observe that 'we say "from Fishguard streets and Cardigan
streets Good Lord deliver us"'.[197] Reverend J Evans, visiting a little later, in
1803, agreed about Fishguard, where the whitewash of the roofs gave the
town a clean appearance 'which… is contrasted by the rugged dirty streets,
with a dung-heap at almost every door.'[198] Although he was more generous
about Carmarthen, which was 'a large, populous, and tolerably built place;
the streets spacious, and many of the houses good… The public buildings
are large, a handsome church… and a new elegant county hall built of free
stone, with colonnades of the Ionic order… the markets large and well supplied'.[199] In 1803 a visitor was also fairly complimentary. 'The situation of
Carmarthen, one of the most wealthy and polite towns in Wales, can scarcely be enough admired'.[200] Sir Richard Colt Hoare, who visited in 1796 was
even more complimentary. 'Caermarthen is a handsome respectable town':
Haverfordwest 'has a magnificent appearance', while the slate houses of
Cardigan were 'upon a par in form and appearance with those of Haverfordwest'.[201] This was despite the fact that he happened to be in Cardigan
during an election campaign where the people were 'swilling in cwrw, (beer)
dead drunk'.[202] A later visitor was not so sure: 'the town is by no means,
interestingly or picturesquely situated… the inn at Cardigan is like most
of the Welsh ones, not too cleanly in kitchen or bedroom'.[203] Carmarthen,
according to Evans on a visit in 1803 was 'a large, populous, and tolerably
well-built place; the streets are spacious, and many of the houses good'[204] but
he noted 'the streets of the town are infested with beggars'.[205]

Malkin's opinion of Llandovery, in 1804, was that 'is the worst in…
Wales… its streets filthy and disgusting'.[206] St. David's 'scarcely boasts a
tolerable house unconnected with the church'.[207] 'Llanelly is a small, ir-
regular, and dirty town; nor does the appearance of its inhabitants, who are
chiefly miners and sailors, contribute to render it more inviting'.[208] Llan-
stephan near Carmarthen he looked on more favourably. It was 'clean and
well built… three or four houses were building when I was there, in a very
good state'.[209]

The Duke of Rutland noted that the roads were as bad as the towns. On
his journey from Tavernspite to Tenby the way was through 'as uninteresting
a country and as bad a road, as I ever witnessed in my life'. The beauty of
the Pembrokeshire coast was rather diminished because 'we got into terrible
lanes, some parts of them so deep that we were fearful of being set fast'.[210]
Another traveller in the same area commented on:

The difficult and dangerous road to Tenby… for the first half mile I
did not think it possible the Horses could have kept their legs, or that

the wheels, tho' strong, could have stood the jolts amongst the rocks. At one time I thought all was over.[211]

The road from Cardigan to Aberystwyth was no better:

After the first ten miles we lost all appearance of good road, and had to proceed many miles upon a track, scarcely passable for a carriage. It did not seem indeed to be intended for that purpose: and sometimes all traces of a road, were lost upon a barren moor. Whenever there was a track, it was narrow stony, and sometimes ran over great patches of solid rock. The holes with which it abounded were deep and dangerous, and once or twice, we were very nearly overturned… The view of the sea was however always cheerful and pleasant.[212]

Yet some 'gentlemen', against some opposition, had arranged for parliamentary legislation to enable the creation of turnpikes. These Rutland would have been surprised to learn, complete 'the communications, from town to town through all parts of the county, below the mountains'.[213] Once again Hoare is more generous He reports the 'roads good in all directions'. And he even lists the view from the road across the Presely hills in north Pembrokeshire as one of the four most beautiful places he has seen.[214]

Sometimes these 'gleaners' give a valuable insight into the lives of the poor. Barber for example, who visited at the beginning of the nineteenth century, found that his party were lost near Pembroke. They called at a cottage, and found a group of miners:

who were regaling around a blazing hearth… the uniform black appearance of this group, their long matted hair half hiding their faces, which caught a ferocious turn from the strong partial light of the fire, was not calculated to inspire prepossession in their favour; but, although in the exterior repulsive as their cheerless occupation, their hearts were not estranged from sensations of benevolence.

One of them asked them to sit down while he finished his 'mess of porridge' which he supposed 'you wouldn't like'. But 'mother can give you a drop of good mead, and some decentish bread and butter' 'Mother' said that she was grateful to Providence for a good harvest, whereas last year 'many of her neighbours died outright of hunger'. At the end it was with difficulty that 'we could prevail on our hostess to accept of a trifling acknowledgement for her favours'.[215] Even such contemporary observers thought mining was a cruel business:

> when we reflect on the various accidents to which colliers are exposed from these and other causes, it is surprizing how men are found to engage in the hazardous undertaking, especially when the smallness of the emoluments and the nature of the employment are compared together. Witnessing some of these poor creatures ascending out of the pits, just emerging ab inferis ad lucem, as black and forbidding in their aspect as the region they had just left, it afforded us abundant reason to reflect on the obligations we were under to a kind Providence, in not being obliged to earn the necessaries of life so far from the surface we trod on, and exempt also from the numerous accidents to which these our fellow creatures are exposed.[216]

On his way to Cardigan, Rutland would have passed near the village of Cilgerran, which is on the borders of the two counties. In a detailed account of the area, Phillips, having commented on the state of the roads, describes the inevitable and 'utmost' opposition by the farmers to improving them, since it would be they who would have to pay for their upkeep. One initiative was notably opportunistic. A local magnate Sir Benjamin Hammett took the opportunity to divert a public road from the front of his house. When 'famine hunger and starvation stared every poor man in the face, and misery was triumphant… almost all the poor people from miles around' were taken on to build a new road. 'Such was this great and good man', Philipps goes on, 'may his name be ever honoured for it'. At the time he wrote, in 1867, 'the roads have been wonderfully improved and are now in excellent repair'.[217] Hammett also built the Llechryd Tinplate and Sheet Ironworks in Cardiganshire.[218]

The picture painted by Erasmus Saunders in 1721 of the Diocese of St. David's adds to the picture of decay and desolation in eighteenth century Dyfed and other parts of Wales, even though one historian defines him as one of 'two largely jaundiced commentators'.[219] The Diocese at the time covered Pembrokeshire, Carmarthenshire, Cardiganshire, Breconshire and almost all of Radnorshire, a large part of Glamorgan, and some of Montgomery: that is, nearly half of Wales. It also embraced some of Herefordshire. The heart of the diocese was symptomatic of the whole, with:

the stately ruins of the bishop's palace, of the college, the schools, the arch-deacon's and the canons houses at St. David's, and the like desolation of the collegiate church and the houses belonging thereunto.[220]

Throughout the area he notes neglected and ruined churches, some of which were rented out as barns or for pens for animals, and some had been taken over by dissenters.[221] His summary sets the milieu for the region which was to remain unchanged for at least the following 150 years: 'the marks of a forsaken poverty and desolation seem to overspread the whole neighbourhood'.[222] Nor had things improved some 170 years later when Bishop Basil Jones, who was bishop from 1874 to 1896, 'used to say: "St. David's is about the largest and poorest of all the dioceses in this realm"'.[223]

The three important occupations in west Wales at the end of the eighteenth century were typical of most of Wales: fishing, mining and farming. Although women shared equally in the work of farming, they did in addition supplement the meagre income by spinning.[224] But in Hassall's survey of Carmarthenshire of 1794 he notes that although 'every woman here knows how to card and spin wool… the manufacture of woollen stockings in the neighbourhood of Llandovery… which was considerable… is much fallen off latterly'.[225]

In Cardiganshire in 1803 the Rev. John Evans reported on the expertise of the women knitters, where 'large quantities are got up, and sent to the English markets'. [226] There were too pockets of tin and quarrying, and in some areas the latter was pre-eminent as an occupation. [227] There were about one hundred slate quarries in Pembrokeshire in the period under discussion. At the end of the eighteenth century Robert Morgan of Carmarthen owned a furnace, forge, rolling mills tin mills and a bank in the county, seemingly with great success.[228] But the usual complaint of contemporary observers, is that all of these resources were under exploited and badly managed.

In an article about fishing, the least important commercially of these, 'Gwinfardd Dyfed', in 1795, deplored the failure of the people in the Fishguard area to improve the fisheries. The season for salmon fishing, for example, could be extended but they will not start to fish until the point 'when the fish almost leap into the houses which skirt the tide'. And this and other failings went unheeded even though the catches were reducing, and fish 'in conjunction with potatoes, constitutes the principal food of the lower orders of the people'.[229] There seemed to be an export in salmon since in 1797 a visitor reported that 'what is not disposed of fresh at market, is salted and dried, and is to be found at the London shops, as Welsh salmon'.[230] But by the 1860s it appears that the rich salmon resources of the river Teifi were

being exploited to the full by the fishermen on its banks. Better communications had, by that time, led to considerable demand for salmon from
England. This led to the complaint that 'it has become extremely difficult
to procure this most delicate fish, at any price, in this neighbourhood'. The
complainant goes on to report that the average price when you could get it,
was eighteen pence a pound. But 'at the commencement of a season, I have
seen as much as five shillings a pound given for the same'.[231] The author
seems an accurate reporter of what he saw and these astonishing figures may
be accepted. Astonishing because at the same time, and in the same place a
ploughman:

> cannot now be obtained under £9 a year, and female servants gener-
> ally get from £4 to £6 a year. Labourers invariably get 9s a week, but if
> they live on the farmer's table they only get from 8d to 10d per day.[232]

On the other hand, while Gwinfardd Dyfed complained, at the same time
Hoare observes approvingly that in Pembrokeshire they exported oysters
from Milford Haven to London and Holland since 'they were found in great
quantity'.[233]

In respect of mining, lead mining in Wales has a long history: 'the first to
attempt lead mining in Pembrokeshire was in the reign of Queen Elizabeth.
This was at St. Elvis, but it was never productive'.[234] There was also a mine
at Llanfyrnach, which was abandoned in 1793, although in the later nineteenth century it was quite productive.[235] Mining had been carried on in
Cardiganshire since the sixteenth century. The position of Sir Carbery Pryse
has been mentioned, but his great mine of lead and silver at Esgair-hir was
bought by Sir Humphrey Mackworth in 1698. The purchase by Mackworth
'the driving force behind the emerging lead industry in Cardiganshire'[236] led
to a boom time in the industry. From 1710 until the 1730s the industry was
in depression.[237] But with the working of Cwmsymlog and Esgair-mwyn
there was 'a marked revival which lasted into the 1760s, during which period there may have been two thousand miners in the county'.[238]

Yet despairing accounts were made of the failure of the people of Cardiganshire to exploit mining. Despite the 'wealth of Potosi', 'I will tell you'
wrote Lewis Morris to his brother in about February 1757, 'a word or two
about Cardiganshire. This the richest country I ever knew, and the one
which contains the fewest clever or ingenious people. I know several persons
as poor as John, Ben Clyttwr, who have veins of lead ore on their lands: and
yet they will neither work them themselves, nor suffer any other person to

do so'.[239] This was a member of the famous Morris family of Anglesey, one of whom, Richard, with the help of his brother Lewis, was one of the founders of the London Welsh Cymmrydorion.[240] Lewis Morris was a very important and controversial figure in the history of mining in Cardiganshire. After the discovery of good quality ore in the county in 1742, and the appointment of a royal steward because ownership was disputed, Morris who had a good deal of experience, was appointed Deputy and afterwards, in 1752 Agent and Superintendent of His Majesty's Mines in Cardigan and Merioneth. He re-opened an old mine, Esgair-mwyn, and its profitability led to a famous dispute with powerful local squires. This culminated in a violent incident in February 1753, when several hundred people, including the sheriff and two magistrates advanced upon the mine and threatened to kill Morris and his workmen. One magistrate, Herbert Powell, pointed a loaded pistol at his head, and Morris was locked up in Cardigan gaol until 4 April.[241] The outcome of the dispute is complicated but Morris was accused of corruption and was dismissed in 1756. Nevertheless he was appointed as a collector of customs, and he continued his mining work.[242]

In 1744 a new and important mine was opened in Cwnsymlog, the landlord being Thomas Pryse of Gogerddan. About 1750 'the old silver vein was discovered, and for twenty years was hugely profitable'.[243] The profits of this and other mines did not, of course operate to the notable advantage of the peasantry. WJ Lewis has written that 'the second half of the eighteenth century has generally been described as a period of great changes, but this did not apply to Cardiganshire'.[244] 'The last decade of the eighteenth century was a period of severe unemployment in the county and the economic position of the labourer deteriorated considerably'.[245] Nor was it to get any better. 'The (Napoleonic) post war period was a cruel and hard period for the people of Cardiganshire, particularly the labouring classes and the paupers, and wages remained stationary for many years'.[246] In Cardiganshire lead mines 'by the 1760s the number (of lead miners) had suddenly risen to 2,000 with the working of the Cwmsymlog and Esgair-mwyn mines'. But '"during the winter months the carriers were poor farmers living near the mines; the poverty of some of these is shown only too clearly by the comment made in December 1766, that the local carriers were then too weak to do much work"'[247] but 'the long-term increase in Wages from 1750 to 1850 was more than offset by the more rapid rise in the price of goods'.[248]

The largest lead mine in the region outside Cardiganshire was in Carmarthenshire. This was Rhandir mwyn in Llanfair-ar-y-bryn, and was owned by Cawdor of Stackpole. By the end of the eighteenth century the owner is supposed to 'have received £300,000 in clear profit'.[249] Hassall reports that 'the great lead mines, which lye some miles north of Llandovery, (belong) to Mr. Campbell, of Stackpole Court', and he notes too the presence of a furnace for making iron and forges which 'give employment to a considerable number of people'.[250] This is an example of how the landowners engaged in early industrial development as is the case of the operation of a forge until 1760 by the Barlows of Slebech.[251] The Vaughans of Golden Grove 'were the first to experiment with the use of coal for the smelting of iron ore, and took a personal interest in the development of the coal industry'.[252] 'By 1755 Vaughans's mines were in production' at Llangunnor, and in 1756 John Vaughan was discussing 'my coal veins' in the Llanelly area.[253] Hoare records how he saw lead mines in Carmarthenshire in 1796 where:

> Large strings of horses are daily, almost hourly, seen in the summer seasons, conveying the oar (sic) to Caermarthen It is carried in small baggs (sic) two upon a horse, and deposited in the warehouses for that purpose to be shipped from thence in sloops to the smelting houses.[254]

To be set against the stunning profits which accrued to the owners are the conditions of the miners and their families. 'Throughout the history of the industry, wages have been low and the success of many mining ventures owed a great deal to the cheapness of the labour':[255]

> The low level of wages, combined with the irregularity of employment, made it necessary for most lead miners to have supplementary sources of income, and one of these was family labour in the mines. The traditional belief was that the family was an economic as well as a social unit [and] was... firmly held.[256]

Lewis Morris believed that people thought that it was sulphur in the ore which produced a sweetish grass which kills horses. He believed that the powder from the ore causes '"a distemper in their breasts, which they feel like a heavy ball and therefore call it in Welsh Y Belen (The Ball)'". He goes on to describe the horrifying effects of contact with the dust on animals: '"to geese ducks and hens it is fatal, and it is in vain to keep any near a Lead mine"'.[257]

In addition the mines were poorly ventilated, so that even a candle could not be kept alight, the dust led to chronic lung disease, and their clothes were generally wet.[258] Lewis, in a sense, defines the last straw:

Yet another tax on the miner's constitution was the use in the vast majority of mines of wooden ladders for climbing in and out of the workings. After eight hours of heavy labour the task of climbing many long ladders to the surface was a great strain on a man's health and caused many deaths.[259]

In a fairly detailed, and more intimate account the Reverend Warner recounts what he saw in the Cwm-yr-ystwyth lead mines in Cardiganshire in 1797. His guide was a former miner who had crushed his arm in a blasting accident. The owner profited from their operation to some £7,000 a year, although the war had reduced this. To achieve this the miner had to engage in work which was 'laborious and dangerous', and where his income was 'uncertain'. He had to buy his explosives and candles, bore, blast, extract, clean and sort the ore: the latter two tasks being carried out by women and children. And he was paid according to how much usable ore he produced. When, inevitably he failed to do so, he had to borrow from his employer. The whole business did not keep him 'above extreme poverty, and even then:

Frequent injuries happen to him in blasting the rock, and digging the ore; and cold, damp, and vapour, unite in destroying his health, and shortening his life.[260]

In Wales coal had been mined since the fourteenth century. When Malkin visited Pembrokeshire, he notes and describes work in Nolton on the Pembrokeshire coast north of Milford.[261] Much earlier Owen noted that in 1600 coal was eighth in the list of exports from the county, and was used locally because of the shortage of timber for domestic fuel, for smithying, and in kilns. By 1700, it had become the main export. By the end of the eighteenth century coal was being used widely in the locality, and was being exported to other parts of Wales, to England and to Europe. This brought some ostensible prosperity. According to Defoe from his observations in the 1720s, Milford Haven was 'the largest, richest and... most flourishing town in South Wales except Carmarthen'.[262] Indeed, the anthracite and semi anthracite coals of Pembrokeshire were amongst the first to be sold outside the region.[263] This despite Howell's claim that 'the relatively substantial mining activity at Hook was worked by just sixty-five to ninety labourers in 1785–86, while a decade earlier sixty four worked at Begelly colliery, thirty eight at Moreton, and seven at Ridgeway' although 'certain of the colliers and carters would have been small tenant farmers. The Picton castle estate leases, for example, bound various tenants to work in their landlord's coalm-ines at the accustomed wages'.[264]

'There were many small concerns operated by workmen adventurers, singly or in groups, which were always desperately short of capital'[265] and some were in the hands of yeomen.[266] In effect the mines were, as might be expected the preserve of the gentry, some of the owners being the Owens, the Philipps, the Wogans and the Barlows. Hassall describes the operation of the collieries, which ran from Carmarthen Bay to St. Bride's Bay. He first of all notes how they are 'checking the progress of agriculture'. Although this was because there were no canals or railways, the coal and culm was taken by carts pulled by oxen and horses to the ports, ruining the roads. Furthermore, the country people are employed doing this for much of the year, and so neglect the land. And in this 'dissipated life' there are 'frequent opportunities of tippling'.

But in this case the failure to improve is laid squarely on the owners, since amongst them 'there seems nothing wanting but a proper spirit of enterprise'. Even his commendation of Lord Milford, a substantial owner, for his attempt to build a canal is tempered by his conclusion that it did not work.[267] In Carmarthenshire, on the other hand a Mr. Kymer 'obtained an Act of Parliament, for making a canal, with proper railways and wharfs' for handling his collieries which were 'rich and extensive'. And in the same county a canal was being developed from Loughor 'through or near the collieries, mines, and lime works of Landebye, to the Vale of Towy near Llandilo' and beyond.[268] As Hassall points out, the collieries are 'extremely rich', but 'none of the rival collieries of South Wales are equal in quality with the Pembrokeshire coal'. There is no reason therefore why, for example steam engines should not replace horses in clearing water.[269] Apart from a few men, none of whom seem to have been gentry, that lack of imagination and incompetence which typified the owners did not extend beyond tak-ing profit. 'But the interest of Pembrokeshire landowners was not enough: in England at this time capital was being poured into the coal industry by progressive merchants'.[270]

There was still little improvement in the county 20 years later. The coal was still excellent. 'It is stone coal, and being sweet, is therefore much in request, and preferred for malting, and in general it is of the best quality'. Not a lot had changed in the years since Hassall wrote:

Canals and railways are unknown in these districts, and all of the carriage of the coal and culm is by carts from the collieries. No coal county has less advantage from mechanical improvements than Pembrokeshire, and none require it more in its present state'.[271]

As late as 1853 Mackworth the Inspector of Mines reported that little had been altered since Owen's day – that is in the early seventeenth century – and that the mines were dangerous and unhealthy. There was, for example, less than the quantity of air needed for the health of the colliers.[272] And the mines may have been, in Hassall's words 'extremely rich', but predictably the miners lived in extreme poverty. In Cardiganshire 'earnings… were lower for most of the eighteenth century than in the north eastern counties of Flint, Denbigh and Montgomery', and in addition 'were paid irregularly', and they had to cope with the truck system. As late as 1843 the poverty was again compared unfavourably with England and nine years later it was reported by an impeccable source, the Inspector of Mines, that they lived in houses of a mixture of mud, road scrapings, and stones with thatched roofs. The two rooms were divided by earth or boards, with constant fumes inside caused by fires which were always alight.[273]

A little distance south, on the borders of Cardiganshire and Pembrokeshire, there were seemingly modest tinplate works in about 1770, and by the end of the century they had come under the control of Sir Benjamin Hammet, like so many of his predecessors a wealthy Englishman. During his ownership over 200 people were employed working the material which was shipped up the Teifi from Cardigan, and which ' various stupendous operations' carried on there were witnessed by the Reverend Warner on his second 'walk' in 1798.[274] After Sir Benjamin died at the turn of the century, in 1806 the works closed. Hammet's mines were recorded in the Report by Lloyd and Turnor and they added 'I know of no other manufactory in the county of Cardigan'.[275] In the same district slate quarrying began at the end of the eighteenth century. This lasted longer than the tinplate works, and by the Census of 1861 between 80 and 100 people out of 1236 in the parish of Cilgerran were employed in the quarries.[276]

The last noticeable commercial activity engaged in by a few of the gentry in the period under discussion was shipping, but this was relatively insignificant, although squires invested in the trade.[277] Haverfordwest exported coal to London amongst other things, and Carmarthen too was a busy port. There is some evidence of export, perhaps on quite a large scale. In 1806 Mavor reported that:

At Aberystwyth a custom-house has been erected, in consequence of the increasing trade. The exports are oak bark, birch ditto, lead ore, blackjack, copper ore, iron, corn, butter, poultry, slates and Welsh ale. The imports are chiefly balk, deals, hemp, pitch, tar, rosin, Russian iron, groceries, flax, porter, cyder, wine, brandy, rum, Geneva &c. The vessels from this port trade to Ireland, Liverpool, Bristol, and some few to London.[278]

Jenkins explains one of the key reasons why Aberystwyth became so important:

Aberystwyth was given a new lease of life when the Customs House was transferred there from Aberdyfi in 1763. Boosted by the considerable herring trade, the port became a major depot in the maritime trade of west Wales.[279]

The herring trade was especially important. In the 1740s 'there were as many as fifty nine small sloops engaged in the herring-fishing trade at Aberystwyth'.[280]

Unlike eastern Wales, which in the nineteenth century saw an explosion of the industry which had its roots in similar early stages of industrialisation in England, in the west the nineteenth century saw a petering out of industry, except in isolated cases. And so throughout the eighteenth and nineteenth centuries the bulk of the population of south west Wales were engaged in agriculture but although it was mainly at a subsistence level, even in the eighteenth century agricultural produce 'was exported in considerable quantities from ports such as Carmarthen'.[281] Yet seemingly the people were very resistant to any suggestions as to how it might be improved. One authority claims that Welsh peasant farming was a century behind that of England, for predictable reasons: isolation and language barriers being two.[282] The general opinion about agriculture in Wales was that it was in the word commonly used, 'defective'. Arthur Young, writing of Glamorgan in the 1760s, believed that 'the husbandry is the most imperfect I ever met with'. Farmers did not fold their sheep which 'is so extravagantly stupid that I was astonished at it', while they ridiculed a farmer from England, and 'thought him really mad' because he grew turnips, and sold them at considerable profit, which left them 'surprised'.[283] Nevertheless Dyfed was an agricultural area, and it was farming upon which the bulk of people relied for their existence.

An important source of information about agriculture in Wales at the end of the eighteenth century is a number of reports to the recently established Board of Agriculture. Its energetic president Sir John Sinclair, and secretary Arthur Young set out to collect information about the state of agriculture in England and Wales, and as part of this process reports for Pembrokeshire, Carmarthenshire and Cardiganshire were submitted in 1794. The report from Pembrokeshire, to which reference has already been made, was by Charles Hassall. In the same year he wrote a report for Carmarthenshire. Thomas Lloyd and the Reverend Turnor submitted the report for Cardiganshire.

Leaving aside the fact that Hassall could have made an interesting change to the course of history by his shooting of the eminent General Sir Thomas Picton in the throat in a duel, Hassall was an expert on agriculture. He was not one of those about whom Cymro might have complained in the *Cambrian Register* – he constantly uses 'our' to describe Pembrokeshire – since he was, at one time, the land steward of the Llanstinan estate in the north of the county, a post from which he was dismissed. His older brother farmed Kil Rhiwau (variously spelled) in the north of the county, and who, in about 1802, got a 'premium' from the Society for the Encouragement of the Arts for reclaiming about 1000 acres 'of high uplands that might with sufficient propriety be termed *mountains*' (his italics).[284] The Reverend David Turnor was active in establishing the Society for the Encouragement of Agriculture and Industry, and he was especially noted for his recovery of boggy land.[285]

Hassall's reports on both the counties with which he dealt are substantially the same. He echoes every account of agriculture in the region at the time, but does so without rancour, and suggests improvements even though 'the slow progress of agricultural improvements in this county, make some gentlemen despair of its being carried out to any considerable length during the present age'.[286] The root of the problem lay in the system of letting the farms, which he estimated as an average 200 acres in size. The land is 'always let at rack rent', and 'the terms of the leases commonly granted upon lands in this district, is for three lives, and the life of the survivor'.[287] In addition the tenant was obliged to repair houses, fences and gates, and to pay all rates and taxes.[288] Furthermore, there were severe restrictions on the operation of the farm. He could not plough meadowland without permission, dung, hay and straw had to be used solely upon the land and not sold, and he could not cut trees, or underwoods, which belonged to the landlord together with mineral rights.[289] The predictable result is most that tenants neglected the buildings, and certainly would not erect new ones. Nor did the system encourage them to improve the land. This seemed to most tenants to be risky, since the lease might not be renewed, or, upon its expiry the rent might be increased. He reported the same fear in Carmarthenshire where 'they are afraid to let the land go out of tillage in good heart, lest their landlord should raise their rent at the expiration of the lease'.[290]

It may have been the fact that this was the disincentive to cultivate well, or ignorance, or fear of the ridicule of their neighbours if they copied 'English fashions' in Pembrokeshire.[291] Or of 'adopting English fashions into their mode of farming, lest their neighbours should laugh at them':[292] an echo of Young's observation in Glamorgan. Although the reputation of the 'English' was not much enhanced when locals saw the results of an experiment to cross a Leicestershire breed with the local Pembrokeshire 'Castlemartin' Black. This produced beasts which were 'sluggish... unfit for labour... slow in feeding... coarse in their flesh.'[293]

And so it was with horses. The attempt to cross the local hunter with full blood Arab horses 'produced a miserable race of undersized feeble animals, that were not fit for any purpose whatever.'[294] There were though successful experiments with cross breeding with working horses, and sheep. In respect to horses, it was reported that Carmarthenshire gentry sent their mares to be covered by the superior stallions of Pembrokeshire.[295] But it is not to be expected that the farmer in eighteenth century Pembrokeshire would be equable in his judgement. As far as arable land was concerned, there was a poverty of production which followed upon 'no systematic rotation of crops' but 'sagacity or caprice' as a policy. It is 'oats-oats-oats, as long as oats will grow'. This 'ends in weeds and disappointment'.[296] All of this despite the claim to 'the character of a better system of management' and where:

> the farmers plume themselves upon a superiority of management; rather than upon a superiority of soil, to which I am inclined to think they are much better entitled'.[297]

In Carmarthenshire 'the prodigious havoc that has been made of late years among the woods is truly alarming' especially since the district is 'in a peculiar manner adapted to the growth of timber'.[298] The Vale of Towy has been 'driven by the plough to the most deplorable state of sterility',[299] and in the same county 'by far the greater number (of farm houses) are in very sad condition... and it would be difficult for an English farmer to conceive the shifts and contrivances made use of, as substitutes for proper accommodations'.[300] Hassall is fair minded enough though to concede that there are some good practices. In Carmarthenshire 'the harvest work of this district is performed with a neatness and security worth noticing – the barley and oats, as well as the wheat, is all bound into sheaves'[301] while: 'just commendation due to many of the farmers of Pembrokeshire, whose minds are open to the obvious advantages of a better mode of husbandry, and whose farms exhibit the pleasing tokens of better management'.[302] In Carmarthenshire he commends 'instances of better management' furnished by the estates of Dynevor and Golden Grove and 'many other gentlemen of the Vale of Towy', while Philipps of Court Henry was 'fast approaching to perfection.[303]

But his overall judgement is that he is describing 'the worst sort of rural management that can be conceived'.[304] In Pembrokeshire he draws attention to the fact that: 'the general manure of the district is lime, which abounds in the southern parts of the county, and is carried by water to the country above the mountains; also by land to the interior parts of the county.[305] Lloyd and Turnor make the same criticism about practices in Cardiganshire. The farmers do not rotate 'but rip out everything'.[306] And in Cardiganshire it is reported that 'I am sorry to observe that these occupying proprietors, are, in general, as backward in their improvements, as any of the tenantry'.[307]

Hassall goes on to describe, and mostly condemn the tools used on the farms. 'The Welch (sic) plough... is in common use... and perhaps a more awkward unmeaning tool, is not to be found in any civilized country'.[308] Again this same point is made by Lloyd and Turnor, 'the ploughs are too bad for description'.[309] Walter Davies too notes that of the ploughs of Dyfed there are no 'models of greater antiquity'.[310] 'They may plume themselves with the idea, that they now use a plough the very *fac simile* (his italics) of that described by Virgil nearly two thousand years ago.'[311] Hassall writes that 'The Welch cart is a bad one' and unsuitable for the roads, and 'the reap hook is a bad harvest tool', which should be replaced with the sickle.[312] 'The spades, shovels, and mattocks used in hedge and ditch work are convenient enough and the labourers here use them adroitly'.[313] While conceding the advantages of using oxen in teams – they are cheaper to keep than horses – he advocates a change to the latter.[314] Hassall says of Carmarthenshire; 'no country exhibits more wretched conveniences for farm uses, than are generally to be seen in this district'.[315] In Cardiganshire Lloyd and Turnor are equally critical, going on to say that 'the implements of husbandry are scarce on a par with the wretched management I have already described[316]... The plough and the cart are particularly faulty'.[317]

There were attempts to improve agriculture both at national and local levels. An Agricultural Society was established in Brecon in 1755.[318] There was the establishment of the Board which commissioned these reports. Fortuitously, its foundation coincided with the outbreak of war, but it was not immediately to have any effect on the escalating shortage of food, and the consequent social disturbances. But before this, in 1784, William Knox,

Hassall's former employer was the patron of 'A Society for the Encouragement of Agriculture, Manufactures, and Industry', which lasted for half a dozen years, and Lloyd and Turnor observed that when they did their report there was an Agricultural Society in Cardiganshire,[319] although in Carmarthenshire 'the slow progress... in a country like this seems to dishearten many of its members and well wishers'.[320] Paradoxically local agricultural societies had been established in Cardigan, Carmarthen and Pembroke before 1775.[321]

As in the discussion about the political and social worth of the squirearchy in Chapter One, it is fair to point to the highly unusual examples of those who tried to develop agriculture in Dyfed. Individual landowners gained reputations as improvers. One such was Thomas Johnes of Hafod in Cardiganshire, who died in 1816. Even allowing for the inevitable hyperbole of his obituary, as well as building decent accommodation for his tenants, he introduced several initiatives to improve agriculture in his 'forlorn county'.[322]

One of Hassall's recommended ways to improve was to encourage more enclosure of land. He takes as his exemplar Campbell of Stackpole (Cawdor), who obtained an Act of Parliament as we have seen, to enclose a piece of fen land of several hundred acres to add to his enormous 16,000 acre estate in the southern, most fertile part of Pembrokeshire; indeed this area has always been regarded as one of the most fertile in the whole of Wales. But, as we shall see, this phenomenon did not benefit the bulk of the people. The landowners' decisions were based solely on self interest. In Cardiganshire Lloyd and Turnor note the adverse effect on sheep: 'Owing to the spirit of enclosing, the flocks of sheep are considerably diminished, as fatal to young growth in the hedges, but never was a soil better suited to them'.[323]

One of the more colourful, and singular features of life in eighteenth and early nineteenth south west Wales was the cattle drover. During his visit amongst the 'virgin descendants of the ancient Britons',[324] the Reverend Warner writes of how:

> as we proceeded, our progress was frequently retarded by numerous droves of black cattle from Pembrokeshire and Carmarthenshire, travelling through the Passage to be transported across the Severn, and driven to the markets of Bristol, and the other large towns of Somerset, Glocestershire (sic) and Wilts (sic).[325]

The scale of the business was considerable. 'Thirty thousand black cattle from the summer and autumn fairs of Wales went, every year, in huge herds through Herefordshire towards south east England.[326] The consequence was that by the time Wales 'had become an orderly country, such wealth as there was consisted largely in cattle'.[327] And it was not only cattle which were exported in such huge quantities. Sheep, pigs and geese were sent. The drover became a legendary figure. Sometimes vilified, usually by clergymen, for alleged dishonesty[328] and heavy drinking.

But the drovers did more than just move cattle, vital though that was. They handled large sums of money and carried out financial transactions for wealthy people. In 1613 Sir John Wynn told the Privy Council that he could pay his bill for his baronetcy 'when the drovers return from Kent'.[329] In a letter to Prince Rupert in January 1644, Archbishop Williams supported a petition from the drovers since they are 'the Spanish fleet which brings us what little gold we possess'.[330] A major financial initiative, caused by the need to avoid carrying large sums of money, was the establishment of banks. The oft quoted example is that of the Black Ox bank, founded by a drover in 1799 in Llandovery, Carmarthenshire. Their role was very important as a conduit of information, gathered from the towns through which they passed:

he reported the trend of political feeling, he had heard extracts from the English papers, and above all from the point of view of the mistress of the house, he would even be able to give her an idea of prevailing fashions.[331]

There was much comment at the time and since, about the context within which the poor of Wales lived. There were the constant battles about the raising of rents. They were at the mercy of the vagaries of the markets, with ever present worries about having enough food. And then there was the huge increase in the numbers of enclosures at the end of the eighteenth and the beginning of the nineteenth centuries. Howell points out that 'before 1797 Enclosure Acts had been passed in only five out of the 13 counties. But between 1797 and 1817 some 75 Enclosure Bills were passed'.[332] Howell is not alone in making the observation that 'tenants felt… insecure and lived in terror.[333] In England Hobsbawm and Rudé observe, discussing the classic work of the Hammonds:

Those who had built a cottage on some patch of common or waste lands keeping a pig or two, a cow and maybe some geese, and to collect firewood or whatnot from them could not but be disastrously hit by their division into pieces of exclusive and fenced-off private property in which they no longer had a share.[334]

As for the habitations of the people, these seemed to be amongst the worse in rural Britain. The English peasantry in the eighteenth and nineteenth centuries also mainly lived in squalor, although conditions did vary from region to region. And 'neither health nor decency could be preserved in the shattered hovels which half the poor of the kingdom were obliged to put up with opined Nathaniel Kent in 1775'.[335] The same source quotes the steward to the Marquis of Bath who concludes that 'there is only one chamber to hold all the miserable beds of the miserable family'.

And Cobbett wrote too of 'hovels made of mud and straw: bits of glass, or of old cast of windows without frames or hinges', and noted the contrast 'with the size and prosperity of the farms'. Hobsbawm and Rudé quote a visiting American in the 1840s as observing that the English country labourer was 'servile, broken-spirited and severely straitened in their means of living… everything conspired to impoverish and demoralise them' and compares their state unfavourably with that of the French.[336] Despite some improvement by enlightened landowners in England in the nineteenth century, Wales remained squalid, as was pointed out by a parliamentary committee in the 1890s: 'bad as the cottage accommodation is in some parts of England, it is far worse in Wales'.[337] Indeed the comparison which is most frequently made is with the rural Ireland of the day. Arthur Young was one who reported that the cottages near Haverfordwest 'were not a whit better than Irish cabins, without an equal show of pigs, poultry and cows'.[338] This was a commonly made observation by visitors to every part of Wales.

The occasional 'gleaner' would detect, in the midst of such squalor, a happy note. The Rev. J. Evans in his observations, describes a Welsh cottage in Carmarthenshire which was as grim as any. But after noting that the 'fine' children were 'almost in a state of nudity', he was invited into the house. It was:

partly formed by an excavation in the slate rock, and partly by walls of mud mixed with chopped rushes… a wall of turfs for fuel served as a partition for the bed-room, furnished with a bed of heath and dried rushes in one corner… The furniture was as necessity dictated: some loose stones formed the grate: two large ones, with a plank across, supplied the place of chairs… (the wife) was as happy as any of the *great folk* (his italics), for that (her husband) loved her and his children, and worked very hard, and they wanted for nothing he could get for them...

She then goes on to explain that she had learned that they should accept 'that state of life in which it has pleased God to call us (and) we shall, after death, change this poor uncertain life for a better, where we shall be happy for ever: and the frequent internment of our friends and neighbours informs us daily this event can be at no great distance.'

The visitor exclaims that he is 'astonished at so much good sense and piety, where I so little expected to find it'. He also observes that 'there did not appear anything like the misery and filth observable in the dwellings of the English poor'.[339] In Carmarthenshire in 1775 a visitor noted that:

The mud houses in these Parts are of most wretched Construction. The Walls do not consist of Lath and Plaister, as in Suffolk, etc., but are entirely of Earth, and that not of Straw wrought up with it, but sometimes with a layer of straw... most of the Cottages are destitute of glass windows, instead of which neat Lattice-work.[340]

Nor were things any different in North Wales:

One smoky hearth, for it should not be styled a kitchen, and one damp-litter cell, for it cannot be called a bedroom, are frequently all the space allotted to a labourer, his wife and four or five children... Three-fourths of the victims of the putrid fever perish in the mephitic air of these dwellings[341]

The standard text on the history of Welsh housing is by Peate. And he is another of those who writes that 'close in all details is the comparison between the cottages of Wales and Ireland'.[342] But his principal interest is in the architecture, and the relationship of dwellings to the life of the community. Inevitably, as is common in Welsh writing of the earlier part of the twentieth century, he manifests a certain romanticism, when he writes:

A less pleasant feature of this transformation in country housing was the introduction, principally after the European War 1914–1918, of 'council houses'. In many instances these replaced old cottages which were native to their environment however much their internal accommodation could be criticised.[343]

A more recent utilitarian view is 'perhaps it is as well that the latter have vanished'.[344] And most certainly the 'internal accommodation' could be criticised, even by the standards of the eighteenth and nineteenth centuries. The style of cottage in west Wales seems to have been unchanging for several hundred years before the middle of the nineteenth century, but there was no major transformation of houses until the twentieth. The traditional cottage was described in evidence to a Royal Commission of 1867, and since the description is so universal, and indisputable, although in this case of 'South' Wales, it is worth setting out in full:

> the state of the labourers' cottages is very bad; badly constructed; one floor and one room on that floor, partly divided by some article of furniture; damp walls; earth floors; smoky chimnies; a small window or two, often no more than a square foot, and never opened; no out-offices, or any accommodation whatever... (it) is a rectangular building about 20 feet by 12 (inside measurement) with walls of mud (clay and straw mixed) or stone about 8 feet high. The mud cottage is almost always covered with straw thatch. In the middle of the front wall is the door with a Small window on each side. Running back from each side of the door for 6 or 8 feet, and almost as high as the door are partitions, often formed by the back of a box bed or chest of drawers, by means of which partitions the inside space is divided into two small rooms, in one of which is a wide fireplace surmounted by a conical chimney. The whole interior is open to the roof, except where boards or wattled hurdles are stuck across heads of the walls to support childrens' beds. The floor is usually of mud or puddled clay. The only outside office is the pigsty, generally built against the end of the cottage. Such is a description of probably four-fifths of the labourers' cottages in the districts I visited.[345]

The Reverend J Evans too wrote of the seemingly exceptionally poor state of the people of both Carmarthen and Cardiganshire when he visited in 1803 writing that: 'Indeed the common people throughout this country (sic) are not only poor but appear completely dejected, as if they had given up every hope of being otherwise'.[346]

It was no better some 40 years later when Thomas Campbell Foster, who reported on the Rebecca riots for *The Times* on 7 October 1843 was horrified by what he saw. And again, his first hand description is so vivid and immediate, that it is worth quoting at length:

> I entered several farm labourer's cottages by the roadside, out of curiosity to see the actual condition of the people, and found them mud hovels, the floors of mud and full of holes, without chairs or tables, generally half filled with peat packed up in every corner. Beds there were none: nothing but loose straw and filthy rags upon them. Peat fires on the floor in a corner filling the cottages with smoke, and three or four children huddled around them. In the most miserable part of St. Giles, in no part of England, did I ever witness such abject poverty.[347]

So the Welsh cottage was based upon a single room, where, in 1797, and for many years afterwards 'the people, cows, asses, hogs and poultry all live in one apartment'.[348] These were the dwellings which the Duke of Rutland saw, describing some as 'a solitary and wretched farm, now and then enclosed with steep and bare turf-banked fences'.[349] Even at the end of the nineteenth century, at a time when many English landowners were raising the standard of accommodation on their estates, this was a 'a tendency notably absent in Wales'. The witness who reported this added:

> It would seem that bad as the cottage accommodation is in some parts of England, it is far worse in Wales. The general standard of accommodation is lower, and there is much less evidence of progress and improvement.[350]

Nor did things improve as the nineteenth century drew to a close. There was a serious agricultural depression in 1885–86, a Land Commission was set up, and some of the evidence submitted to it will be discussed in the Epilogue. Thomas Gee, a pioneer publisher through whose endeavours the Commission was called into being had pointed out 'the desperate plight of the Welsh Farmer'. Once again comparisons between England and Wales were central in the evidence. Between 1815 and 1889 the total rent in Wales increased by 70 per cent, compared with 5 per cent in England. By 1890 in Wales there had been a reduction of 5 per cent, 'while that year saw a reduction in England of 20 per cent'. There was also lowering of the price of corn and a devaluing of the price of stock as well as that phenomenon so well re-membered in the folk tradition of west Wales 'the game nuisance aggravated by the organised terrorism of English gamekeepers'.[351] It is not surprising, in the light of such conditions that there is an almost complete absence of description of life by the poor themselves. As Colin Thomas points out in his excellent effort 'to rescue from oblivion an even more humble social stratum, that of the agricultural labourer', there has to be reliance on the employer as a source of information'.[352]

The principal variant on the one room cottage was the long-house. This was a solid stone based or entirely stone built building, which by the early nineteenth century provided living space for people in one half, and cattle and other animals in the other. These were separated by a door, through which there was a feeding walk. At different times and in different places the house might be divided into a kitchen, living room or parlour, and a dairy. There might also be stairs leading to a loft, where people would sleep. This pattern of dwelling, together with the cottage formed the most typical and widespread rural, fairly prosperous housing in Wales until the twentieth century. Even during the course of that century smallholders lived in build-ings which were recognisably long houses, even though the door dividing animals and people may have been taken away, and hearth fires replaced by stoves and ovens. Peate points out that during his research in the 1930s there were still 'a fair number of long-houses in Cardiganshire, and that 'sev-eral good examples of long-houses survive in Carmarthenshire'.[353] The farm-ers' houses were rather better throughout the eighteenth and nineteenth centuries, but were only more elaborate versions of the same basic design.

In the eighteenth and nineteenth centuries the farmers, labourers and the small number of industrial workers of west Wales lived in abject pov-erty. In the mid eighteenth century the poverty of the people of Dyfed was described, from first hand observation by Griffith Jones of Llanddowror, a description which was repeated over the next 150 years. And, it may be noted, he is here talking mainly of farmers:

> What I humbly suggest concerning the growing poverty of the low people, at least in these parts of Wales (notwithstanding the affluence of some) may appear from the many tenants that break yearly, the many untenanted farms, and the general complaints of most landlords for the very bad payment of their rents. These are very undeniable testimonies that farmers are very much reduced in their substance, owing, partly, perhaps, to the stagnation of markets for passing away their cattle. This being the case, their dependents, the day labourers,

who cannot be imployed by them as usual, and the many that cannot labour, but lived in benevolence, must be extremely reduced; yes, too many of them are reduced to the want of their daily bread.[354]

One of Jones' severest critics a clergyman John Evans attacked this account, saying that he had been 'to a very judicious farmer in Wales to know the truth of this; and he assures me, that Welsh cattle never passed away in such large quantities, or at so great prices, as they have ever since the distemper among the cattle of England'.[355] Such hunger was found throughout Wales:

> For dinner you will see a small farmer have half a salt herring, with potatoes and butter-milk (very poor food for a working man); his wife and family must content themselves with butter-milk and potatoes or perhaps after the farmer has finished his part herring, there will be a scramble amongst the youngsters for the bones to suck as a treat.[356]

A similar diet is described by Hassall in Pembrokeshire, where the labourers lived on cheese, bread, milk, and vegetables, herrings and poor quality veal in season. In 1801, 15 per cent of the Welsh lived on wheat, compared with England and Wales as a whole where 65–70 per cent lived on wheat.[357] Even the barley and oats which they grew did not help them much. This was partly because the farmers did not have granaries in which to store the corn – another example of the improvidence of which Hassall despaired – and the consequence, which was that they had to sell to corn dealers for whatever they could get. The questions which he might have asked were about the rent system, and whether or not it was worth it, and whether the damp climate in Pembrokeshire made the storing of corn impossible. The best people could hope for was barley bread, rarely wheat bread, and oat bread was out of the question 'except for porridge and flummery'.[358] By midsummer, he wrote, the barley is finished, and imported grain is so expensive that the labourers are 'reduced to a state of distress, which call aloud for the assistance of the affluent'.[359]

As to meat, despite the vast numbers of good quality cattle which were sent to England for fattening, the common people very rarely ate beef. Cobbett, having encountered two thousand cattle en route from Pembrokeshire to Sussex, observed that 'most of them were heifers in calf, the very thing… for a cottager'.[360] Although the labourer might keep a pig, it was generally to sell it.[361] Although labourers' diet was marginally better by the 1870s in the south west – they ate more wheaten bread for example – they could still not afford butcher's meat.[362] But overall not much had changed.

The diet was similar in Cardiganshire where potatoes with barley bread was 'the chief sustenance of the poor, and are 'universally cultivated'.[363] Lloyd and Turnors' summary was that 'the earnings of the poor are certainly of late years inadequate to their expences (sic).[364] In the same county Lloyd and Turnor report that 'their pay bears no proportion to the price of provisions, or the labour they perform' Their chief food is barley bread and few of them have cows. They go on to list the other features of peasant life, and after the usual depressing recital conclude 'you will be able then to judge of the real condition of our peasantry'.[365]

In the case of Cardiganshire, which merely exemplifies the position in Wales, by 1794 'the price of barley was considered exorbitant'. In the next year Lord Lisburne was informed that 'the Lower Class… (were) much discontented and restless at the present exorbitant Price of all Grain in the County'.[366] The end of the Napoleonic wars saw a series of bad harvests because of the weather, and combined with a period of 'severe agricultural depression, as in the years 1816 and 1817, the result was calamitous'.[367] The farmers of course suffered too, but the worst off were the labourers. In 1817 it was reported that labourers in some of the Cardiganshire parishes were 'from the scarcity of fuel, clothes and food combined… reduced to the last extremity of wretchedness, want, and misery'.[368]

Yet even in such wretched circumstances the people maintained some degree of religion and a concomitant culture. Erasmus Saunders, a Pembrokeshire born priest working in England, wrote of west Wales as early as the 1720s that: 'There is, I believe, no part of the nation more inclined to be religious, and to be delighted with it than the poor inhabitants of these mountains'. He describes how they travel 'over cold and bleak hills' for three or four miles on foot to attend services 'often to be disappointed' (by the non appearance of a clergyman). One of his more remarkable reports is how, in the absence of any Welsh schools, and only an occasional English one, they teach each other to read and 'it is by this means that most or all of them do attain the knowledge of reading and writing in their native language'. Even more arresting is his account of how 'they are naturally addicted to poetry', and they compose *halsingod*, which were carols 'of a religious or moral character'. Indeed singing seems to have been an integral part of their lives at home and on public occasions. When, for example they visited graves they would kneel, put candles on the graves and sing *halsingod*.[369]

Despite such glimpses of dignity, the fact is that when it came to the basic matter of survival, nothing would improve, although there were exceptions during the nineteenth century. There were pockets where conditions became better, usually temporarily, and there was slight improvement in the 1830s, but more common were the reports of, for example, 'the distressed condition of many of the inhabitants of Cardigan and its district'.[370] Indeed it would not be until well into the twentieth century that there would be any substantial improvement in the lives of the common people in Wales.

During the eighteenth and nineteenth centuries those lives, in material terms were as poor as any in Europe, and a good deal poorer than some. In contemplating the description of the turbulence which follows in the next chapter, a central mystery must be why there was not much more.

3

THE EXPLOSION OF PROTEST

Cym'rwch Fara i chwi yn Drych
Ni chewch ond edrych arno.
Now distant view the bread you
see but must not dare to taste.
John Jones (Jac Glan-y-gors)[371]

In the eighteenth and nineteenth centuries many parts of Britain were the scenes of violence. Protests 'appeared all the time on the pages of the local press – (the peasant) protested all the time and most of the time very effectively indeed'.[372] This is how Peacock describes rural life in eastern England in the late eighteenth and early nineteenth centuries. He adds that:

> no year in the first half of the nineteenth century was a quiet year in the east. Every year was violent, and the amount of violence that took place was very great indeed.[373]

Some of the causes were:

> enclosures, bad housing, ill health and the sight of increasing prosperity among the farmers as the fens were improved, the sight of which made men 'doubly poor' as George Crabbe said – these were the constant background to half a century of violence.[374]

Such discontent in one region of England was replicated throughout Britain. Nor was discontent and rioting about corn a new phenomenon which appeared for the first time in the eighteenth century. Beloff notes that 'such

years as 1527, 1551, 1587, 1596, 1622–23, and 1630 saw widespread disorder and attacks on dealers and others suspected of hoarding corn'.[375]

In Wales there were riots in 1709, 1713, 1728, 1740, 1752, 1757–58,
1765–66, 1778, 1783 and 1789.[376] Yet at the same time some extraordinary
claims have been made about the peaceable nature of the Welsh. In 1820
it was claimed that 'although England, Scotland and Ireland had riots and
commotions, Wales remained faithful to the government'.[377] 'Alun' in the
North Wales Chronicle of 7 August 1832 observed 'the tranquillity of Wales
"in these days of sedition and threatened anarchy"'.[378] This latter comment,
for one, is startling in view of the fact that there had been major riots in both
Carmarthen and Merthyr only the year before, in 1831. In reality Wales had
never been an exception and throughout the country there were incidents
which the authorities sometimes had great difficulty in controlling. More
typical than people like 'Alun' would like to admit was the small village of
Prendergast, nowadays part of Haverfordwest, which had an especially fear-
some reputation. In 1771 an attempt to arrest a man in a public house for
debt led to the arrival of a mob who threatened to murder the complainants
and the bailiffs. A second attempt, this time with armed men, also failed.
The cry went up from the mob that 'Prendergast was not so easily managed!'[379]

The coast of west Wales was especially lawless.[380] There was, for example,
a major riot in Newquay in Cardiganshire in 1704, albeit over smuggling.
It was described as 'a very mutinous riot' in which a man was killed and
an 'official indicted for murder'.[381] Almost 100 years later things were the
same along the coast. In 1801 Lady Cawdor wrote a letter in which she
describes how her husband and three others, having heard that a vessel was
coming into Freshwater East with contraband spirits, tried to intervene.
They were badly beaten, and 'Lord C has been very ill in consequence'.[382]
Another visitor in 1811 noted how Manorbier castle 'has been appropriated
to smuggling, on a most daring scale… the person concerned… used to
fill the subterranean apartments and towers with spirits.[383] There was also
widespread wrecking where:

> they strip even children and females, when dead, cut off their fingers,
> and tear their ears for the sake of the clothes and jewels! And leave
> their naked bodies exposed on the beach, for interment (sic) to the
> returning ocean![384]

In the Pembrokeshire Spring Assizes of 1769 five yeomen from Castlemartin were indicted for stealing from a ship wrecked in Freshwater

bay.[385] Despite such violence, there is a view that smuggling should be included as a variety of 'political' protest deserving the status of one 'of the traditions of resistance, carried on by the poor, to the laws and institutions of their rulers'.[386]

The question as to whether there was any common denomination between such activities, and whether they were of political significance is the quintessence of this book. Can they be related to events such as those described in a letter from Swansea dated 6 February 1793[387] and signed by the Sheriff and a number of justices? During disturbances it was said that although the people are well paid, they seem to be acting in solidarity with those they "ignorantly suppose" to be suffering elsewhere. 'Several hundreds' gathered forcing their way into farmers' houses to insist upon a fixed price for corn. The effect of a rising of such numbers, it was noted, would be disastrous in neighbouring counties. They begged for two troops of horse or at least something. On 10 February the Sheriff acknowledged the despatch of a detachment of dragoons. Also at the same time a resolution was passed by the people about corn and bread in which they sneered at the 'very fine Tongued Gentry'.[388]

On 1 October 1800 it was reported from Merthyr, in later years to be the scene of momentous disorder, that 'the riot is at an end'.[389] But there was more trouble in April 1801 when the 'workmen of the Iron works on the Hills' put out an address which proposed that they should extricate 'ourselves and the rising Generation from the Tyranny and the Oppression of the times', and that they should 'be of one mind as one man', which came close to the cry of the Hook miners discussed below. Two Merthyr miners were hanged on that occasion.[390] The Glamorgan county magistrates offered £50 for the name of the writer of this 'inflammatory address'.[391]

In the south west there was a long history of radicalism, discontent, violence, and the catch-all 'sedition'. Jones records several early examples in Pembrokeshire, including that of a Yeoman Morris who was indicted in Haverfordwest in 1613 for publicly stating, upon the death of Prince Henry, that he hoped the next news would that the king 'may be poisoned also'.[392] And Pembrokeshire had its share of recusants. In 1613, and 1620 a number of them were paraded before the Sessions, and in 1625 two men from Tenby were sent to prison for 'speaking disloyall words'.[393] Later in the century, in 1642, Quakers and dissenters were charged with holding unlawful meetings.

The civil wars in the meantime produced a substantial amount of violence, with charge and counter-charge as the centres of power shifted. The accession of William III provoked several important Pembrokeshire squires to assemble in Narbeth 'armed with swords and pistols, tending to disturb the peace'. They included members of the families of the Barlows, Laugharnes, and Wogans. The same families were prominent in an action in 1693 when, having been appointed magistrates, they refused to take the oath.[394] Thus the persisting pro Stuart empathy remained.

In the late eighteenth and early nineteenth centuries protest in Wales had many causes, of which the most important were resentment over enclosures and simple hunger. The turn of the century saw the culmination of the deterioration which had been going on for some years. Its central feature was a lowering of the quality of life of poorer people. During the second half of the eighteenth century 'more and more of the sharply rising population entered the ranks of the poor'.[395] Above all 'the year 1801 thus marks the peak of a period of acute inflation in the prices of arable products'[396] – the most striking movement – of annual wheat prices for England and Wales… was the very large rise during the revolutionary wars.[397]

Hobsbawm and Rudé go on to point out that the farmers by then were used to making a lot of money, and determined to continue to do so, by depressing wages, restructuring the method of remuneration, and reducing staff. In Wales at the end of the eighteenth century and especially during the wars 'there was a passion for raising rents, shortening leases, consolidating farms, and enclosing land hitherto little used'.[398]

The effect of all of this can be illustrated by events in Carmarthen. This had been an important town for centuries. It was described in a chantry certificate of 1548 as 'a fair market town, having a fine haven, and the fairest town in all South Wales', and it was important enough to be described as 'the commercial capital of the south west'.[399] It was also the site of a very influential Dissenting Academy, set up by the Presbyterian Trust which was attended, amongst others by the pioneer educators, Thomas Charles of Bala and Griffith Jones of Llanddowror. A visitor in the early part of the eighteenth century described Carmarthen as 'the London of Wales'.[400] But from the middle of the eighteenth century its commerce was often interrupted by violent confrontation. During that period, and for many years afterwards, it was necessary to station troops in the town.

In 1796 an MP was illegally elected and there was a gun battle in the streets and the people barricaded themselves in their houses.[401] In March 1798 the Pembrokeshire militia was in the town, and they were there again in April 1800. At about the same time it was reported that 'a number of colliers were coming to cause a riot (which) created great consternation in the market. Drums beat to arms, soldiers were called out, which kept them away'.[402] On 2 May 1800 Spurrell wrote that the 'town full of soldiers,

seventeen different recruiting parties here at the same time'.[403] On May Day
of the following year, 1801:

> the town was full of soldiers – amongst them were the West Glamor-
> gan Volunteers, Swansea and Gower Legion and two battalions of the
> Carmarthenshire Volunteers… not until 1804 did the town begin to
> become normal, and the military were gradually withdrawn.[404]

Many sets of thanks were given to the troops 'for their very orderly, peaceable and soldierlike good conduct during the time they were on duty in
this borough'. Thanks were to be expressed in the newspapers and tangible
thanks were expressed by giving dinners to the officers in the several hotels
in the town. The motives of the protesters have been the subject of much
controversy. Broadly, on the one hand the claim has been made that these
were non political events, and on the other that they were charged with
deeply political motives. This will be discussed in the next chapter, but at
this stage the nature and extent of the unrest will be reviewed.

The riots associated with elections in the eighteenth century have often
been described, and no town was more turbulent than Carmarthen. On 7
August 1740 the Common Council Order Book records that:

> great riots have been committed in the night time: for several weeks
> past, to the great detriment as well the disturbance of many of the
> inhabitants of the same. John Rees a labourer is to be prosecuted for
> shooting at Richard Lewis gent.[405]

This cannot perhaps be set in the context of that political ideology or awareness for which historians of disturbance look so avidly, but there is no doubt
that this was an expression of class hatred.

At the centre of the turmoil for much of the century in Carmarthen was
the Whig Griffith Philipps of Cwmgwili. It was probably his defeat by Sea
Serjeants in 1741, which he disputed, which led to the famous 'cut and slash
in the Dark Gate' episode.[406] But in 1747 he used a mob to ensure the election of an alternative Whig corporation in Carmarthen to ensure his power
base. And in the bizarre manner which characterised Carmarthen politics
there were *two* corporations.[407] In further violence in December 1753, a
note written by '100' threatened those who 'have exposed our Worthy May-
or Capt. David Edwards'. If prosecutions continued then 'your house shall

be Burnt to the Ground and your Hearts Blood given to the Dogs. So we
will serve Everyone of your Party, for We will Die hard'.[408]

A period of especially serious violence took place at the end of 1755,
when, in a letter written by the Sheriff to the Member of Parliament on 24
November he warns that he expects to see:

> the town in flames every minute – there are five hundred separate fel-
> lows come to town from Pembrokeshire and other places, arm'd with
> firearms and quarter pieces, and, I am told, ship guns with a great
> number of gentlemen – such as they are, and who you know, together
> with some Pembrokeshire gentlemen I verily believe to do mischief.

The Sheriff goes on to say that lives and properties are in great danger 'as
the mob and rioters are publickly supported by a lot of gentlemen, some of
whom are of the Sea Serjeants Club, and I am positive, disaffected to the
government'.

The Sheriff wrote again on the 4th and the 11th of December describing
the continuing rioting. He had been shot, and believes 'the inhabitants of
this Place – will be massacred'. A bookseller, John Lewis died of his wounds:
'the lives and limbs of those Pembrokeshire desperadoes are many'.[409] The
Gentlemen's Magazine of 1755[410] reported that the cause 'tis said by the
election of magistrates – violence of party, and a dislike to the Jacobites'. The
Pembrokeshire people were based at The Red Lion, but even before they had
arrived, the local people 'had for some time with impunity, maimed several
persons – and beat out the brains of a barber at The Red Lion, and tried to
demolish it'. On 10 March the MP received another letter, in which it was
reported that the mob engaged in 'tirannical Outrageous and Rebellions in
opposition to Justice and Law, and in Defiance of Heaven itself'.[411] Lewis
Lewis the agent of John Vaughan of Golden Grove discusses the uproar in
Carmarthen, 'complaining that he could not collect the rents for "they are so
much arms in Carmarthen that it is dangerous to go there"'.[412]

Carmarthen is only an example of such scenes of political violence in
Wales. In 1796 Sir Richard Colt Hoare, in the course of a visit to Wales,
stayed in Cardigan. It had been mentioned that an election campaign was
taking place, with 'Welsh blood boiling with drink and party feuds and
flowing plentifully from their broken pates'.[413] Fairs too, when drink flowed,
were riotous. Again in Cardigan, at a fair in 1729 several people were 'beat-
ing one another with cudgels', and the attempt to arrest the ringleader led
to a confrontation between JPs and the deputy mayor.[414]

In Pembrokeshire too there was political violence. In 1701, for example, a challenge to Sir William Wogan who had been the Member for Haverforwest since 1685, was attended by physical violence which stopped his supporters voting, and resulted in him losing his seat.[415] In Pembroke in 1734 the defeated candidate, Rawleigh Mansel, a Sea Serjeant, complained that his supporters had been prevented from voting 'by a great number of persons, who were placed on the stairs leading to the said hall, armed with pitchforks, and other offensive weapons' while others 'stood at the head of the said stairs with their back-swords or scimitars in their hands'.[416]

Enclosures were another potent cause of riots. One judgement is that enclosures in Wales by Act of Parliament were 'accepted remarkably peacefully',[417] although in fact this claim is difficult to sustain. As indeed is the claim by Walter Davies that in the decade 1750–60 'whole parishes were enclosed by common consent'. As Howell goes on to point out 'actual documentary evidence for this area is difficult to unearth'.[418] And there was criticism at the time. A friend of Hassall's sent a rebuke when Hassall praised the enclosure of Tenby marshes with the rhyme:

It is a sin in a man or woman
To steal a goose from off the common
But who can plead that man's excuse
Who steals a common from the goose?

Hassall replied:

He stands in need of no excuse
Who feeds an ox where fed a goose
… witness the marshes near this town,
so lately clad in dreary brown,
But now are always to be seen,
in gay and everlasting green.[419]

The truth is that enclosures brought disturbances to many parts of Wales including Caernarvonshire, Flintshire, Carmarthenshire, Cardiganshire and Pembrokeshire. Enclosure riots occurred on Hirwaun Common, near Merthyr in 1791 and Llanrhystud (Cardiganshire) in 1812:[420]

Eighteen enclosure acts for Wales and Monmouthshire before 1793 gave the go-ahead for enclosure of nearly 35,000 acres, some eighty-five between 1793 and 1815 legislated for enclosure of at least 213,000 acres. This period, indeed, saw the most feverish activity.[421]

In Dyfed however only two enclosure acts were passed during the eighteenth century. One, of 1786, allowed Knox to enclose 2,450 acres,[422] which action, as we shall go on to see led to him being denounced as an Irish wolf. The other previously mentioned was that by Cawdor, and commended by Hassall, which made a bog of 274 acres 'into the most fertile land in Castlemartin'. Howell goes on to make a very serious criticism of some of this activity:

> The encroachments made by landowners in that (eighteenth) century sometimes had nothing to do with the margin of cultivation. They were blatant acts of robbery motivated by the desire to own the mineral wealth lying beneath the soil.[423]

DJV Jones begins his account of disturbances in Cardiganshire in the early nineteenth century with the claim that 'it would be fair to say that no Welsh county was more disturbed in the late 1810s than Cardiganshire'.[424] And much of this coincided with the fact that it was between 1793 and 1815 when 'the Welsh enclosure movement was at its height'.[425] 'Parliament authorised the enclosure of some 10,000 acres in Cardiganshire'.[426] There were several serious incidents in Dyfed, especially in Cardiganshire. This led to much protest, especially since it undermined the Welsh tradition of *tŷ unnos*.

There are many examples of protest, which added to the rioting provoked by the execution of writs. By the summer of 1814, attacks on the officers attempting to carry out legal duties were regular, an example being in June 1816 in Aberystwyth, when soldiers of the 55th regiment fired on a mob who refused to disperse after the reading of the Riot Act.[427] At about this time the authorities began to worry even more when 'opposition to the execution of all writs spread to the lead miners of the county, and talk of a concerted rising of the "lower orders" of west Wales was in the air'.[428] There were frequent and serious attacks on officers trying to carry out enclosure legislation. One especially unpopular figure was warned that if he kept on 'he had better bring a bag with him in which to carry his bones'.[429] There had already been trouble over enclosures in Carmarthenshire. There is a letter from a woman on 28 March 1789, in which she reports that:

A mob has destroyed and lay'd waste all the enclosures of the commins about the town this last week. I am afraid it will end seriously if there is not a stop put to it. The first rebellilon (sic) that ever happened in Carmarthen was about enclosing the commins. I hope it will not end now as it did then.[430]

But it was the scarcity of food which provoked the most disturbance throughout the eighteenth and early nineteenth centuries. Riots happened throughout England and Wales. And these, especially at the end of the eighteenth century, had overtones of political discontent and radicalism. As we shall go on to see, although historians have debated whether or not they were provoked by a wish for political change, or were a statement about 'class' divisions, many contemporaries were convinced that they were.

In 1740 there were food riots in Denbigh, Rhuddlan, Rhyl, St. Asaph and Prestatyn. In Dyfed colliers, like colliers all over Wales, engaged in violent protests over corn, in this case, as in many instances to come, over its exportation at a time when there were shortages in the district. In Pembroke a ship carrying corn was attacked, the corn removed and taken to the market, where they demanded that it should be sold at a fair price. They also threatened to burn the town. The mayor claimed that corn in Pembroke was cheaper than anywhere in England, a claim which was made often in the welter of riots throughout the period. The arrival of 20 members of the militia from Carmarthen stopped further trouble, but 'much care is taken by the owners of the collieries to supply the men with corn to keep them in order that no disturbance can happen for the future'.[431] The same tactic, that of boarding a ship and removing the cargo was to be repeated at Lawrenny near Milford Haven in February 1757.[432] And the same precaution was taken once again in Pembroke after riots in December 1795 'where greedy farmers' were 'brought to their senses... having "become alarmed and promised a constant supply"'.[433] Sometimes there is evidence of trouble, but very little documentation has survived. On 20 February 1778 James Hughes of Carmarthen acknowledged receipt of £68.9s.4d 'for the prosecution of the Prendergast rioters'.[434]

On 17 June 1757 in Carmarthen there was one of the most serious events of the whole period. 40 colliers and bargemen broke into a corn store. The 'Proclamation' was read, they refused to disperse, and four were shot and killed. Upon which the rest 'took to their heels and fled'. Spurrell in a report, probably upon the same event, states that six colliers were killed in Spilman Street.[435] The correct number seems to have been five, since on 2 September 1757 Mayor John Evans was tried for their murder. In his evidence he said that he had read the Proclamation, and had offered them corn at a reasonable price, but had had to withdraw. He ordered the military to fire. He was acquitted without the jury even leaving the court.[436]

In *The Gentlemen's Magazine* of 1757[437] 'AB', clearly a local man, in the process of deploring the trial of the mayor, paints a grim picture of events in the county:

> There were some hundreds of colliers, miners, ironwork men, and other disorderly persons, having left their works for several weeks, to live upon free booty plundered storehouses, warehouses, and vessels at Kidwelly, Llanstephan, and Laugharne, of all the corn and meal they could come at, and afterwards they had the boldness to enter the town of Carmarthen.

And he was not the only one to be convinced and 'confidently affirm that some persons of figure and influence are always acting behind the scenes' and 'that the real mob are only the tools of those who are led by either principle or interest to wish for a general confusion, in order to overturn the government… no friends to the present royal family and the Protestant interest'.[438]

Later, on 7 August 1795 two men, William Derbyshire and William Thomas were charged with riotous assembly with others, and breaking the Winchester Measure belonging to Carmarthen market. They were acquitted.[439] This was a new measure of corn and earlier, in February, at a time of shortage, had been the object of attack in a riot in Bridgend, when in asking for the military to be called in, it was claimed 'constables rather lean to the country people'.[440]

Cardiganshire too had its share of violence in the eighteenth century and beyond. One of the most extraordinary centred upon the operation of the lead mine at Esgair y Mwyn. The man in charge was none other than Lewis Morris, of the family so much admired for their work for Welsh culture. There was a major dispute about the ownership of this mine, and the seriousness of the dispute can be gauged by an event in February 1753 when magistrates, a sheriff, and a 'mob of several hundred armed people' threatened the lives of those they believed had usurped their authority, even though that authority was the Crown itself. One of the ringleaders, a Justice of the Peace, presented a cocked pistol at Morris' head and threatened to shoot him. In the event Morris was imprisoned in Cardigan for several months.

The year 1795 was an especially troublesome one for the authorities throughout Wales. A magistrate, Thomas Griffiths wrote from near Mold on 2 April 1795 to Portland of the mob breaking into the house of a man:

> who buys corn in this country for the use of Cheshire and Lancashire and forced him to sell it to them somewhat under the market price. But had they taken it for nothing, they were in too great strength for us to have attempted to oppose.

He pleaded for 'some troops to be quartered within our reach', since:

> should the numerous body of Colliers and miners again assemble, the property of the whole country might be laid waste and destroyed before assistance could be procured.[441]

The newspapers on the borders reported rioting in several parts of Wales, because of the price of corn 'and the apprehensions of a further advance'. In February 1795 the *Salopian Journal*[442] described how:

> the colliers and poor people in the neighbourhood of Conway and Bangor Ferry, Carnarvonshire, assembled last week in a riotous manner and stopped several vessels laden with that article for Liverpool.

They appeared frightening, and the military were sent for. The appearance of the Somersetshire Fencible Cavalry, under Lieut. Colonel Strode, subdued the rioters without bloodshed. But 'the neighbouring gentlemen have entered into a liberal subscription to enable the poor to purchase corn at a reduced price'.[443] The next day the same regiment travelled through mid Wales to Aberystwyth where miners were involved in rioting. As in other areas, miners were at the forefront of trouble. Lead miners had, for example, rioted at Aberystwyth in 1783 because of the price of corn.[444] On this occasion, in 1795, they had entered the town:

> in the dead of night, plundered and abused the inhabitants, broke open the storehouses and took away the corn, urging as an excuse, that the monopoly of the dealers had caused the present scarcity and high prices of grain in the country.[445]

On the arrival of the soldiers, it was reported, 'the miners dispersed and quietitude was restored to the inhabitants. Some of the ringleaders were apprehended for breaking open a storehouse and taking away some corn'.[446] A few weeks later it was reported that the troop of the Somersetshire Fencibles that arrived from Ludlow on the 27 February to quell the riots, had to go to Carmarthen to assist the magistrates there in restoring order. But another troop of the same regiment arrived in Aberystwyth:

> on which a liberal subscription was entered into by the gentlemen in this town and neighbourhood, to aid the innkeepers in the burthen occasioned by this necessary protection. It is but justice to say, that the miners employed by Messrs. Smith, Bonsall, Pierce and Sheldon at their respective mine works were not in any manner concerned in these riots.[447]

At the same time, in 1795, other Somersetshire troops were sent to Abergavenny 'to assist the Civil Magistrates in keeping peace and good order in that neighbourhood'.[448]

A similar disturbance happened at Narbeth but 'by the immediate assistance of the Carmarthen Yeomanry Cavalry the insurgents were brought to a sense of their error, after the apprehension of some of the ringleaders, soon after which everything wore the appearance of tranquility'.[449]

There are several, often lengthy accounts by educated people who felt that the condition of the people was so wretched that they had to draw the attention of the public to the fact. They often felt too that physical protest was the only option open to them, and the only way of forcing improvements. Such an account was the result of a visit to Fishguard reported in 1795. The writer refers to an allegation that the Fishguard Troops had been involved in collusive behaviour with protesters, a matter to which we will return. The account of Gwinfardd Dyfed appears in the *Cambrian Register* for 1795:

> The price of labour here bears no proportion to the advance which all the necessaries of life have of late experienced, for even these last two years the rate has continued the same – parochial business is managed here in a very slovenly manner by a junto (sic) who claim a sort of hereditary right to lead the parish by the nose, a set of people, insolent and arbitrary like all usurpers, yet in whose assumed authority, and

unresisted decisions, the herd, who are either too ignorant or too indolent to put things on a better footing, tamely acquiesce – the authors of their misery, the forestalling merchant, and the avaricious farmer, by whom, in a great measure, the melancholy scarcity was occasioned, or without even permitting their distress to find a tongue, till lately, at a time of impending famine.. in consequence of those confederated blood-suckers attempting to whip off a cargo of corn and butter, with its destination strongly suspected, a number of the poor labourers and peasants of this and the adjoining parishes instigated by actual want, and the unsatisfied clamours of their children and families, met to remonstrate in the most moving and peaceable manner with the enemies of their species, who, far from relenting, have not only pronounced the meeting tumultuary (sic) and riotous, but, by the dint of the most impudently, as well as ignorantly fabricated affidavits, are labouring to represent the conduct of the magistrates, and the commanding officer of the fencibles, who attended most humanely on the occasion, from a wish to mediate between the parties, and satisfy both, with as little violence as possible to either, so as to involve them in a charge of the foulest calumny, saddle them with a persecution (for prosecution is too mild a term) and fix a stigma on the country. In a case like this, where the voice of nature and of policy calls so loudly for it, it is to be regretted, that the arm of magistracy was not strengthened to be an over match for such harpies.[450]

There was continuous trouble in Pembrokeshire throughout 1795, and as we shall go on to see for several years afterwards. In March 1795, for instance Lord Dynevor wrote to the government about bread riots in Haverfordwest and Narbeth, fearing that the shortage of barley might 'encourage disloyal agitation in the towns'.[451] Later in that year the miners of Hook in Pembrokeshire rioted also in Haverfordwest, an episode about which we have an unusual amount of information since a detailed account was sent to the Duke of Portland, the government minister accountable for the control of these events.

The port of Haverfordwest was very active at the time and could handle ships of 200 tons. On 24 August 1795 The Reverend Dr John Philipps (sic) of Williamston wrote to the Duke of Portland.[452] This man was a member of an influential Pembrokeshire family, an important magistrate, and one of three who presided over the Quarter Sessions. At the time of the riot he was about 65 years of age, and Rector of the small village of Burton near his home. Williamston at the time was a well respected estate, but like so many in Dyfed it deteriorated, becoming a farm and eventually a nursing home in the twentieth century,

On 17 August 1795 Philipps reports, he was told that Hook colliers were 'determined' to board a sloop with butter on board which was to sail from Haverfordwest for Bristol. This would happen as the ship passed Hook colliery which was some six miles down the river Cleddau. He 'applied' to Captain Longcroft the Regulating Captain of Milford to order a tender to escort the sloop. The tender drew too big a draft to go higher than Hook, but he said he would meet it there and conduct it down to the sea. Philipps then sent a messenger to Pembroke to Mr. Bushell, the Commanding Officer of a company of The Carmarthenshire Militia and begged (sic) him to bring troops to Haverfordwest the next morning. By seven o'clock the next day 50 men armed with 30 rounds of powder and ball were in place.

As the militia entered the town, the women told them 'that they knew they were in their hearts for them, and would do them no hurt. They replied that they should do their duty'. Now two problems arose. The first was that the sloop had to sail that evening or she would miss the tide, and the captain was afraid, insisting that the owners came with him, so that the colliers would see that he was forced to sail. The merchants did not know what to do. At about 12 o'clock Philipps was in High Street talking to some gentlemen when 'one of them suddenly cried "Doctor have care, the colliers coming"' (sic). He saw 'a great crowd of men women and children with oaken bludgeons coming down the High Street bawling out "One for all, One for all".' He:

> darted into the middle of them and seized two of the men and asked them where they were going. They said they thought there was no harm to walk the street. I told them it was very criminal to be guilty of a Riot and if they did not go peacefully home they would be shot by the soldiers and whoever escaped being shot would be hanged. They made no reply but stood still.

He grabbed two more. The women 'were putting men on and were perfect Furies… I had some strokes from them on my back' but 'luckily for me' a stout young fellow 'happened to come into the street and ran immediately behind me and kept the women off. A lawyer Mr. Bateman seeing the danger tried to take a 'a great oaken bludgeon' from 'one of the foremost and stoutest of the colliers'. Another collier tried to knock him down, but a young curate took the bludgeon away. This episode lasted about two or three minutes, but 'at last Bateman and Summers proved victorious'.

'Several ladies screeched out that I should be murdered, and sent what men they could muster to my assistance'. In the meantime the drum beat to arms and the militia ran together and formed. Mr Bushell had a blow on the head, and one of the militia ran at the assailant with his bayonet and would have killed him had it not been for a clergyman who 'begged he would not kill him'. The Riot Act was read and the Militia ordered to 'ram the balls well that every shot might do execution'. The colliers ran away and warned others that the militia 'were determined to fire'. Two of them were put in prison, saying they had only come because they had been sent for by the people of Haverfordwest.

There was another body of colliers who 'lay on their bellies' near the quay waiting for those who had come through the town, and had they joined up they 'would have gutted the sloop'. Learning 'their brethren' had been defeated they ran off. 'During the riot a woman said "that in less time than a twelvemonth she would see the downfall of all clergy and of every rich person"'. The merchants asked if it would be a good idea to unload the ship. He said that 'at all events the ship must sail'. The ship weighed anchor about 9pm with a merchant, a magistrate and 20 militia on board. The ship got down to the tender next morning. The sergeant asked that he and his men be landed at Hook quay where there was a large body of colliers. They landed and 'marched quietly' to them and asked which was the road to Pembroke, and one of the colliers went 'very readily' to show the way.

On the Wednesday Philipps went again to High Street, and there was a group of eight or nine of 'the common people'. They told him of a collier who had come from Hook to complain that he had been beaten by a lighterman in Hook the night before for refusing to join the marching colliers. Had not the master of a ship intervened, he believed he would have been killed. There was in Haverfordwest at the time a Regulating Captain, whose job was to conduct the press gangs, and Philipps ordered the press gang to arrest the lighterman, who at that moment landed in Haverfordwest. In less than three hours the man had been escorted to Pembroke guarded by 30 militia, and put on board a tender, presumably 'pressed'. Philipps adds, seemingly without irony: 'He happened to be a very good sailor'.

It was now dangerous to leave Haverfordwest without a military presence, and so he asked Colonel Knox to bring down his Fishguard Fencibles which he did before the militia left. All was then quiet and 'I dare say there will be no further disturbance. The colliers are most heartily frightened, and declare they will never stir again, let butter or corn be ever so dear'. He imprisoned two of them until the Friday evening and then released them. Had they unloaded the vessel he claims that they would have taken all the corn at the Saturday market 'and correcting various abuses' (sic). Philipps, like AB in Carmarthenshire in his article in *The Gentleman's Magazine* in 1757 about the rioting there earlier, was sure that the trouble was concerted and organised:

They were certainly set on and sent for by some People of Property in Haverfordwest who assured them that the inhabitants would join them and that the militia would lay down their arms. I cannot get at the knowledge of the persons who were at the bottom of this Riot.

It was his opinion that a notice should appear in this form:

Whereas it is currently reported and generally believed that some Person or Persons of Property resident in the town of Haverfordwest did stir up – for encouraging the colliers of Hook and the adjoining collieries to come in a body armed to the said town of Haverford-west on the eighteenth instant in order to take the butter out of the sloop called the 'Haverfordwest' bound to the port of Bristol, and did likewise assure the said colliers that the inhabitants of Haverfordwest would join them. This is to give notice that a reward of – will be given to any one who will discover the offender or offenders so that he or they may be brought to justice.

He suggests that it be put in *The Gazette*, and *The Evening Mail*, *The Sun*, or *The Star* and in *Farley's Bristol Journal*. These papers, he points out, are all read in Haverfordwest. He repeats that:

I am perfectly satisfied in my own mind, tho' I cannot prove it, that a man of considerable Property (an enemy of the present Constitution) along with others of the same kidney was at the bottom of the riot. The cry about butter was a mere pretence; the real design was to distress Government. There is a quantity of butter in the warehouses at Haverfordwest, and the merchants engage to retail it to the country at seven pence halfpenny per pound, whereas it stood them seven pence by the cask.

Some idea of relative prices may be gauged from the fact that in 1777 colliers were paid about eight or nine pence a day and women four pence. By 1806 this had risen to a shilling for men and six pence to eight pence for women. One observer in 1806:

> expressed amazement at the low levels of pay in Pembrokeshire, contrasting them with those between two shillings and four shillings paid in his own area.[453]

Another contemporary observer shared his surprise. Speaking to one of Lord Dynevor's gardeners:

> I learnt that the wages in this country are astonishingly low, Ld. Dynevor not paying his labourers either in the garden or farm more than seven shillings a week, which is the general custom of the country, without any perquisite of beer or anything whatever.[454]

Such figures made pathetic the cry of the rioting Hook women quoted by Philipps as especial evidence of the danger posed by the riot that 'they would have fresh butter as well as the Gentry, and would live as well as the Gentry'. Philipps claims that the people were profligate, rather than hungry, by pointing to the example of:

> one man about three weeks back went into the shop of Mr. Warlow (?), who sells wine and spirits. He complained that butter was so dear he was not able to purchase a pound; but at the same time he bought a bottle of brandy.

Philipps concludes his letter: 'I flatter myself, that your Grace will not disapprove of my conduct. I certainly acted to the best of my judgement, and at the hazard of my life. In 1800 Philipps wrote a much less assertive letter to the duke, in which he pleaded for help since the magistrates had received letters threatening to burn down their houses, and 'they really now are afraid of their lives'.[455]

Later in the year and at the beginning of 1796, the area around St. David's was the scene of 'disturbances and tendency to riot' over the shortage of corn. This was so alarming that Lord Milford called a meeting of the county magistrates on 27 February 1796 to discuss what could be done to prevent a repetition of such 'dangerous and illegal proceedings' This meeting had repercussions which will be dealt with later in this chapter. The agitation in Pembrokeshire remained unabated for several years. One of the more notable cases was the charge laid against John Ladd, the Mayor of Newport who was committed on 4 February 1801 for promoting an unlawful assembly. In an Order sending Ladd to Haverfordwest Gaol it was noted that:

> by his own confession of having on Friday last the thirteenth day of January 1801 (being marketday at Newport) collected and joined and headed a mob of more than a hundred people unlawfully assembled together for the purpose of lowering the price of corn.[456]

He went to Llyngwair, an estate nearby, to speak to the Justices, but could not find any. When the mob got back to Newport Ladd addressed them. If they wanted the price of corn lowered they should assemble on the following market day 'and to bring three times their number'. If they brought money he would supply corn out of the storehouses: barley at five shillings the Winchester and oats at two shillings and four pence the Winchester. Anybody who refused to assemble would be fined 20 shillings. Ladd said he should be locked in since 'he declared that if he was not left alone and excused, he would yet do more mischief'. He was tried on 11 April, and this seemed to have stopped the agitation.

On the same calendar is John Stephens, aged 24, committed on 24 September 1801 'for a riot'. He was from Carew, near Pembroke, and 'together with fifty other persons unknown – with swords sticks staves and other offensive weapons assembled at the house of George Look in St. Florence, and threatened to demolish it unless he gave them corn'.[457] Look seems to have been a notoriously unpopular and ruthless exporter of corn, and the Home Office had been warned seven years before that unless he was restrained a 'mutiny' would occur.[458]

On 23 December 1800 'a great number of persons' assembled at Blackpool Mill, which is near Haverfordwest one of whom was Rowland Hugh (sic). Hugh, a labourer from Narbeth was charged in the following March, together with Daniel Williams with taking 'with force and arms' 50 pounds weight of butter. Some measure of the turbulence may be gauged by the fact that considerable precautions had to be taken to keep order at markets. At the Quarter Sessions held at the Guildhall in Haverfordwest on the 17 April 1801, payment was authorised to eight petty constables for two, three, and four days attendance in the cornmarket for preventing disturbances there.

Milford wrote to Portland on 4 October 1800 in despair that:

> There is scarce a week that does not produce some treasonable papers
> at Haverfordwest and every means that could be devised has been used
> to detect the writers of them but without success.[459]

'Tumults' went on for years in Carmarthen too. On 25 September 1818
a 'numerous and tumultous assemblage of inhabitants of Carmarthen' prevented the shipment of a cargo of cheese. The mayor and a magistrate tried
to stop them but they went on board and took the cheese back to the warehouse. 'From the increasing violence it was deemed prudent to detest (sic)
for a time shipping any more cheese'. Three days later:

> Another effort was made to ship cheese at the port. The consequence
> was the populance (sic) again assembled and became more infuriated
> than on the former occasion. The vessel was completely ransacked and
> the cheese again taken back to the warehouse.

The Lord Lieutenant 'instantly ordered the Carmarthen Yeomanry and Militia to assemble in the town – From a published letter it is gathered that
the opposition was due to complaints by inhabitants of certain persons mo-
nopolising cheese and butter for exportation, when it might be sold in the
town and district. The writer states that two or three farmers refuse to sell
their cheese even at advanced prices to persons engaged in exporting the
product, and that they are an example to others to do likewise'.[460]

At the same time throughout the region the small farmers in particular
sank into increasing debt, and were unable to get out of it. An eye witness
wrote that labourers tried:

> to prolong life by swallowing barley meal and water – boiling nettles,
> etc. – and scores in the agonies of famine have declared to me this last
> week that they have not made a meal for two days together.[461]

The consequence was that by 1814 'the mountainous north-eastern corner
of the county (Cardiganshire) was represented as being lawless'.[462]

The question arises, and it is one which will be discussed often as to
whether this unrest was inchoate or whether it was at all politically inspired.
A report to the government from Lord Dynevor in March 1795 confirms

that seditious literature was circulating in Haverfordwest.[463] Further evidence of concern is in a letter to Portland from Lady Milford dated 30 December 1795 explaining that Lord Milford could not write himself because he had gout. He had the Bills for the security of His Majesty's person in the prevention of seditious meetings which he sent to the Chairman of the Quarter Sessions.[464]

One of the most notorious trials for sedition created a furore at the time, partly because of the anti-Nonconformist overtones, partly because of the popularity of Thomas Evans, and partly because of the severity of the sentence. It was held in Carmarthen in 1801. Three men were charged: Daniel Evans, Daniel Jones, and the most eminent, the Reverend Thomas Evans, wrongly called Evan in some of the court documentation. He was a Unitarian minister, and the three men were from Brechfa in the county of Carmarthenshire. Their trouble began in March of that year, when a group of neighbours met to draw lots for a watch, seemingly a common practice. When the winner was announced Daniel Evans objected to the way in which the lottery had been conducted 'in very strong terms', and he and others insisted upon another draw. Another neighbour, George Thomas, later to be the principal witness for the prosecution, and who had been involved in the draw, was highly offended. It was during the jollification afterwards that the alleged offences were committed.

There was a sing song, which included 'a lyrical version in Welsh of Gray's Elegy in a Country Churchyard, and a Welsh song to the tune of the Marcelois hymn which had been printed in a Welsh magazine in May 1796'. The authorities seemed not to object to this song, and indeed in the course of his tour in 1797 the Duke of Rutland wrote approvingly that the French prisoners in Haverfordwest castle 'sung the Marseillois Hymn, really in fine style'.[465] At the auction party Daniel Evans and Daniel Jones and others then sang a song 'of a strictly satirical nature, and severe on such immoralities as some imagined George Thomas had been guilty of'. He was outraged, and 'supposed' that the Reverend Evans had written it. But their offence lay in the allegation that they had sung an 'English song assumed to be a translation from the French song called Carmaghol (modern Carmagnole). This was a revolutionary song, one verse of which runs:

And when upon the British shore
The thundering guns of France shall roar,
Vile George shall trembling stand
Or flee his native land,

With terror and appall.
(dance)

Vile George was, of course, the king. Three weeks after the lottery the three men were charged with singing it. Affidavits were sworn from a large number of people testifying that they had not sung the song, and there were very many demonstrating the good character and loyalty of the minister. It was sworn that he had 'expressed his abhorrence of the bloodshed and cruelty that had lately been exercised in France, and his hopes that nothing of the kind would ever occur in this country'. Furthermore, after the French invasion of Fishguard in 1797, 'he wrote a Welsh song in celebration of ancient British valour and his abhorrence of the French designs'. Appeals were launched to Unitarian congregations throughout the country to help financially since he had a wife and nine small children. The main thrust of his defence was a series of counter allegations against his accuser George Thomas. Of him, many people said that he was an atheist, and that he had been seen to 'alter the form of prayer', and sent it to the defendant. This episode had upset the Bishop of St. Davids and his clergy, and 'it was supposed by most' that it had been done by the defendant, and this 'drew on the said Thomas Evans unmerited reproaches and imputations of disaffection to Government'. George Thomas had in fact sung the Carmaghol frequently, and 'he rummaged his own stores of sedition for wherewithal to charge these persons who were by him falsely and maliciously accused'. In addition he had tried to persuade others to give false evidence, especially those who could 'understand English tolerably'.

Worse was to come. A number of people claimed that during the winter of 1800 George Thomas had suggested to them that they should break into the arms store of the Tivyside (sic) Volunteers in Powel's castle, and give weapons to the colliers and miners who were threatening Carmarthen saying 'he himself would lead that insurrection and become their leader... it was a pity such brave fellows were not encouraged'. David Morgan had read a letter from Thomas, in Welsh, threatening the lives of the mayor and his family unless the price of corn were greatly reduced. In addition to all this, he was a horse thief. Another prosecution witness, John Jones, was described as 'an abandoned and bad character', who had said that he would swear 'anything they might happen to ask me to swear. I cared nor what'. His reward was £5.0s.6d.

Such attacks on the integrity of the prosecution witnesses were fruitless. This is not surprising since Evans was no ordinary minister. He is known as Tomos Glyn Cothi, well known as a sympathiser with the principles of the

French Revolution, a poet and a writer of political and social pamphlets. The authorities were probably not much interested as to whether he had committed this particular offence: it was a good opportunity to make an example of what was regarded as a dangerous faction in Welsh society. Upon conviction Judge Lloyd, addressing the defendant, admonished him that:

> to aggravate your crime, you have brought together a great many witnesses in your favour to foreswear themselves, for I have not the least doubt but that they were all of them suborned by you – you are a man of a very bad and dangerous disposition'. He went on to say that 'I have no doubt but that of (sic) your disposition were to have its course it would break out in murder and bloodshed'.

It was nothing to do with Evans' 'religious sentiments', although 'I cannot help lamenting that the country is divided into many sects'. The judge then dealt with the family: 'as to your wife and nine small children they must suffer. I cannot help it. It's the consequence of your own conduct'. Evans was sentenced to two years imprisonment, to stand in the pillory in the market place in each of those years for one hour each time, and afterwards to give security for good behaviour for seven years.[466]

Earlier there had been even more serious charges brought against local people in the aftermath of the French invasion of Pembrokeshire in 1797.[467] There were about 1300 men in the invasion force: Americans, Irish, British and French, though when the Irish patriot Wolfe Tone saw the Legion Noir reviewed, he wrote of 'about 1800 men', 'and sad blackguards they are'.[468] Tone was very involved in the preparations for this invasion, and at one time seems to have contemplated joining it himself, 'convinced that an invasion of England would unite all'.[469] Tone eventually joined an invasion force for Ireland in 1798 which he had always dearly wanted, but was captured and sentenced to death. He managed though to commit suicide. Tone says that he recruited about fifty Irish and ten English prisoners of war.[470] The French General Hoche, a very successful soldier wrote of the force that there were 'six hundred men from all the prisons in my district', which he had secured on two islands 'to obviate the possibility of escape' and 'six hundred picked convicts from the galleys, still wearing their irons'.[471] The chef de brigade (colonel) was an American, William Tate. He was about seventy.[472]

The popular histories of this invasion are replete with stories, many of questionable veracity. There is Jemima Nicholas, an Amazon who supposedly armed with a pitchfork rounded up twelve French soldiers and brought

them in as prisoners.[473] Then the story is told of how the French were de-
ceived about the size of the enemy by numbers of women parading in traditional red flannel.[474] And there is the belief in the bravery of the defending
troops, and the local people. But the overwhelming truth is that the local
forces were lucky. There was a good deal of looting, at least two rapes, and a
number of people on both sides were killed. The invaders were certainly ill
disciplined, and because of drink were very quickly beyond control. But it
is not correct to describe the events as a 'comic opera landing'.[475] When the
French surrendered some observed that their equipment was of good quality, and the Duke of Rutland reports that:

> About six hundred of these were as fine men, and as fit for service, as
> any that were ever employed in any country. The grenadier companies
> consisted of men all above six feet, and they were well armed and
> equipped.[476]

He goes on to report that:

> had they attacked Lord Cawdor, there was every probability of their
> being successful, and the most serious consequences were to be appre-
> hended from the smallness of the English force, and the little depend-
> ence that was to be placed upon the country people who had joined
> them. Those, although armed, nevertheless kept themselves aloof, and
> would certainly (had affairs come to that crisis) have united them-
> selves with the strongest side, which ever it might be.[477]

Some of the French waved 'as if to invite the country people to join them…
they did not wish to frighten the peasants, and several of the latter rode up
and conversed with them during the day'.[478] Certainly 'that they expected
to be joined by a considerable body of peasantry is evident from the orders
given to the general, as by the quantity of ammunition they brought with
them'.[479] He does go on to single out 'instances of particular courage'.[480]
But the reports of the time that the 'peasants many thousands having assembled armed with pikes scythes' and repeated, for example in a letter from
Milford to Portland,[481] must be a fabrication taking demography alone into
account. More convincing is the statement of a French sergeant major at
the trials of local people that 'he had seen many country people around the
camp'.[482] Nor were the 'gentlemen of the county' any more reliable, since
they 'would certainly not have come forward as they did, had it not been

for Lord Cawdor's appointment'.[483] This is confirmed by Milford in another letter to Portland on 1 March 1797, when he writes that 'I don't find that any of the officers on Half Pay in this County have shown any readiness to serve except Ensign Hodges'.[484] Cawdor on the other hand drew the attention of the Duke of York to 'the merit of the officers on the half-pay list who contributed to the service'.[485] Rutland's report was probably accurate since he can only have received the account first hand from Cawdor, and in fact he specifically credits 'this interesting information' to discussion in 'the course of dinner'.[486]

The duke then sets out – again he must have been told – what the root of the trouble was: 'When I talk of the disaffection of the peasantry, I must be understood to mean those all around the place where the enemy landed. They are chiefly anabaptists, and some men were afterwards taken up for having communicated with the enemy'.[487] There is other seeming evidence that local people were not unquestionably loyal. John Owen, master of a sloop which was on its way to Fishguard, was captured, and questioned by the Commodore of the French fleet. While he was on the ship he recognised James Owen, who had been a servant at Trehowel, later to be the French Headquarters.[488] He had supposedly been convicted of horse stealing, and been transported.[489]

At the conclusion of these activities, it was decided that the behaviour of the commander of the Fishguard Fencibles, Thomas Knox, should be questioned, and that there had been collusion amounting to treason by a number of local people. It is likely that the attempt to discredit Knox was initiated, and perhaps orchestrated by Charles Hassall, reference to whose agricultural reports has been made often in this book. He had been dismissed from his post on the Llanstinan estate by William Knox, father of Thomas. The three men were Irish, and not local, and it could be that the case was fuelled by jealousy of the position of power the Knox family had accumulated in the county. William, it may be remembered, was one of those who had drawn the attention of the pitiable state of the poor to the authorities in London, and it has been written of him that 'intellectually he was far ahead of any one else in the county'.[490]

Although the Duke of York eventually indicated that the matter should be dropped, the Knox family did not give up trying to clear their name, and the father took up residence in London so that he could continue the battle. A number of Pembrokeshire gentlemen signed a letter in which they stated that they would under no condition serve under Knox, although the officers of his regiment sent a memorial supporting him. Despite the persistence of expressions of confidence in his behaviour from the highest quarters, Knox was forced to resign the command of the regiment which his family had created and equipped. Cawdor was seen by Knox as a particular enemy, and in May 1797, Knox challenged him to a duel. Although arrangements were made, it is not clear whether the duel took place. The whole sorry episode was a disaster for both Knoxs, with the father being ruined financially, and the son seemingly finishing his life in a state of insanity.[491]

Less eminent people also suffered from the strange welter of recriminations. One of these was Thomas Williams, who had escorted two French officers to Fishguard with proposals for surrender, and another was a farmer William Thomas. Neither of these was charged, but a number of dissenters found themselves in very serious trouble. Of the anabaptists identified as a threat Rutland adds, in a somewhat ambiguous phrase, that 'in Carmarthenshire, and other parts of Wales, they would have risen en masse.' A visit to Haverfordwest castle to view the 'state criminals' caused him to say that one '(an Anabaptist) seemed as desperate and determined a criminal as ever was seen'.[492] To him this was not surprising in view of the fact that 'this part of the country is very much under the pernicious doctrines of Methodism… like wolves dispersed all over the country… they are pests to the community'.[493]

This was the atmosphere in which four men were sent to trial, all from the north of the county. They were Thomas Davies, John Reed, a weaver, Thomas John, a farmer and a Baptist and another farmer Samuel Griffith, who was an Independent. Nearly all of the witnesses against them were, incredibly, French prisoners of war. It may be for that reason Rutland seems to have been very sympathetic to the French, and commented approvingly on Cawdor's 'severe lecture' to some of the guards who had ordered prisoners off the fives court so that they could play.[494] This was just one example of very odd behaviour concerning prisoners who had just invaded, behaviour which in part was due to the contempt in which the peasants were held by the squirearchy.

At the subsequent hearings, ending up at the Great Sessions in Haverfordwest in April 1797, and the Assizes in September of that year, it was variously alleged that three of the defendants – the case against Davies was dropped – had given information about the size and disposition of the local troops, advised that there would be a lot of local support, that there had been conversations with the French commander, Tate, and generally that they had 'joined' themselves 'to a certain large body of Frenchmen, and did 'counsel comfort encourage and abet them'.

By the time of the Assizes,[495] Reed was no longer charged, but in any case the prosecution case had collapsed, substantially because the French had made new statements admitting that they had lied and been bribed. Subsequent accounts do not reveal the names of those who bribed, but there is evidence which shows that they were well educated, since they spoke French when they visited the prisoners in the castle so that the debtors would not understand what was being said. The one admission Griffith made was that at one point when the French were handing out muskets to the locals – which by the way they willingly accepted – he tried to get one. But although John and Griffith were freed, they had been put to huge expense, one estimate in John's case being £200, and they had spent seven months in appalling prison conditions.

The threat of a return of the French remained for some time. The Times reported on 15 April 1797 that shipping seen off Pembrokeshire was not an invasion fleet as had been feared, but British merchantmen. More ominously, especially after the experience of the invasion, it was reported from Haverfordwest in the early part of 1800 that a French invasion was expected, and the 'People are upon the Eve of rising in Mass'. Meanwhile newspapers in Wales pointed out that 'an artificial scarcity of wheat' had been 'one of the chief instruments in bringing about the French Revolution'.[496]

The point has been made earlier that there were at least some in authority who were sympathetic to the plight of the poor in the period under discussion, and tried to ameliorate their condition. Some of these attempts were, of course, made in their own best interests and because of alarm at the unpredictable and violent behaviour of large numbers of their neighbours. Portland received plenty of notice of trouble and advice as to how to avoid it from all over Wales. In north Wales The Reverend Holland Edwards, Rector of Llanrwst, warned Portland:

> of the risk likely to be attended with serious consequences as… occasioned by certain persons who buy up corn and potatoes – at very depressed prices – for exportation – in a manner smuggled to the riverside where it is shipped under pretence of being carried for the supply of Lancashire and other places along the coast.

Is it possible, he wrote, to put a stop to this? Especially since the conduct of the people was 'exemplary and proper'.[497]

In August 1795 when wheat and barley 'had at least doubled in price since the previous September – the Cardiganshire magistrates spoke for the authorities of most Welsh counties when they declared that the working classes were 'much discontented and restless at the present and exorbitant price of all grain in the county'.[498] They wrote again in December that: 'in the opinion of the magistrates, the only certain mode of reducing the grain to a fair and moderate price is to stop all exportation from the county. Unless this is done there will be riots'.[499]

But it must be the case that at times the concern which was expressed was principled. One of the quintessential and sober statements which reflected the more sophisticated analysis of unrest was made in a debate in the House of Lords in 1737. In this debate most of the time was taken up with a discussion of a devastating riot which had taken place in Edinburgh, and a speech from Lord Carteret was a rare example in the history of the Lords for its understanding both of the plight of the people, and the complexities of the issues.[500] Indeed, it is identical in tone with that of Lord Byron on the Luddites in his maiden speech in February 1812.[501]

Carteret points out that the rioting seems not to have been directed at the government, but the government had to be concerned since 'governments have been overturned by Tumults which at first seemed insignificant'. If the constant calling upon the military did not stop and the Law used, then it would be the end of civil government. Of turnpike riots in the west of England, he is 'apt to suspect that those tumults proceeded, not from any want of Power in the Civil Magistrate (sic) but from some other Cause, perhaps from some real Injustice or Oppression brought upon our poor People by means of these Turnpikes'. He goes on to say that the People 'seldom or never assemble in any riotous or tumultous Manner, unless when they are oppressed, or at least imagine they are oppressed' and until that oppression is removed, and the oppressors punished severely, hanging and shooting would achieve nothing. 'I shall never be for sacrificing the Liberties of the People, in order to prevent their engaging in any riotous proceedings'. Another speaker pointed out that riots 'have in some Manner spread over the whole Kingdom', and he expressed the familiar view 'that mobs were manipulated by those who are prompted by their Malice or Revenge'. The Duke of Newcastle thought it was very simple. 'The People – are often the worst Judges of their own real interests'.

At a local level in Wales there is some evidence that there was sympathy with Carteret's views, which were translated into action. In an account of food shortages in Pembrokeshire as early as 1757, the Council of the Town and County of Haverfordwest met to discuss the problem and interestingly, to do something about it. It was reported that corn had been bought up and shipped out, with the result that the 'poorer sort of people are already pinched, and much distressed thereby'. The Council had already set up a fund to buy corn to be sold at a moderate price, and they now invited 'the several Gentlemen who are of the Common Council of this Town and County and are not inhabitants of the same, to contribute to so good a work'.[502]

Sheriff Foley wrote from Pembrokeshire to the Home Office in January 1795 and begs for help because 'the most favourable account does not calculate above a month's short allowance to be in the county. The harvest promises to be late, consequently the distress for six weeks will be extreme'. He reports that the poorer families have been relieved but the whole stock is exhausted. 'The people who have risen up to supply themselves are colliers, and they have been quieted by the most indigenous families being supplied with barley at four shillings a Winchester when the market price was six'. The inhabitants of Pembrokeshire 'shall be found to be in the greatest distress'.[503]

On the 14 July William Knox wrote to Portland that 'By the judicious application of very large subscriptions, we have been hitherto able to supply the laborious (sic) poor of Pembrokeshire with corn at a moderate price, but the stock is now exhausted' He asked for 1,000 Winchester bushels from Scotland, adding that 'I will be answerable for the first cost'.[504] This is the same William Knox discussed earlier, and who is commended in *The Cambrian Register* for 1795[505] for setting up a school in Fishguard at his own expense, even though it was failing. Such benevolence did not how-ever stop one critic of his enclosures from describing him as: 'an Irish wolf who have not the look of a man' engaged in 'tyrannical barbarous proceed-ings'.[506] There were instances of caring landowners, such as 'Mr. Mirehouse and other gentlemen, who furnished their cottagers with necessary articles at the ordinary rate during the scarcity, but resisted the advance of wages'.[507] This Mr. Mirehouse, the visitor goes on, 'is esteemed one of the best gentle-men farmers in the kingdom' and in 1800 had been awarded a gold medal for improving waste moors by the Society for the Encouragement of Arts, Manufactures, and Commerce.[508] As mentioned earlier, this was done in collaboration with Lord Cawdor.

Another Pembrokeshire landowner Major Dudley Ackland protested about the possibility of being brought to 'the disagreeable necessity of firing on our poor creatures'.[509] It has even been suggested that he resigned his commission in the Castlemartin unit of the Pembrokeshire Yeomanry.[510] He was also at the centre of an attempt to limit prices, and on 10 March 1796 he sent a 'resolution' 'signed by all the principal people here' to Cawdor from Pembroke in which the price of a number of commodities had been pegged. Cawdor disapproved, and indeed wrote to the mayor of Pembroke to protest.[511]

On 29 March Joseph Adams wrote to Campbell from Pembroke. His letter was courteous enough, but firm. He wrote that the position in the district was serious. After setting out the alarming rise in the price of commodities (barley had risen from six shillings to six shillings and sixpence in a week), he admonishes him that: 'the channel you have chosen to convey your sentiments to the public was not the best through which you would have them stated with candour and impartiality'. 'Your letter' he goes on to say 'has certainly occasioned no small degree of agitation and irritation amongst us'.[512]

Cawdor did though in the autumn of 1799 open a successful subscription for the starving people of Pembrokeshire,[513] while in February 1801 the Common Council of Haverfordwest allocated £20 for making soup for the poor.[514] In the same year Cawdor allowed the poor to plant 23 acres of potatoes on his land 'to their great relief'.[515] The historian Richard Fenton bought corn for the poor in Fishguard. In June 1800 another subscription was opened in Haverfordwest to buy corn for the poor, miners being especially singled out. 'The gentry raised £320 on the spot.'[516] Hassall, with his characteristic advocacy of improved farming practices, believed that:

> Grain is frequently exported when cheap, and imported when dear… the great cause of this injurious traffic is, the bad state of our farm buildings, and the want of granaries for those farmers who can afford to keep a stock of corn upon lands, to lay it up in the summer. The buildings are so bad that a farmer who has to thresh in the winter to get straw for his cattle has nowhere to keep his corn. He has to sell it to dealers for whatever he can get. If they can they will keep enough for their own families to use during the summer, but the poor working people, are driven to the most deplorable distress.[517]

Hassall here touches upon the root cause of the trouble because there was little mystery about the reasons for this starvation. Apart from the vagaries of the weather and consequent bad harvests, and the effects of the wars, the problem was that the farmers and merchants cornered markets, and artificially inflated prices. A vivid and detailed description of the system in operation was written in 1803 by a visitor to Haverfordwest. Since it provides an excellent summary of the practice throughout the country, it is worth discussing the report in some detail.[518]

In the district around Haverfordwest he reports that the price of provisions were 'nearly as dear as those in England, and of inferior quality.' The country was now 'labouring under dearth and scarcity, and numbers of poor creatures of this and the neighbouring districts literally fell victims to the poverty of their country and the artifice of man'. Like Hassall he describes how the small farmers sell their corn, of necessity to dealers with ready cash, 'without reserving a supply for their families'. The dealers had a monopoly and kept such control 'as to keep the country in perpetual dread of famine'. When a vessel arrived, they the masters might sell grain at below the price it should have been. The 'poor starving inhabitants' had no money to buy corn even at this reduced price, and the merchants raised the price.

Another example he gives is that of a situation when there was a prospect of a good harvest in England, and the English merchants wanted to empty their warehouses. They knew that the Welsh were starving, and in due course a vessel from Sussex carrying barley arrived in the Cleddau (Haverfordwest), and it was offered at nine shillings a bushel: it was selling locally at 12 shillings. The dealers knew that the market was falling, and offered seven shillings. The owner was 'disgusted', and hearing that 'at Cardigan the people were starving to death' decided to go there. The merchants sent agents to Cardigan so that when the ship arrived they could corner the market at six shillings per bushel... he would be forced to return to the Cleddau, and to sell at seven shillings. The barley was then sold on at 11 shillings... 'such withholding of corn (is) a general curse'. And how can these men 'hope to evade the heavy curse denounced against those who wilfully withhold the corn from the poor'. One is left bewildered, in the light of this account, by the comment of another contemporary visitor who writes of the same area that 'corn (was) of course as reasonable as in the cheapest town in England'.[519] Or that of another who records though that 'the price of provisions and the rate of labour are much lower than in any part of Wales, or probably in England'.[520]

A rare defence of the merchants is made by Hassall when he points out that the numbers who need to buy corn is small because the bulk live on the land. So farmers have difficulty in selling it; the dealers buy at a price below that of the open market in autumn and winter. They buy to export. But, Hassall points out, it must be remembered

> they have to store it, transport it by sea, insure it, deal with the middleman and get a profit. And because the corn is likely to be damp, if the ship is delayed it will be ruined.[521]

The response of the authorities to profiteering was less analytical, and much less sympathetic. There was rioting in St. Davids in 1795 and in response Lord Milford convened a meeting of the County Magistrates on 27 February 1796. A number of resolutions were passed, some of which cut across what was the course of crude supply and demand. Some of these were: that the export of corn from Pembrokeshire should be stopped: that the Collector of Customs at Milford should be told to use every legal means to impede any vessel exporting corn: that people going round farms buying corn for export are 'enemies to the country and the real authors and instigators of the riotous disposition of the people', and that they 'are amenable to and punishable at Common Law'. The Clerk of the Peace was to take opinion, and to move with 'the utmost severity of the Law. These resolutions were to be displayed in public places throughout the county.[522]

The resolutions were sent to Portland whose reaction was predictable, since he was absolutely convinced of the merits of a free market and became hysterical by any interference with it by reformers who 'like quacks in other professions, will destroy their patients in the course of the cure'.[523] He was furious and considered their actions 'highly improper'. They were contrary to the Parliamentary wish for free trade in corn, and 'meet with the unequivocal disapprobation of His Majesty's confidential servants'. They would do 'mischief', and something must be done 'to do away the impressions they must make upon the people in that neighbourhood'. He deplored the meetings and the resolutions 'in the most unequivocal manner'.[524] Portland held so strongly to this view that he was firm, even when he wrote to someone as eminent as the Duke of Marlborough about the matter, courteously but insisting upon 'the folly and injustice of this false policy to which is to be attributed the assumption of a right to set prices on commodities brought to market'.[525] This was Portland's normal reaction to any attempts to interfere with the markets, and he sent the same message on many occasions.

The Duke of Portland was at the centre of all the civil crises of the time. He was the recipient of all reports of treason and sedition, and his cardinal belief was, in his own words, in 'a religious observation of the respect which is due to private property'.[526] George III regarded him as 'a true lover of order',[527] and it was not surprising that he 'never flinched from suggesting the use of armed force'.[528]

At their meeting on the 29 March to discuss and reply to Portland's letter, the magistrates were unrepentant. They explained, for example that their advice to the Collector of Customs was intended, amongst other things, 'to prevent smuggling, and to satisfy the people (inflam'd with apprehension)'. Most important, they pointed out, 'disorder and turbulence have entirely ceased in the neighbourhood of St. Davids and that no ill impression appears as yet to have been occasioned by the Resolutions'.[529] The crises continued in Wales. In Cardiganshire:

> In February 1817 many people went around the Cardiganshire countryside begging food and work at the houses of the gentry. The London Association for the Relief of the Manufacturing and Labouring Poor sent money, clothing, and food to help those who were starving. A local branch of this association was formed in the county, but it seems to have collapsed from lack of support.[530]

There are a number of certainties about the situation of the lower classes in Wales at the turn of the eighteenth and nineteenth centuries. The first is that they were desperate. The second is that they were the victims of what would today be called racketeering such as what was then called badgering. Racketeering took several forms. Merchants could 'forestall', which meant buying before the product was available for general sale. Then there was 'engrossing', which was buying as much as possible so that 'regrating' could take place. This was selling on at a profit. And the third is that the government, although apprehensive about violence and the threat of violence, chose to use force rather than to engage in positive steps to deal with the problem of hunger. And all of this was dominated by the intransigence of Portland and his mulish belief in a policy which was manifestly not working.

There are two phenomena which have been insufficiently stressed about the social unrest which has been described. The first is the prominence of miners, and the second is the role of women. Dodd is one who emphasises this, drawing an interesting comparison with an earlier time. To peaceful town dwellers the cry of 'the colliers are coming to town' was as terrifying in the eighteenth century as the cry of 'the beggars are coming to town' had been in the sixteenth.[531] It was a view that was shared by John Vaughan of Golden Grove in a view expressed to his agent in 1758 that 'all Colliers have been looked upon to be great rogues and require good looking after'.[532] And, of course, in much of the protest which has been described in this chapter miners have played a central part: lead miners in Cardiganshire, and coal miners throughout Carmarthenshire and Pembrokeshire, Glamorgan, and in north Wales. It was miners who were shot in Carmarthenshire, and miners who threatened to burn down Picton castle.

In her excellent article on the role of women in Welsh mining history Angela John sums up the neglect of the contribution of women to social protest: 'Women's history in Wales can be said to be a history of omission'.[533] For many hundreds of years women throughout Britain had taken a share, and sometimes the lead in rioting. Southey was not without evidence for his 1807 opinion, however much of a overgeneralisation, and however unfortunately expressed, which was that:

> Women are ever inclined to be mutinous; they stand less in awe of the law, partly from ignorance, partly because they presume upon the privilege of their sex, and therefore in all public tumults they are foremost in violence and ferocity.[534]

In November 1693 there was serious rioting in Northampton, and there, as in Oxford earlier, women 'took a prominent part – great numbers of them coming into the market with knives stuck in their girdles "to force corn at their own rates"'.[535] Women were in the forefront again in May 1709 where in Essex 'mobs of women amounting to hundreds were on the move, and had threatened to "fire divers houses, and shoot several persons, by reason they have been dealers in corn to London, on pretence they make the same dear"'.[536] In a riot in Poole in 1737 '"the Numbers consist in so many Women & the men supporting them"'. In 1740 'the mob was raised' in Stockton by a "Lady with a stick and a horn"'.[537] During the Highland clearances '"deforcement", that is of mobbing sheriff's officers to prevent them from serving the formal legal writs of removal... were generally the work of the women of the township, and they were almost always spontaneous'.[538]

Women were to the fore in protests in Wales too. In Haverfordwest in September 1644 'the poorest sort of women' attacked the government officials who were trying to collect taxes on food.[539] In June 1740 'a crowd comprising mainly women unloaded wheat from a vessel about to sail from Flintshire.[540] Women played an important part in a march from Llangyfelach to Swansea in 1793 where 'they were amongst the most vocal and extreme members of the mobs'.[541] They were prominent too in August of that year at Hay. 'Indeed 1795 has been called 'the year of – the revolt of the housewives'.[542] On the night of 23 August that year, 1795, at Hay, a number of women stopped a wagon loaded with a few bags of flour and took the bags into the market-house to be divided out the next morning'. 'For a similar offence early in 1796 in the parish of Hawarden, in Flintshire, Ann Catherall, aged thirty two, and Elizabeth Huxley, a widow of twenty-nine were each sentenced to transportation for seven years'.[543] And we have seen how the women of Hook were to the forefront in 1795. Later in March

1800 women were prominent in a march from Llangattock to Beaufort. A few years after that in the studied struggle by Cardiganshire peasants to obstruct the carrying out of the 1812 and 1815 Enclosure Acts in the middle of 1815:

> A mob comprised solely of women, and armed with dripping pans, came down upon John Hughes and his helpers 'like a rolling torrent' – They directed his attention to a pit which had been dug for the internment of every surveyor who approached their 'rights'.[544]

Once again it is useful to examine a case in rather more detail, and one especially vivid account concerns events in Swansea in 1801. On 20 April a tax collector reported that 'a number of poor women with two Girls of the Town at their head assembled and paraded the streets, and being joined by a number of poor children whom the women encouraged to holla and scream – the whole body proceeded to a corn warehouse – and forced open the door, but did not attempt to take any of it away'. The Cardigan Militia were called out, the Riot Act was read and the women dispersed. 'One or two of the ringleaders were taken into custody and delivered to some of the Swansea Independent Volunteers, but as the females were of the Cyprean Corps, the Independents suffered them to escape'. This is a euphemism for prostitutes, but it was surely used to denigrate the women, prostitutes or not. It might also excuse the behaviour of the Independents, who perhaps felt sympathy towards their plight. After all most of the militias and their kindred organisations, as we will see, were unreliable. The collector goes on that on the Saturday before 'which was much more serious than this day's proceedings' with rumours of 'a large mob of miners colliers etc.' intending to assemble, 'Col. Morgan, (Steward to the Duke of Beaufort and reputed King of Swansea) found himself so intimidated that notwithstanding he could call out 600 Volunteers of Horse and Foot' sent to Cardiff for some of the 'Iniskillings (sic), as it was rumoured that a large mob of miners colliers & meant to assemble that day'. This is one of many reflections on the unreliability of the militia. On the 21 April 1801, twenty Iniskillings arrived and 'everything is quiet at present'. On Wednesday 22 a witness to the events of the previous Saturday said that the 'avowed purpose' was to have corn at a rate 'as to keep them from starving', and that 'the distress of the labouring poor is unparalleled'. There might be a revolution because 'he had heard many of the lower orders call his Majesty a Dam German Butcher, that he delighted in blood, and that they would not be starved under such a <u>Whelp</u> i.e. <u>Guelph</u>'.[545]

As may be seen from the recital of these events, Wales was a place which was, not surprisingly, of concern to the authorities. The debate remains as to whether the protests were systematic, or had their origins in an intellectual base, or were studied, or random. We now go on to explore the degree to which the people of Wales knew about, or were influenced by, the wider political issues and upheavals of the time.

4

AN INTELLECTUAL BASIS OF PROTEST?

'The Printing-press, so say the wise, is the Candle of the World, the Freedom of BRITAIN'S Sons'.[546]

Having discussed the extent and variety of social disturbance, this chapter will consider several aspects of the circumstances surrounding these events. These circumstances are the subject of much controversy. The questions focus on whether or not the riots were spontaneous and devoid of political motivation or background. Or whether, especially after the American and French Revolutions, they were the expression of studied political discontent, which in some cases at least were underpinned by radical political theory. If the latter is the case, then the question of the role of the written word in propagating such ideas must be examined. As part of this question, there must be taken into account the levels of literacy, the nature and growth of printed work, and the highly speculative contribution which the spoken word may have made to the political awareness of people at an especially troubled period. These difficult questions are compounded by the fact that while we are considering Britain, we are concentrating especially on Dyfed, which was, as we have seen, a notably backward and remote area.

Analysts of the turbulence of the lower classes, especially in the eighteenth and nineteenth centuries very broadly have two opinions. On the one hand it is possible to take the view that 'it has been rightly asserted that the riots of the eighteenth century were almost exclusively the mere impulse of an untamed people, mob outrages on a large scale excited by some local and temporary grievances'. And that there was in these riots 'no intermixture of sedition'. There is too the parallel of view of GM Trevelyan that although there were huge differences in the distribution of power and wealth 'there was little or no social discontent'.[547] Others agree:

There is no evidence that, in spite of a constant animus against the clergy and a growing one against the farmers and gentry (at least in some parts) the movements sought any subversion of the social order. They sought its regulation. No doubt the general moderation of their atmosphere was partly, and paradoxically, due to the fact that they were movements of an agricultural proletariat and not a peasantry. Peasants, however unrevolutionary, want land, and lack of land is against natural justice. The remarkable characteristic of the proletarianised labourer was that he no longer wanted land, but higher wages and good employment.[548]

In Britain as a whole, Wells detects the same 'conservatism'.

> Contemporaries commonly detected what they interpreted as 'levelling' principles at the popular level; in fact, most of these manifestations were theatrical... the crowd's activities were primarily conservative, be they a reduction of food prices, resistance to the turnpiking of roads or to the erection of new workhouses. The crowd was never mobilised against an economic structure.[549]

With respect to Wales, Wager is an example of a writer who sees the Welsh as hardly sympathetic to notions of rebellion or revolution and refers to the 'innate conservatism' of the Welsh people: 'one has only to compare their hostile reaction to the radical societies with their immediate enthusiasm towards the pro-government loyalist associations of 1792'.[550]

It should be remembered though that such evidence as there is about 'conservative' views in Wales derives, as we shall go on to see, from the statements of chapel leaders, and the massive support given to the Establishment and the royal family by the London Welsh and their several organisations. The recorded views of the poor in Wales are very sparse, and the best evidence comes from their actions, as set out in the previous chapter.

DJV Jones writes that there was little ideological struggle, especially during the momentous struggles which were to come between workers and owners. The corn riots of the years from 1792–1801 in Wales:

> did not represent a conflict between capital and labour – only in the Swansea and Merthyr disturbances did the demand for higher wages appear – it was about 'supplier-consumer conflict' – moreover the riots were not directed against the existing political order, although there were hints of political motive behind the disturbances.[551]

But it can be argued that this is something of an overstatement, since he goes on to list what he defines as seditious acts.[552] Certainly there was much talk of so serious a matter as sedition; seditious literature, talk and even songs. And people were accused, tried and convicted of seditious offences, as we have seen with the notable case of Jac Glan y gors. And finally Jones concludes with an opinion that 'with greater unity and better leadership the corn riots of the years from 1792 to 1801 might have helped bring about a revolution'.[553]

Such views – that the insurrections were inchoate – are not especially new. Nor is another claim that the writings of some of the most prominent Welshmen were not influential in the formation of public opinion new or revisionist. Thomas Evans writing in 1936 of Dr. Richard Price, claims that:

> it is very doubtful whether they exercised much influence on the Welsh masses except very indirectly. They all visited Wales, but their stay was usually of short duration, and their points of contact with the people were not such as to ensure a lasting influence (One should doubt) the existence of a strong public opinion among the ordinary Welshmen of the day as a result of the English writings of these Welshmen of the revolutionary period.[554]

The alternative interpretation could not be more in disagreement: 'the influence which Dr. Price had exerted during his visits to Wales, in the late summer of each year, was widespread and lasting'.[555] Gwyn Williams draws attention to the fact that 'Richards Price went home to Wales every summer and his kinsfolk were radical colonisers of the Welsh mind'.[556] And Beloff, despite the earlier quotation, goes on to point out many examples of where there was 'the rumour – one not apparently without foundation – that political discontent was at the bottom of the whole affair'. In this case he writes of rather earlier disturbances of March 1668, such as the occasion when the famous apprentices opened the prisons in the midst of rioting which needed the military to restore order.[557] Again in respect of Wales Howell reports that:

> a perceptible change in the chemistry of food riots was to occur in the 1790s for, as we have earlier observed, with the heightening of radical consciousness food riots in Wales as elsewhere in Britain were sometimes driven, in part at least, by Jacobinical sentiments'.[558]

There is also the case of a woman called Hannah More (1745–1833) who 'broadcast throughout the land a myriad of small tracts' designed to counter both the trivia of traditional popular literature and revolutionary ideas. In a letter of 1794 she wrote:

> When we consider the zeal with which the writings of Priestley, etc., are now brought within the compass of penny books, circulated with great industry, and even translated into Welsh, I begin to fear that *our* workmen and porters will become *philosophers* too, and that an endeavour to amend the morals and the principles of the poor is the most probable method to preserve us from the crimes and calamities of France (her italics).[559]

The question as to how far these riots were 'political' and systematic has been addressed often. With regard to Wales a representative view of the 'political' context is that of Gwyn A Williams. He is perhaps one of the principal advocates of the notion that the disturbances which happened in Wales were in some way inspired by the American Revolution, seemingly subscribing to the view that '"politics" in Wales begin with the American Revolution':

> The American example, charged now with French styles, drenched every radical and protest movement in the turbulent Wales of the 1790s – in books, leaflets, journals and graffiti.

Furthermore the volume of reading material was impressive: 'From the 1790s the number of political texts in Welsh had multiplied sixfold'.[560] He also makes what some might regard as extravagant claims:

> a political thread of Jacobin democracy runs through everything, weaving in and out of the crowd actions. It is present in the slogans of the Swansea colliers in 1793, in the speeches during the great Denbigh riot of 1795 in the crowd protests in Merioneth and Llanbrynmair.[561]

Wager adds that:

> copies of Henry Hunt's Spa Fields speech were sent to Methyr in December 1816 and translated into Welsh. Similarly, at Neath and

Merioneth, extracts from Cobbett's *Political Register* were translated into Welsh.[562]

The thrust of Williams' argument is an insistence that pre-industrial Wales was not naïve, and so by the 1790s radicalism was a potent force in Welsh life. Davies and Edwards hold similar views claiming that:

> Though Wales still remained much more backward than England, the spirit of change was abroad, the old established order began to break up and even in remote places the fiery breath of the French Revolution seared, or quickened men's minds, according to their interpretation of it.[563]

And can it be true that the poor people or 'Patriots of Swansea in 1793 spoke of France as a warning?' And that reports from Haverfordwest about a mass rising were not true?[564] It seems difficult to believe that such statements and their concomitant actions were not part of a coherence, which as we shall go on to see was certainly identified by the government.

As the rioting increased in the 1790s one can ask how far Wales was involved in the new groups which came into being in the wake of the two Revolutions. The London Corresponding Society was founded in January 1792 by Thomas Hardy and a group of tradesmen, mechanics and shopkeepers:

> It is not known for certain if any branches were formed in Wales, although it is clear that some contact was established – The minutes of a general committee meeting of the Society on 26 December 1793, for instance, record that a letter from Wales was read. There were certainly individual members of the Society in Wales, such as John Jones of Anddren, near Bala, who in 1792 had resolutions of the Society printed in Welsh.[565]

Although there is no question about the radicalism of the London Corresponding Society, it had to be discreet. When an opposing organisation charged it with demanding 'no king, no parliament' it repudiated both propositions with equal vigour.[566] 'The Hamden Club, a London society founded in 1812 to organise reform petitions, circulated literature to many parts of Wales',[567] and there is no reason to suppose that Dyfed and other distant counties, remote though they were from the rest of the country, were immune from such influence. Indeed Williams goes on to cite Dyfed as a case of especial difficulty. As late as the 1830s and 1840s:

South west Wales (was) in quasi-permanent crisis – Cardiganshire was the most disturbed county in Wales – the Galicia of Wales – Carmarthen (was in) a kind of secession from public order – shaping itself behind a language and religious line which was also a class line. There was a rooted populist radicalism in Carmarthen, fed by its neighbour villages, which could make it a 'sans-culotte' sort of place. In a sense, it served as a staging post between the south-west and the industrial complex; Chartism in Wales was appropriately born there.[568] Williams insists upon the coherence of early radical organised working class resistance. He dismisses what he terms 'the related notions of isolation, backwardness and "primitive rivals"', and claims that 'that complex in south Cardiganshire/north Carmarthenshire/ north Pembrokeshire… was the human matrix of so many working-class movements'.[569]

One episode which Gwyn A Williams[570] regards of deep political significance, and an indication of a greater degree of sophistication than is generally supposed, are the events surrounding the affair which has come to be called *Rhyfel y Sais Bach* (The war of the little Englishman). The scene was Mynydd Bach near Llangwyryfon in Cardiganshire, after the passing of an Act (55 George III, c81) in 1815. This authorised the enclosing of about five thousand acres in Cardiganshire, and in 1819 an Englishman, although he was described as an Irishman or a Jew, Augustus Brackenbury, bought some 850 acres of the enclosure. The land was rough, and was used by local people to cut peat. In 1820 Brackenbury built a house there, and in a very short time there was gunfire, seizure of the owner, and the house was burned. Magistrates meeting in Aberystwyth offered a reward, to no avail. By 1826 Brackenbury had built another house, and had started preventing locals cutting turf. On 23 May he spent the night in Aberystwyth, and the next day a well organised mob attacked what seemed to resemble a castle, and destroyed the contents. According to one writer the attacks were more frequent than the three usual described.[571] There followed arrests and trials the course of which has left experts puzzled. Brackenbury still did not give in, and probably in 1828 he built a third house. He was now left in peace, but sold up and left the district two years later. Brackenbury wrote of himself as 'an example in the nineteenth century of a Subject of this Realm, without the means of prevention or redress, deprived of a valuable Property by open and lawless force'.[572] The reason he could get no redress is almost certain to have been the notorious incompetence of the magistrates or their considerable fear of the peasantry, or both.

The question which now must be addressed is the degree of literacy in Wales, since upon that substantially depends the possibility that the literature of revolution, in sophisticated or naïve forms was accessible. The gentry were of course, not only literate, but some, even in the eighteenth century had a serious interest in the collection of books and the building of libraries. One gentlemen 'Richard Morris, who worked in the Navy Office, was regularly called upon to comb London for books required by his family and friends back in Wales. Bristol booksellers supplied Welshmen with catalogues'.[573] Thomas Johnes of Hafod was a regular customer. Not everyone however is convinced that the bulk of the population was literate, or able to exploit available material:

> It is one thing to publish, and quite another problem to read, discuss and understand. The proportion of Welsh people who could read and write was low, and even *'Y Cylchgrawn Cymraeg'* could not enlist more than a thousand subscribers. It is probable that the same copy was circulated among many readers, still, it is not likely that there was enough reading to justify a belief in their deep and widespread influence.[574]

As early as the sixteenth century it appears that there was an expectation that the people of Wales could read. In a book published in 1631, called *Car-wr y Cymru*, Oliver Thomas 'urges the clergy to encourage their parishioners to buy Bibles and to read them'.[575]

There is considerable evidence that by the seventeenth century substantial numbers of the Welsh were literate. Geraint Jenkins sets out the case that yeoman farmers and tradesmen and others 'of middling sorts' had 'a growing appetite – for pious literature'. He describes a small parish in Cardiganshire where, in the 1690s the people were 'perceptive and literate men', while 'in rural Carmarthenshire "the middling sorts" – were reputedly so well read that Methodist evangelicals hesitated before crossing swords with them'.[576]

The SPCK at the end of the seventeenth and the beginning of the eighteenth century reprinted Welsh books, and new ones were translated. These included Sion Rhydderch's translation of Dr. Woodward's pamphlets (around 1701) while a new edition of the Welsh bible in 1718 sold 10,000 copies, with a second edition appearing in 1727.[577] And there was plenty of evidence of scholarship:

our knowledge of the past would be immeasurably poorer had not a small group of scholars deliberately striven to preserve our priceless literary treasures by rescuing, copying, and preserving ancient manuscripts.[578]

One of the more remarkable of these was James Davies (Iaco ap Dewi) who in Carmarthenshire at the end of the seventeenth century spent his life copying ancient manuscripts, and translating the works of people like Bunyan. And then there was the 'towering scholarship of Edward Lhuyd', who 'stimulated the curiosity of whole generations of Welsh antiquarians, historians, archaeologists, and philologists.[579] And although Jenkins' caveat (about the book) is probably wise, it is nevertheless a fact that *Lhuyd's Archaeologia Britannica* was regarded as 'worth all your labour and pains'.[580]

Theophilus Evans wrote a popular history of Wales, *Drych y Prif Oesoedd*, republished in 1740 which 'it is scarcely an exaggeration to say – became the most popular history book in Welsh prior to the twentieth century'.[581]

The main purpose of publication was though to save souls: 'the overwhelming majority of books published in this period (late seventeenth, early eighteenth centuries) consisted of practical works of piety couched in plain, intelligible language'.[582] There was much admonition to eschew drunkenness and cursing, and much advocacy of the sanctity of the sabbath, which was to be a central plank for Welsh politics well into the twentieth century. Blame for pestilence, such as the diseases which hit Wales from 1726–29 was blamed squarely on sinning. Thomas Richards published a translation of Advice to persons recovered from sickness, and:

4,000 copies… were distributed in 1730 to sick people who had experienced both the goodness and the severity of God.[583] Humble yeomen-farmers and craftsmen formed a sizeable proportion of the 689 subscribers to *Trefn Ymarweddiad Gwir Gristion* (The order of the living of the true Christian 1723–24).[584]

And books such as *Canwyll y Cymry* (The Welshman's Candle), written by a native of Llandovery, Rhys Pritchard, were widely accessible because 'charitable bodies like the Welsh Trust and the SPCK published sizeable editions at cheap rates and distributed many of them free of charge to the deserving poor'.[585] Others 'offered a view – later echoed by many Methodists – that a heart full of grace was a greater asset to an individual than a head full of knowledge'.[586] This ominous and philistine doctrine was to be promulgated by the Nonconformists, notably in the turbulent 1790s and in the succeeding years.

When it comes to other than the gentry, the initial discussion can usefully focus upon two much lauded educators, one in the south, and one in the north, respectively Griffith Jones of Llanddowror, and Thomas Charles of Bala. Both were natives of Carmarthenshire, both were clergymen, and both were at work at the middle and end of the eighteenth century, Jones before Charles.

Jones (b. 1683) was the pioneer of Circulating Schools. This was a system which involved the recruitment and training of teachers who moved around the countryside, most notably in west Wales, and through the medium of the bible taught both children and adults to read and write Welsh. English however, was the medium in English speaking areas such as south Pembrokeshire. A fact of some significance is that apart from Sir John Philipps of Picton, his brother in law, and Madam Bevan, he received very little support in Wales:

> The movement prospered because Griffith Jones came to know a circle of wealthy and philanthropic English people who supported his efforts – not one of them had any connection with Wales, by birth or residence.[587]

There were some who attacked his work in very disparaging terms. One John Evans of Eglwys Cymmin, a clergyman, wrote a book in 1752 which was 'a bitter personal attack upon Griffith Jones and a condemnation of his schools.[588] And he later wrote that he 'would not have ventured to offend a man of his revengeful temper, and one armed at all points with so much dirt, as I have already found him to be',[589] while Howell Harris wrote in 1736 that 'the clergy hate him for his singular piety and charity to the dissenters'.[590]

Charles (b. 1755), used the medium of the Sunday school, but both men had the same goal. It was to teach literacy, and thus develop Christian ideals. Jones predictably believed the purpose was not 'intended to make their pupils "gentlemen, but Christians and heirs of eternal life – not to elate their minds, but to make them by the grace of God good men in this world and happy in the next"'.[591] One apologist suggests, without saying how, that this perfectly clear statement 'is an aim capable of a variety of interpretations'.[592]

Charles would have subscribed to this, probably only adding how important the Methodist dimension was. And it is generally accepted that the Sunday schools' contribution to literacy in Wales in the eighteenth and nineteenth centuries was immense. His initiative 'proved to be profoundly significant and enduring'. The effect of the work of both:

> was to allow the majority of the people of Wales to read their own language and to attain, for members of their class, an unprecedented knowledge of theological issues and the ability to deal with them in intense and mature manner, unlike anything achieved by their peers in England. We have the evidence of the 1847 report of the education commissioners to testify to that.[593]

It is a truism of educational experience however that it is impossible to restrict the use of literacy to some narrow and specific end, and if the Welsh were as literate because of the efforts of these men as is generally claimed, then the potential for the dissemination of *all* kinds of information must have been enormous. This was a commonly expressed fear:

> There is a risk of elevating, by an indiscriminate education, the minds of those doomed to the drudgery of daily labour above their condition, and thereby rendering them discontented and unhappy in their lot.[594]

Charles was a prolific writer and publicist, and was an important influence in the formation of the British and Foreign Bible Society. Jones too encouraged several reprints of the bible in Welsh. The scale of the operation of both men, even allowing for hyperbole and exaggeration, is impressive. In 1804 Charles' organisation had caused the distribution of 20,000 copies of the bible, and 5,000 copies of the new testament to be distributed across Wales.[595]

As to Jones, with whom we are chiefly concerned because the centre of his operation was the south west, there has been debate about the scale, details and accuracy of his claims. It is claimed in 'Welch Piety' that, from 1737 to his death in 1761, 3,495 schools had been set up, in which 158,237 pupils, excluding adults had been taught. Glanmor Williams claims that the 'true totals would seem to have been 3,325 schools in just under 1,600 places with 153,835 scholars'.[596] The article on Jones in *Eminent Welshmen* puts the overall figure rather higher at 158,000,[597] while another claims some 3,000 schools in 1,600 places.[598] Kelly's estimate is that there were 'over 3,000 schools in about 1,600 centres with over 150,000 day scholars and about the same number of evening scholars'.[599] Sir Thomas Philipps writes that at his death 'the schools had increased to 218' and that '150,212 persons had been taught, in twenty four years, to read the Welsh Bible'.[600] Twiston Davies writes that by his death 158,237 pupils had received teaching[601] while Howell as an estimate 'perhaps as many as 250,000'.[602]

Glanmor Williams' summary is that Jones' claim that two adults were taught for every child 'seems too generous a proportion'. His opinion is that the 'most critical estimates of recent years put the numbers in the twenty five years at 200,000', and that out of a population in Wales of between 400,000 and 500,000. It is difficult to disagree with his summary that 'this is, by any standards, an immense achievement'.[603] For the purpose of this discussion it is important to note, in addition, that these numbers are mainly drawn from the south, and especially the west since 'the circulating schools of Griffith Jones had not enjoyed great success in north Wales'.[604] As an illustration of the level of literacy is Jones' claim in *Welch Piety* that 'The great cry and most incessant application, that is now everywhere in these parts for Welch bibles, which yet are distributed among them with all convenient dispatch, shews, that the number of Welch readers is of late years greatly increased amongst them'.[605] Henry Richard adds to the usual admiration for the work of Jones by using him as another weapon in his relentless attacks upon the Established Church, when he claims that Jones was discouraged by many, including the bishops.[606] The distribution of bibles in Wales was not new in the eighteenth century. There seems to have been a sizeable demand before then. In the decade after the Restoration as well as a large-scale attempt to diffuse Welsh bibles for private use, a small number of Catholic devotional books 'slipped through' including *Allwydd neu Agoriad Paradwys i'r Cymru* published in 1670.[607]

Other claims are made for the levels of literacy in Wales. Beddoe is one who in her study of nearly 283 Welsh convict women who were transported between 1787 and 1852 to Australia, reports the remarkable fact that the records show that those who were 'exclusively Welsh speakers could also read and write in Welsh'.[608] This is an interesting commentary on literacy in Wales, since convict women are the last group who could be expected to be literate. Similar claims were made by contemporary observers. One such was made by one of the witnesses, a Mr. Rees, to the Education Commissioners of the 1840s:

> The Welsh peasantry are better able to read and write in their own language than the same classes in England. Among them are found many contributions to Welsh periodicals. I publish a monthly periodical myself *(Yr Haul)*, and have many contributions from this class.[609]

In the 1790s a visitor reported that:

> In our way through the town (Machynlleth) we looked into its church…where thirty or forty boys, the lads of the town and neighbourhood, were instructed in writing and reading both Welsh and English, during the summer months.[610]

Another remarkable claim is made in a discussion of the Morris brothers who, it will be remembered were from Anglesey, and have been credited with a major contribution to Welsh antiquarianism:

> Still less did it occur to them (the Morris brothers) that Methodism, which they all three hated so cordially, was to bring healing in its wings – to give the language a new and a long lease of life – to multiply the Welsh reading public to such a point that when the initial and exclusively religious phase of the Revival was spent, and when the Circulating schools of Griffith Jones and the Sunday Schools had taught the Welsh masses to read and to <u>think</u>, their reading could (and did) embrace not only the Tudor Bible but also the popular poetry and even (in cheaper reprints and at a later date) the 'classical' poetry of the Morrisian circle itself.[611]

In the view of Eiluned Rees, the results of all such literacy efforts is that there emerged a peasant culture probably unique in Europe:

> country people hitherto prevented by illiteracy from immortalising the poetic sentiments that came so easily to them were now able to pour out expressions of their faith in prose and verse, and revel in the works of those more talented than themselves. [612]

She goes on to enumerate the occupations of those who were on subscription lists of Journals. These range from grocer to tanner to glover to innkeeper to carpenter. In addition there were farmers, ministers and schoolmasters and 'a fair number of women'.[613]

There is evidence too of printing businesses which further support the existence of a reading public. After 1695, when there was more freedom for the press, Thomas Jones, who had already published in Welsh in 1680, from his base in Shrewsbury from 1695 'spread the reading habit simply by adapting his material to popular tastes – no one did more in this period to ensure that literacy was no longer the preserve of the affluent and leisured classes'.[614] As early as 1718 Isaac Carter established the first printing press in Wales near Newcastle Emlyn. The first book printed in Carmarthen was in Welsh in 1723. The printer was 'probably Nicholas Thomas from Cenarth who was the second printer to set up business in Wales', who printed 'at least three other books before the end of 1725'.[615] Yet another Carmarthen printer John Ross 'dominated' the Welsh printing trade in the second half of the century.[616] Again in Carmarthen 'as far back as 1724 there was a market for second-hand books – when Crispianus Jones advertised that he had for sale several second-hand school books',[617] and the advertisements 'prove that Carmarthen catered most competently for bibliophiles'.[618] In 1734 Shon Rydderch's almanac for this year was the first almanac printed in Wales. 'Some of the best poetry of the age may be found in the almanacs' which proved to be a very popular form of reading at the time.[619] Perhaps the scale of the activity in Carmarthen is indicated by the fact that there were some nine printers there at the end of the eighteenth century.[620] Also in respect of remarkable Carmarthen 'by the 1790s globes, telescopes, microscopes, mathematical instruments, and an electrical machine were as much in use in the Carmarthen academy as were works of divinity'.[621] Then, in 1803, Thomas Johnes of Hafod set up the first private printing press in Wales.

For those who were literate in either Welsh or English or both, what was available? Leaving aside religious material, there were first of all the writings of those who to some degree, and at varying times, were impressed with the Revolutions in America and France. 'Approximately 40 per cent of the contents of the *Cylchgrawn Cymraeg*, for example, was a translation of English and American works'.[622] These were the works which were deemed by commentators such as Thomas Evans to have made little impact. Whether or not this dismissal can be sustained in respect of Wales, there is no doubt that in Britain, and for that matter in America and France, the Revolutions were very much *the* topic of public discussion.

The first writer to be discussed, and without any doubt the most influential was Richard Price (1723–91). One of the remarkable features of the historical evaluation of the period and his role in the development of the ideas of the age is that he so little discussed, except by a small group of (notably Welsh) devotees.[623] He was a Welsh born Unitarian minister, principally of the chapel in Newington Green, London, and a relentless supporter of the American and French Revolutions. When America became independent, Benjamin Franklin-Price's close friend – Arthur Lee, and John Adams 'were specially deputed by Congress to invite Dr. Price to give his assistance in regulating the finances of the New Republic'.[624] In July 1790 at a meeting presided over by Lord Stanhope a toast was proposed by Price. In it the hope was expressed that there would be an alliance between Great Britain and France for perpetuating peace, and making the whole world free and happy – 'it was so warmly approved, that it was resolved to send it to the Duc de la Rochefoucauld – it was read twice in the National Assembly, all the members standing uncovered'.[625] Price was 'pronounced by Lord Lyttleton to be one of the clearest thinkers of the age, and by Condorcet to be one of the formative minds of the period'. It is even suggested that it was his idea to throw the tea into the sea in Boston.[626]

Richard Price achieved fame in several spheres, including financial matters and philosophy. In respect of the former he wrote a very influential book, first published in 1771 entitled *Observations on writings on Reversionary Payments,* which was revised and republished throughout his life. But it was as a political theorist that he is best remembered. His writings were not mere abstractions, since they were grounded in the momentous events of the American and French revolutions. In respect of the first he wrote three works which advanced the cause of the colonists: *Observations on the Nature of Civil Liberty, The Principles of Government, and The Justice and Policy of the War with America (1776).* This sold over 1,000 copies in two days, 60,000 in six months, was translated into German French and Dutch, and was published in America. Then came *Additional Observations on the Nature and Value of Civil Liberty and the War with America (1777)*, and *Two Tracts on Civil Liberty, the War with America, and the Debts and Finances of the Kingdom (1778).*[627] Typical of his views were those expressed in a discussion of Montesquieu in *Additional Observation:*

> We may learn from it that we have nothing to fear from that disposition to examine every public measure, to censure ministers of state, and to be restless and clamorous, which has hitherto characterized us.[628]

Such writing predictably created huge controversy. The Archbishop of York, in a sermon, spoke of 'mischievous opinions… I consider them as relating, not indeed to the rebellion itself, for that rests upon wickedness only, but to the specious fallacies by which it is so shamelessly defended'. One does not have to look far to find other what can only be described as violent attacks. John Lind (1737–81), lawyer and friend of Bentham, political adviser to Lord Mansfield wrote:

On that perusal they seemed to present to me what I had expected,
abuse of terms, confusion of ideas, intemperate ebullitions of mis-
guided zeal, gloomy pictures of a disturbed imagination; all the effect
I apprehended from the book arose from the opinion which I was told
the public had of the author.[629]

For these, at least to the Establishment, inflammatory views, he was given
the Freedom of the City of London in 1776. Of this honour Lind wrote that
they 'bestowed upon the writer of a sixpenny pamphlet what was thought
an adequate reward for the services of a Pitt'.[630] Less surprising, but even
more distinguished, was his award of an honorary degree from Yale in 1781,
on which occasion the only other recipient was George Washington. It was
the first of many national and international honours. The offer to him of
American citizenship was turned down although his interest in, and his influence on, American affairs was undiminished. It is not surprising that this
offer was made since Price commonly defended the revolution in uncompromising terms:

But among the events in modern times tending to the elevation of
mankind there are none probably of so much consequence as the recent one which occasions these observations. Perhaps I do not go too
far when I say that, next to the introduction of Christianity among
mankind, the American revolution may prove the most important
step in the progressive course of human development.[631]

And in one of his letters to Franklin he remarks:

(In America there has) terminated in a state of society more favourable
to peace, virtue, science, and liberty (and consequently to human happiness and dignity) than has ever yet been known.[632]

Washington, in what seems to be profound respect wrote in 1785:

G. Washington presents his most respectful compliments to Dr. Price.
With much thankfulness he has received, and with the highest grati-
fication he has read, the doctor's most excellent observations on the
importance of the American revolution, and the means of making
it a benefit to the world... For the honourable notice of me in your

address, I pray you to receive my warmest acknowledgements, and the assurance of the sincere esteem and respect which I entertain for you.[633]

This relationship was in marked contrast to the ostensible views of the Welsh people 'which were manipulated by local politicians'. These politicians, who were, of course, members of the squirearchy, organised the presentation of Loyal Addresses in 1775, all from the south west, that is from Carmarthen, Carmarthenshire, and Haverfordwest. It was not until the war was proving to be failing and expensive that Welsh landowners began to protest, especially because the government proposed an inquiry into the diminution of royal revenues in Wales. The landowners saw that this 'would reveal long term encroachments on royal lands in Wales'. This was quickly claimed to be 'an attack on liberty and property in Wales'.[634]

In his classic *A Discourse on the Love of our Country* (1789) was a sermon in which Price hailed the beginning of the French Revolution with fervour, and with his usual convincing logic. He was also as uncompromising as ever:

Be encouraged, all ye friends of freedom and writers in its defence! The times are auspicious. Your labours have not been in vain. Behold kingdoms, admonished by you, starting from sleep, breaking their fetters, and claiming justice from their oppressors! Behold the light you have struck out, after setting AMERICA free, reflected to France, and there kindled into a flame that lays despotism in ashes, and warms and illuminates EUROPE![635]

Edmund Burke, although he had famously supported the Americans, was so angry at Price's words that he published his *Reflections on the Revolution in France* (1790). Burke in turn provoked Thomas Paine to answer *him* in his *Rights of Man* as a response, the opening words of the Preface underlining a critical change in Burke's affiliations:

from the part Mr. Burke took in the American Revolution, it was natural that I should consider him a friend to mankind... it would have been more agreeable to me to have had cause to continue in that opinion than to change it.[636]

All of the well known supporters of the French revolution discussed in this chapter became disillusioned after the Terror. Price did not live to see it take its course, and it would have been interesting to see what his attitude, which was so adamant, would have been. Certainly Price's even more radical nephew George Cadogan Morgan (1754–98) never lost any of his revolutionary fervour.[637]

We have seen the allegation that Welshmen such as Price made little impact on resident Welsh people. Gwyn A Williams, as has been shown, hotly disputes this, with his claim, already mentioned that the kinsfolk of Richard Price were 'radical colonisers of the Welsh mind', and that 'David Jones, the Welsh Freeholder, preached the doctrines of the Unitarian democrat Dr. Joseph Priestley as a way of life'.[638]

In February 1793 a letter was received in the Home Office from an informant in Cardiff. As we shall go on to see, the government relied on a variety of informants and spies to keep abreast of what was going on. This writer reports the fear felt by the community: not panic, for that would be to demean the 'tough' descendants 'of Cadwalleder'. He writes of the threat to write 'in gore'. And most interesting he claims it 'is known to be a certainty that a Welchman of great talents is translating Tom Paine's book in Welch & very industriously doing mischief thro' the strong espousal he has given the French cause'.[639] It is not clear whether this man of 'great talents' was John Jones (Jac Glan-y-gors) (1766–1821).

He was born in Denbighshire, was a publican in London, and active in several of the Welsh societies which were established at the end of the eighteenth century. And it was he who published the ideas of Tom Paine in two Welsh volumes: *Seren Tan Gwmmwl* (A star under a cloud) in 1795, and *Toriad y Dydd* (Daybreak), which introduced those who were happier reading Welsh to some of the most threatening ideas of the age. After Price, Jones was the author who produced the most radical and uncompromising attack on society. In *Seren Tan Gwmmwl* he launches a savage attack on kings from Nimrod to Louis XVI, detailing how they had heaped misery upon their people because of their ambition. The system of hereditary kingship, he declares, makes no sense, because there is no guarantee of the inheritance of quality. and 'expressed surprise at the blindness of the Israelites of old, in persisting in having a king'. As an illustration of the ignorance of monarchs he points out that William and Mary were made king and queen even though 'neither of them knew more about the laws and regulations of the kingdom, than a mole knows about the sun'.[640] Bishops and clergy were 'greater oppressors of their parishioners than ever Nero was at Rome'.[641] The money that went to bishops 'would do far more good in teaching the poor children of Wales, who were then kept in a cloud of ignorance'.[642] Next he dismissed the House of Lords using as one example the injustice of the tax on beer. Since the Lords brewed their own, they did not have to pay the tax. A strange choice of target until it is remembered that he was a publican. He goes on to attack the Commons and Pitt, in passing observing 'the silence of the Welsh members'. Then comes a virulent attack on the extravagance of the Prince of Wales. And naturally there was the inevitable praise of America – 'the morning star of liberty'.[643] *Seren* 'was widely read in Wales, and created a great stir throughout the Principality'.[644]

Toriad y Dydd (Daybreak), published in 1797, lists the same kinds of complaints; that the people had to consent to the government, that primogeniture was wrong, and that there were similarities between Henry VIII and Pitt. Both had to be obeyed. 'Henry VIII wanted a new wife often: and Pitt wanted a new tax even oftener than that'. This book 'bears evident traces of the main argument and contention of Thomas Paine's *Rights of Man*'.[645] Whether or not people could read the original Paine in English or the 'versions' by Jac Glan-y-gors, it was certainly believed that these ideas were circulating. Jac Glan-y-gors was in fact forced to leave London after the publication of *Seren Tan Gwmmwl*.

There can be no doubt of the certainty that Paine's ideas were circulating in Wales. An informant wrote to the Home Office on 19 December 1792 about dangerous people:

> infusing into their minds the pernicious tenets of Paine's *Rights of Man*, upon whose book, I am told, public lectures are delivered to a considerable number in the neighbourhood of Wrexham, by a Methodist. The pernicious effects of them are too evident in that parish.[646]

Another hugely widely read and influential book was Volney's *Ruins of Empire* (1791). This became, 'as an exercise in revolutionary fantasy or science-fiction, a standard text of working-class intellectuals for three generations was available in Welsh in 1793, just after the first English version and earlier than the first popularly effective version in English'.[647] And so the important claim is made that the essence of Volney was now available in Welsh. Furthermore, Morgan John Rhys' published translation 'was reprinted, word for word from his journal, in *Udgorn Cymru,* the Chartist newspaper of the 1840s.[648] Volney's ideas would surely appeal to the desperate with their assurance that nothing was immutable:

> And now a mournful skeleton is all that subsists of this opulent city, and nothing remains of its powerful government but a vain and ob-

scure remembrance!... the opulence of a commercial city is changed into hideous poverty. The palaces of kings are become the receptacle of deer, and unclean reptiles inhabit the sanctuary of the gods. What glory is here eclipsed, and how many labours are annihilated! Thus perish the works of men, and thus do nations and empires pass away.[649]

In Montgomeryshire, it is declared in the Education Commissioners' report (The Blue Books) that:

I ascertained, by a careful inquiry amongst the persons best acquainted with the condition of the working classes, that even at the present day low and unprincipled publications, of a profane and seditious tendency, are much read by a class of the operatives; that private and secret clubs exist for the dissemination of such writings, by means of which the class of operatives have access to the writings of Paine and Volney, to Owen's tracts, and to newspapers and periodicals of the same pernicious tendency. It is also stated that many persons who read such works also attend Sunday schools, from their anxiety to obtain a knowledge of the art of reading, which they cannot otherwise acquire.[650]

The solution was 'intelligent publications on general subjects within the comprehension of the working classes, by the help of reading societies and circulating libraries, at terms which the operatives would be able to afford.[651] The parish of Llanidloes, for example, 'has been infected with infidel and seditious principles. The writings of Paine and Carlile are read, and societies exist for teaching and discussing their theories'.[652] There seems to be no doubt that those in authority were convinced, and very concerned that such influences were present, and were widely subscribed to by people.

Samuel Homfray, a well known iron master and Magistrate in Merthyr, was another who expressed concern. He 'had little doubt that political principles had influenced the minds of the working classes who were rioting at Merthyr Tydfil'. He attached considerable significance to the appearance in the town of John Thelwall, a leading member of the London Corresponding Society, which had been suppressed in 1799. He had been living since 1798 in Llyswen in Brecknockshire from where he had carried on treasonable correspondence and attended regularly a society of Jacobins in Hereford.[653] Although he was a well known poet of his time, he was also a strong supporter of the French Revolution and in 1794 had been imprisoned because he was considered dangerous.

Apart from the towering figures of Richard Price and John Jones, there were other Welsh writers and activists living and writing at the end of the eighteenth, and the beginning of the nineteenth centuries, who are commonly regarded as radicals, and who generally are discussed as such. It is now appropriate to consider, briefly, the work and influence of some of these. Their complex relationships to radicalism will be considered in a later chapter.

David Williams (1738–1816) was a very active supporter of the French revolution in its early stages. According to Brissot, who was a major figure in the Revolution, he was 'one of the foremost political thinkers in England, and the least tainted with national prejudices, as he had embraced the cause of humanity'.[654] One of the French agents in London 'considered his understanding of the French Revolution far more profound than that of Burke, and spoke of him in higher terms of admiration even than the philosopher, Richard Price'.[655] It was decided to confer the title of French citizen upon a number of foreigners, and he was one. 'He accepted the honour in a letter in which he expressed very pronounced republican ideas'.[656] This is not surprising since in *Lessons to a young prince* in 1791, of the Revolution he wrote that it is 'an event the most beneficial to humanity in all the records of mankind'.[657] There was also a lot of pressure on him to put his name forward for the Convention. But unlike Paine, he thought that was going too far, arguing that he did not know enough about French affairs.[658] And he was important in the negotiations before war broke out. This is a complicated matter, which is the subject of David Williams' article, but outside the theme of this book.

He wrote a *Treatise on education* (1774) which 'attracted the attention of Benjamin Franklin', and together they founded the Thirteen Club, a group of deists for whom Williams wrote *Liturgy on the universal principles of religion and morality* (1776) This was 'politely accepted by Frederick II and received high commendation from Voltaire, while Rousseau considered that it "realised one of his highest wishes"'.[659] He wrote a defence of the American colonists – *Letters on Political Liberty* – which was translated into French.

We have already encountered Thomas Evans (Tomos Glyn Cothi) (1764–1833) for he was the minister pilloried in Carmarthen. As well as everything else he made an crucial contribution to the religious life of Wales since he 'is justly regarded as the pioneer of Unitarianism in Wales'.[660] He edited the first number of *Y Drysorfa Gymmysgedig* (The Miscellaneous Repository) in 1795. Such publications 'provided space for other writers, to present their views to the monoglot Welshman'[661] which comment under-lines the certainty that someone must have been reading them. His first publication was a Welsh translation of *The Triumph of Truth* which was an account of the trial of Edward Elwall for publishing a book in defence of the Unity of God in 1793, and which had a preface written by Joseph Priestley His admiration for Priestley led to him being nicknamed 'Priestley bach'.[662] The first issue of *Y Drysorfa Gymmysgedig* has a 'Hymn to be sung on the Fast Day'... which is a reflection of the sentiments which widely prevailed in Wales.[663] It speaks of 'the rapacious spoilers that waded in blood' a peti-tion that God would 'hurl headlong from their high seats, in one brief hour, those world-oppressors; and scatter the people who had fattened on human blood'... there would be an end to the fattening of 'odious plunderers'... and much in the same vein. In the same issue was an address from the Dam-many Society of America to Priestley: 'You have fled from the rough arm of cruelty; and you will find a refuge in the bosom of Liberty, in the bosom of Peace, in the bosom of America'.[664]

In this first issue is also pointed out that the French soldiers sent by the king of France to fight for America returned with unwelcome ideas about liberty.[665] This what can only be called adoration of America is a constant theme in Welsh writing of the period, since that country was the apothe-osis of freedom: 'The long and bitter struggle between Britain and America stirred the thoughts of men': [666]

Ballads of the period reflect these facts vividly, especially in relation to the war with America, when the people of Wales sympathised very largely with America rather than Britain. [667]

Life was 'well nigh intolerable in France' the Journal goes on and the Revo-lution was 'a welcome relief to the nation'. We also see an important, per-haps the most important theme in the writing of Nonconformists: hatred of the Roman Catholic church. The church was 'filled with immoral clergy: who withal had adopted infidel creeds, that fitted in with their lives – they reserved all their enthusiasm for the persecution of Protestants'.[668] Thomas Evans also published hymns, sermons, dictionaries and poetry. He trans-lated some of the works of Joseph Priestley in 1792, and second and third editions were printed in 1812 and 1824. In 1808 he translated a work by Benjamin Franklin.[669]

The next activist to be considered is Morgan John Rhys. He was born in Glamorgan in 1760, and died in America in 1804. In 1791 he went to

France 'as he believed the Revolution had opened an important door for the preaching of the Gospel, and the circulation of the scriptures in France', and he was welcomed in the French Assembly.[670] Amongst his activities was a campaign for funds for bibles to send to France. We shall go on to emphasise that anti Catholic ideology was a major, if not the most important, platform in the writings of this group. In 1793 he published the third number of *Cylchgrawn Cynraeg neu Drysorfa Gwybodaeth*. This contains a summary of an English book by Bicheno on *The signs of the Times, or the overthrow of Papal Tyranny in France, the Prelude of Destruction to Popery and Despotism, but of Peace to Mankind*: a book the popularity of which 'is undeniable'.[671] Bicheno (Rhys translated it into Welsh) developed a case that there was 'a correlation between biblical prophecy and the Revolution itself' – the French Revolution was portrayed as the work of God. Its purpose was to undermine Christian corruptions generally and Popery in particular'.[672] Such was the speed of Rhys' translation that Welsh readers were aware of the work before the first review appeared in an English periodical.[673] Rhys' 'role was both that of the publicist and the pedagogue', and like so many Dissenters 'Rhys agreed substantially with Bicheno's anti-Catholic interpretation of the French Revolution'.[674]

The Signs is a weird book, very much located in some of the more obscurantist religious concerns of the Age. Bicheno proposes 'an identification of the second Beast of the Book of Revelation with Louis XIV and the Capet family of France. The Beast was also 'associated with the despotic institution of monarchy characteristic of the *Ancien Regime*'.[675]

The 'resurrection' in Prophetic language marked the ending of the Second Woe and the beginning of the Third Woe when the Seven Angels would pour out the Vials of Divine Wrath upon Anti-Christ. The fall of the tenth part of the city, the French Revolution, was not the end of God's retributive justice; other anti-Christian institutions, and in particular the Papacy, would perish.[676]

And the analogies go on. 'The Jacobins were God's agents in so far as they were the opponents of Popish despotism'.[677] The association of divine revelation with the Revolution was to have serious and interesting consequences. For if the architects of the Revolution were 'doing God's will', then they must be supported. But such support, to put it mildly was in direct conflict with the disapproval of the British government which was to lead to war with France.

Dissenters like Rhys, Priestley, and Bicheno delivered, and published sermons which 'all focused on English hypocrisy and profligacy and defended the French Revolution against the charges of "atheism" levelled against her'.

Bicheno in a Fast Day sermon 'A word in season' spoke of the 'national crimes' of Britain.[678] 'Britain', he went on, 'was not the providential instrument to punish France for her excessive sins, rather Britain would be punished by France'. In February 1794 Rhys published an anonymous Fast Day sermon *Cynghor Gamaliel* (The Counsel of Gamaliel) in which he pointed out 'those who fought against France were also fighting against religious and civil liberty, and were fighting for the cause of Tyranny and Popery'.[679] In the issue of 3 August 1793, he attacked the government for policy towards France, and pointed out that Pitt had been declared 'an enemy of the human race' by the French parliament.[680] And in an oration delivered in Ohio in 1795 he addressed the INVINCIBLE FRENCHMEN! (his capitals). Urging them to 'go on!... The Popish beast has numbered his days!'[681] Small wonder then that the government, and supporters like Burke reacted so strongly to a studied opposition, one of the most worrying features of which was the strength it derived from scripture. But like so many Rhys became increasingly worried and disillusioned at the excesses of the French. 'He himself strongly protested that he was loyal to the British Government; and in the second number of *Y Cylchgrawn* he expresses his fervent wish that Providence might keep the family of Hanover on the throne'.[682] But he did in the magazine advocate press freedom, and education – especially so that people could read the bible. It is commonly supposed, and generally accepted, that he was pursued by the government, and he left for America. Like many Welsh he regarded America as:

> a new State, in which 'dwelleth righteousness' established by God on earth – a country, bestowing privileges upon its cities, in the enjoyment of as good a Government as was ever instituted on the earth.[683]

We shall go on to see that generations of Welsh people were to believe this and act upon it. For his part Rees went to America, and set up a colony which he called Beula, a reference to biblical Isaiah 62, and changed his name to Rhees.[684]

David Davies of Holywell (d. 1807) was the editor of *Y Geirgrawn* (The Treasury of Words, 1796), the first Welsh magazine to be published after those of Morgan John Rees.[685] The nine numbers were advertised as being intended to spread 'Knowledge, Justice, Love, and Peace throughout Wales'. It supported both revolutions, and for good measure carried a Welsh version of *Le Marseillaise*.[686]

The first issue contains a letter from Morgan John Rhys 'urging Welsh-men to make a settlement on the River Ohio'. But the 'chief feature' of the magazine was discussion about *Seren tan Gwmmwl*.[687] 'Antagonist' engaged in 'a vigorous, and somewhat abusive criticism of the author of *Seren*'.[688] A rather remarkable feature of this savage attack was that 'Antagonist' was a man called Edward Charles who was one of Glan-y-gors' closest friends. Indeed he composed odes in praise of the public house kept by Glan-y-gors, which was the meeting place of the *Gwyneddigion* Society. In the June 1796 issue 'Peris' also attacked the translator of Paine, saying that Paine's followers were 'mad, and hard visaged'.[689] In the July issue Carwr Rheswm denied that John Jones was a follower of Paine! Or that *Seren* was a translation.

Then there was Thomas Edwards, (1738–1810) whose nickname was Twm o'r Nant. He was born in Denbighshire. Unlike some of those who have been discussed he was not an especial advocate of the principles of the revolutions, but was for justice and liberty and condemned the failure of the rich to help the poor. He wrote something entitled 'Interludes'. These 'were a type of metrical play' performed by strolling players. For various reasons they were disapproved of by religious leaders.[690] He has been distinguished from some of his contemporaries, because although he did not attack roy-alty he was better than the other Welsh bards who 'were content to sing the praises of the House of Hanover, and generally bore no witness to social ills'.[691] An example of the latter was Dafydd Ddu o Eryri whose 'delight was in rule and law: contentment, to his mind, was the duty and happiness of subjects'.[692] There was 'sickly repetition of the fawning flattery, that was never wanting on the lips of the great majority of the great majority of the bards of the time, to the House of Brunswick in general, and the then King George in particular'.[693]

Religious people must have noticed that the Revolution was strongly atheistic. The dissenters were able to console themselves because they also detected enormous animosity to Rome, which they shared. This atheism was difficult too for the Established Church, but this was compounded not least because of their duty to support the throne, from which, quite rightly, they believed their authority derived. There were a very few exceptions, of-ten quoted because of their rarity such as Bishop Shipley of St. Asaph and Bishop Watson of Llandaff. It should be noted however that their ostensible sympathy with the French revolution was mild, selective and temporary.

Shipley was appointed to St. Asaph in 1769. For his part he publicly op-posed the war with America, preached against it, and voted against it in the House of Lords in 1778. He was a close friend of Benjamin Franklyn. Yet he remained loyal to the constitution and royalty, but he was always regarded as an ally by the Welsh because he supported the cause of the dissenters.[694] Watson was appointed to Llandaff in 1782. Despite this, and not unusually for his day he actually lived in Westmoreland as a prosperous farmer and forester. In his 'charge to his clergy' in 1791 he describes the French Revolution as 'this wonderful struggle'[695] so it was 'not surprising' that 'his splendid vindication of Nonconformists 'was speedily translated into Welsh'[696] and was 'greeted in its translated form by monoglot Nonconformists throughout Wales'.[697] There will be closer analysis of such opinions in the later chapter on the role of religion as a controlling mechanism.

More typical of the attitude of the church hierarchy to revolution and religious dissent was to be found in the pronouncements of Bishop Samuel Horsley of St. David's (later of St. Asaph). His attitude is well summarised by Thomas:

> History, according to Horsley, supports the judgements of the prophets and theologians because the sufferings and misery that follow rebellion against established authorities are worse than the miseries that are caused by tyrants.[698]

Such views led to a famous attack from another Welsh Unitarian who had incidentally been a student in Price's Hackney College. In 1791 David Jones (1765–1816) published a second letter to the Bishop – the first had been an attack on the church – and in it he quotes from a letter of support he had received. The Bishop thought that:

> the reward of his distinguished prowess, would afford him an undisturbed retreat: where he should recover from his wounds, and have still an opportunity of employing the remainder of his strength, in attacking the feeble and unresisting Dissenters of Wales. Easy he might think would be the conquest. Herein you must have convinced him of his mistake.[699]

Jones' Letter was such a success that it went into a second edition. Jones also wrote *Reasons for Peace* a condemnation of the war with France, in which he deplored the alliance of Britain with tyrannical regimes such as Prussia. He also defended Joseph Priestley against the public and physical attacks on him, deploring the magistrates addressing the rioters as *friends and fellow churchmen* (his italics) when they were committing capital offences.[700]

The last of these Welsh writers to be discussed is the remarkable Edward Williams, called Iolo Morganwg (1747–1826) who arrogated to himself the title of 'The bard of liberty'. He is generally included in a discussion of 'radicalism' although there is considerable controversy about his activities. When in London he became acquainted with some of the political leaders of the day, and at the house of his friend, David Williams, he met many who shared what some suppose to be his own revolutionary opinions – Talleyrand, Franklin, Horne Tookey, Priestley, and even Paine himself.[701] It is the case that he did compose a song in 1789 'in which he bade Liberty lift up her voice in a sweet song, and cling to it, for its resounding music, would yet, like heaven's mighty thunderings, awake the world, as she lifted up her cry, for the Rights of Man'.[702] Some would even go so far as to say that 'Iolo's *The Dawn of Liberty* was a companion to Paine's *The Rights of Man*.[703] It may be claimed, with equal force that this was the act of a poseur, and certainly he has a place in history as a major liar and forger. Famously he wrote poetry, some of which was acknowledged to be his own, and some of which he ascribed to Dafydd ap Gwilym (who was a real person and poet) and Rhys Goch ap Rhiccert, whose name occurs only in genealogies but was employed by Williams to prove the existence of medieval Welsh troubadours.[704] This practice led to an excoriating criticism from Thomas Parry: 'his forgeries, or what some would call his fabrications, confused Welsh scholars for more than a century, thus impeding the development of a true history of Welsh literature'.[705]

Such bizarre behaviour is sometimes attributed to his lifelong addiction to laudanum. A more serious charge is that he was a principal in the deflection of the energies of the Welsh, especially those with influence, away from the desperate situation of poor people towards a fantasy world of pseudo history and culture. With regard to his attitude to the powerful, Davies quotes a letter from Professor Ifor Williams in which he states that 'Honest Iolo, the Republican, got Dukes and Duchesses, Lords and Ladies, to subscribe to his poems, lyric and pastoral, which he dedicated to His Royal Highness, George, Prince of Wales, by his most humble servant'. The extent of his skill as a liar may perhaps be measured by reports of how the poet Southey's wife wrote 'Bard Williams is in town: so I shall shake one honest man by the hand'.[706] A quite remarkable comment on arguably the best known liar of his generation.

Many would forgive him all of this because of his revival of Welsh 'culture' especially his resurrection of the mythology of druidism and its attendant *gorsedd* and *eisteddfod* 'offering them – a democratic organisation of their intelligentsia, a cadre of People's Remembrances, as its instrument'.[707]

And so here is an early example of the deflection of energy which might have been used by the powerful to improve conditions in Wales into language, for the most part a cause which could be applauded, was socially non threatening, and yet was a challenge in some vague way to an Establishment. It was manifestly a deeply conservative cause.

Eiluned Rees points out that although:

> the commercial press was non existent in Wales before 1718 – by 1800 practically every town of note could boast of at least one press – the book trade invades every aspect of Welsh social life in the eighteenth century because books were no longer the prerogative of the privileged few; developments in the trade were necessarily linked with social changes.

She illustrates this by reference to the increase in the number of books printed annually in Welsh. These 'rose from about ten in 1710 to about forty in 1790'.[708]

Apart from the writings of such major figures as Price, as Rees points out, there were other sources of information and opinion, such as newspapers and magazines. As has been noted in the account of the Hook riot, Philipps suggested that a reward should be offered for information. He suggests that it be put in *The Gazette*, and *The Evening Mail*, *The Sun* or *The Star*, and in *Farley's Bristol Journal*. These papers, he points 'all come to Haverfordwest'. This fact, at least about one of these, is confirmed in a notice dated 15 November 1796 about recruiting soldiers and sailors where it is noted that Sarah *Farley's Bristol Journal* is 'usually circulated in this county'.[709] The Farley family had a more direct connection with Wales since it was they who set up a printing establishment in Pontypool.[710] More evidence of the existence and influence of newspapers can be gauged from the 'Advertisement' to his *A letter to the Right Reverend Samuel, Lord Bishop of St. David's* in 1791. Our 'Welsh Freeholder' says that this letter was rejected by an editor of 'a country paper of considerable circulation in the diocese of St. David's'.

Newspapers made the connection between riot and the potential for more serious troubles. Some pointed out that an 'artificial scarcity of wheat' had been on of the chief instruments in bringing about the French Revolution.[711] The events at the end of the eighteenth century were widely reported in the press *The Times* for example carried lengthy reports on events in France – and important speeches by major figures such as Hunt and Cobden were translated into Welsh.

The extent of reading material is set out in a quite invaluable summary by D Lleufer Thomas as a contribution to the Royal Commission on Land of 1896.[712] He begins with 'The earliest of Welsh magazines' which was *Trysorfa Gwybodaeth neu Eurgrawn Cymraeg*, of which there were 15 numbers fortnightly from March to September 1770. He lists, of course, The *Cylchgrawn Cymraeg* (Welsh magazine), which has been mentioned in this book, or to give it its full title *Cylchgrawn Cymraeg neu Drysorfa Gwybodaeth*, and there were five numbers quarterly in 1793 and 1794. 'It paid great attention to the social and political questions of the day'. As we have seen the editor was Morgan John Rhys.

He goes on to recount that 'several other periodicals were started in the early years of this century, but they were either short-lived productions or, if not so, were of a purely denominational character'. One short lived publication, which dates from 1798, was Thomas Robert's *Cwyn yn erbyn Gorthrymder* (Protest against Oppression), which was 'the most specifically Welsh of all the Jacobin texts'.[713] 1814 saw the publication of *Seren Gomer* (Star of Gomer) which was published until 1983, albeit with gaps in the early period, and from 1880 was the official journal of the Welsh Baptist Union. The founder was a Pembrokeshire man and minister from Llantydewi. This was an important voice, since there is at least a glimmer of sympathy for the hungry. Lleufer notes that in the issue of October 1819 of the formation of an Agricultural Society in Monmouthshire:

> We regret to see that of similar institutions throughout this country most, if not all, have petitioned the Government against the importation of corn until the price of the home-grown grain has reached a fixed minimum. The only result of this will be an increase in the price of bread. We know that farmers have heavy payments to make, and they have a right to combine and support what petitions they agree upon... But if farmers are groaning under their heavy burdens, why should they desire to place them on the shoulders of their neighbours... we cannot support them in their petition.[714]

There was also a number of libraries. In 1703 a committee of the Christian Knowledge Society was appointed:

> for considering a proper method for establishing lending libraries in Wales where they are extremely wanted. – Sir John Philipps, on the 19 July 1705, reported a resolution 'to promote Welsh libraries; desired

an Act for buying in impropriations, that good books should be translated, the lives of good men supplied, and a serious treatise of advice
to schoolmasters drawn up' – Accordingly, in 1711, books to furnish
four such libraries were sent to Carmarthen, Cowbridge, Bangor, and
St. Asaph.[715]

Walters points out that there was a library at The Pembroke Society which
is likely to be at least as early as 1741:

> which is not ante-dated by many such societies in England – There
> are two printed library catalogues of 1776 and 1791 – 419 volumes in
> 1776 – 531 volumes in 1791.

There were as well as some works of law, religious works and science books,
but heading the lists were current periodical literature, travel memoirs and
other topographical works. Walter's summary is a remarkable piece of evidence to be set against the notion that Dyfed was entirely devoid of literacy
and culture:

> Here, in the somewhat isolated south-west of Wales, was a literary
> society comparable in significance with the book clubs which were
> such a unique phenomenon in the eighteenth-century English social
> scene.[716]

At such troubled times there was a huge amount of ephemeral material
which was intended to encourage loyalty. Travellers sold:

> broadsides and ballads, pamphlets, primers, and sermons, portraits
> and caricatures, song-books and story-books, and Chap-books togeth-
> er with the latest issues of a formidable array of monthly magazines
> like the *Gentlemens'*, the *Universal*, the *London*, the *Town and Country*,
> and many others, all of them dealing with the topical questions of the
> day, and reproducing the New Year's and birthday odes, together with
> other popular and patriotic effusions.[717]

It is at least arguable that if there was a market for such material, then
there may well have been more subversive material in circulation. As for

information about current affairs the '*cerdd* (ballads) in Wales carried out the function of the modern newspaper for a whole century in Wales'.[718] And since:

> Wales had no vernacular newspaper press in the eighteenth century, these ballads; formed the chief means for the distribution of local and foreign news.[719]

A selection of ballads reveal that:

> over fifty – relate to foreign affairs, such as pestilence and wars outside the British Isles – there are six ballads on the Fishguard invasion in 1797, eight on the war with America – fifteen on the militia of various Welsh counties, and these give interesting particulars. Twelve on the hardships of farmers, and about twenty on the hard times and the wretched lot of the poor and the scarcity and the dearness of food.

The variety of subjects is endless from drink to tea drinking by women, from the press gangs to Welsh history, from murders to the suffering of British prisoners in France:[720]

> Ballads dealt with popular themes like birth, love and death, they reported current events, especially horrific tales of murder, and in keeping with the atmosphere of the era, they usually contained a moral   A century of printing within Wales strengthened the power of the written word. No longer merely an additional channel for expressing contemporary ideas, the printed word was developing into a weapon that proved formidable in the political and religious battles of the nineteenth century – The book trade had changed from being a useful adjunct of spiritual life to being an integral part of everyday life in all its aspects.[721]

There was also a significant link between the Welsh and English clergy, which would cause ideas to be brought back to Wales:

> Denominational connections were equally important for the dissemination of 'modern' ideas in Wales. The Welsh Baptists, in particular, enjoyed close connections with their English brethren. Several Welsh

Baptist ministers received their ministerial training at Bristol Baptist Academy, and a few took up pulpits in England.[722]

In the countryside there was much informal learning. From early times there was much listening to those who could read. Geraint Jenkins recounts how:

> during the 1680s the youths of Llanfihangel Tre'r Beirdd in Anglesey used to flock to the home of the only literate parishioner, Sion Edward, a cooper, in order to learn to read books published by Thomas Jones the almanacker.[723]

It was, of course, not necessary to read to learn. There were other less formal ways of getting information one of which was singularly Welsh. And since the Revolutions were, in their time the main subject of conversation everywhere, and the focus of political interest they must have been a common topic of conversation. One of the main sources of information were the drovers:

> The drover was sometimes a rough customer, but it was worth their while for the squire and his lady to come out to the kitchen regions when he was being entertained there on his way home – he had usually picked up a considerable amount of information on his way home from the English towns through which he had passed.[724]

Colyer also makes the case for the drover as a source of information, even more strongly and at great length:

> A great deal has been written about the contribution of the drovers to the cultural and social life of Wales. This is rightly so, especially before the nineteenth century when mobility was restricted and a relatively small proportion of the working population had the opportunity of travelling far beyond their home villages. The drovers enjoyed the advantages of extensive contact with English culture, social life, farming systems and financial matters, besides representing an essential communications link with England.[725]

He goes on to list drovers' contributions to Welsh publications, which shows that there were amongst them cultured and wealthy men.

We are left with the question with which this chapter began. How far the disturbances were informed by ideas and ideology, and if they were, what the role of writing was in their execution? Especially because of the dominance of the recorded views of the powerful, and the diminutive voice of the poor the matter must rest on the balance of probability. But surely it is inconceivable that the unrest did not draw inspiration from literature, which in turn drew ideas from the two Revolutions. What is certain is that social discontent was contained and we now go on to examine the processes by which this was achieved.

5

THE MACHINERY OF CONTROL

'They replied that they would do their duty'. [726]

In the final analysis all the riots, disturbances, and social anger were contained, and this chapter will discuss how this was achieved. The ostensible methods ranged from the crude exercise of force, through penal legislation and by the creation of an extensive espionage network. But there were other more subtle factors at work, such as the failure of important and influential groups of Welsh people to associate themselves either with the desperate plight of their countrymen, or with their protests. And other singular phenomena must be taken into account, most especially the isolation occasioned by the inability of many to speak English, and the fact that many of the best quality of men chose emigration as a way out of their misery, thus reducing the pool of those with enough intelligence and energy to fight.

But first of all the successful containment of social unrest and serious political radicalism in the late eighteenth and early nineteenth century must be set within the context of what was happening at the time. And as has been made clear, the dominant theme was the French Revolution and its aftermath. The initial enthusiasm by sections of British society was much tempered by the 'Terror' regime of 1793–94, when the world received 'a shock of horror',[727] although key politicians such as Fox and Sheridan never gave up their advocacy of peace. But later Sheridan was to join the campaign for loyalty with an Address to the People headed Our King! Our Country! And our God. It finishes with the words: 'tell them too, we seek no Change; and, least of all, such Change as *they* would bring us' (his italics).[728]

The next factor which inhibited any rebellious inclination was the wave of anti French sentiment after the breakdown of the Treaty of Amiens signed in 1802 and broken in 1803, and the seemingly real threat of invasion. By now the famous sympathies of people such as Burns, Southey, Coleridge and Wordsworth had evaporated. Instead Burns joined the Dumfries Volunteers, and wrote a patriotic song for them.[729] Wordsworth in turn wrote some exhorting and excruciating lines to the men of Kent which began:

> Vanguard of liberty, ye men of Kent,
> Ye children of a soil that doth advance
> Her haughty brow against the coast of France,
> Now is the time to prove your hardiment![730]

There was a massive appeal to loyalty and fear with many songs, plays, political pamphlets, and speeches designed to demonise Napoleon and the French:

> It is no exaggeration to say that the loyal songs in vogue between 1796 and 1805 may be counted by thousands… every town, village, and outlying farm or cottage was promptly flooded with literary and pictorial satire on the common enemy, as well as with timely reminders of the possible consequences of his success and of our own military and naval achievements in the past.[731]

Very often these would appeal to men to protect their women and children against the unspeakable barbarity of the invaders, if they were successful.

In North Wales in 1804 there appeared one of the curiosities[732] of Welsh literature: 'The horrors of invasion; a poem addressed to the people of Great Britain, in general, and to the Chirk Hundred Volunteers, and all Welshmen in particular' by Holland Price. In it he calls for the spirit of the Welsh who fought the Saxons and the Normans now to use their might against the French, in other words to support those who had so recently oppressed the Welsh. The verse is however no worse than that of Wordsworth quoted above:

> The shrieking virgin from the spoiler flies
> And fills the valleys with her piercing cries,
> He heeds them not, but seizes on his prey,
> And bears in triumph the poor maid away.[733]

While a song of the Cowbridge Volunteers ran:

From Rapine's mad soul what oppressions are hurl'd
What huge depredations that deluge the World!
See whelming wide regions the rancours of Hell!
Haste, grasp the keen blade! And those furies repell![734]

In August 1803 the Bishop of Chester expressed the view that in the event of an invasion the clergy would be 'most actively and suitably occupied' by looking after the 'female parishioners and children left behind; by his weight and influence he might, in some measure, protect the former from abuse or alienation, while he would be constantly at hand to administer comfort and assistance to the latter'.[735]

Like the Church, the Law brought all its weight to bear. In Cardiff in 1803, for example, Mr. Justice Hardinge addressed the Grand Jury with these words:

Brave and generous hearted Britons!… promptly decide to die gloriously rather than tamely and ignominiously to *crouch to the grand Enslaver*, be enfettered by his *galling* chains – remember all lies at stake, LIFE, LIBERTY, AND SAFETY – (the enemy regard) JUSTICE, and the observance of Good Faith, as Plebeian virtues, deserving no place in *the glorious new order of things*'. (his emphases)[736]

There was allegedly great success in that appeal. An example is the rhyme about Napoleon designed to frighten children, the middle verse of which runs:

Baby, baby, he's a giant,
Tall and black as Rouen steeple;
And he dines and sups, rely on't
Every day on naughty people.[737]

But despite the recital by so many historians of the manner in which people rallied round and supported king country and government, it is difficult to be know what poor people thought. What does seem to be the case is that that even that most insistent of rebels Jac Glan y gors became subdued, and 'in due course his animus against the Hanoverians abated'.[738]

For those in authority, the reality was that the disturbances had to be put down, even if the simplistic solution to the riots in Northampton in 1693 was, even in the 1790s unacceptable. There, it was said, the trouble was not about corn, but 'to satisfy an idle and thievish humour the mob was at present possessed withal out of which they must be well whipped.'[739] So how was control maintained?

Firstly the government passed penal legislation. Outstanding in this area were the Treasonable Practices Act and the Seditious Meetings Act of 1795 – the famous 'Gagging Acts' – described by one writer as 'notorious'.[740] The first made it much easier to be a traitor, since now any action, speech or written material which threatened the king or brought political pressure on the king, for example to change his ministers, was now an act of treason. The second included the banning of political meetings of over 50 people to discuss political matters without the permission of two magistrates. 'Many were bewildered at the government's proposals'.[741] Then there was the suspension of Habeas Corpus, manifestly a very grave step, even if, as Duffy points out, it was limited to 'those suspected of treasonable offences and limited to nine months, with renewal requiring further parliamentary approval'. It was suspended in May 1794 and again in April 1798.[742]

Duffy however underlines the threat posed by those who so actively sympathised with France, and Wilkinson draws attention to the real threat from Irishmen, and their organisations.[743] And after all there was a rebellion in Ireland in 1798. Duffy submits that Pitt was conscious of the need to carry such legislation only as far as was absolutely necessary, if he was not to enable a contrast to be made between such measures and the alleged freedom enjoyed by the French people. And Wilkinson goes on to point out that during Portland's period in office 'only twelve men were tried for treason in England' and only one was executed.[744] And of prosecutions for sedition 'there were fewer than two hundred prosecutions for either treason or sedition during the 1790s'.[745]And in any case as Francis Place, who was far from being a Pitt supporter said, there was widespread support from the people who 'may be said to have approved them without understanding them'.[746] But Place still 'regarded 1797–1801 as an era of terrorism: men were imprisoned for laughing at the awkwardness of Volunteers at drill'.[747] Pitt also sponsored an 'Association for the Preservation of Liberty and Property against Republicans and Levellers – primarily to deter and prosecute sedition'.[748]

Of great significance was the Aliens Act of 1793. The Aliens Act stated that travellers from the continent had to explain the reasons for their visit and get a certificate before landing. This led to the creation of an Aliens Office which was of the greatest significance in the work of counter espionage and the suppression of organised resistance to the government.[749] The London stipendiary magistracy, established in 1792 also set up a network of informers which was extensive, and quite apart from the ostensible reason for which the organisation was instituted.[750] This stopped at least the open toasts of the democrats such as 'may our liberties never be swallowed in a Pitt'.[751]

Whatever the apologia which are offered, the fact is that the Duke of Portland did set up an elaborate system of espionage. Portland was a critical element in the control of dissidence, and he and Pitt together 'certainly played a significant role in the prevention of revolution in Britain'.[752] It was Portland who was the 'fountain head' of the spying system,[753] and he 'dealt with all reports of sedition and treasonable reports of sedition and treasonable activity.[754] He demanded, in his own words, a 'religious observation of the respect which is due to private property',[755] and to ensure this he 'never flinched from suggesting the use of armed force'.[756] And of course, he was totally out of sympathy with any demand for social change: 'I hardly know of any act or measure *vulgarly or commonly called* popular which has not originated in a bad cause, and been productive of pernicious effects' (his italics).[757] Small wonder George III called him 'a true lover of order'.[758]

Some of Portland's spies were very successful. An especially notable example is James Powell, who 'worked for years at the heart of the London Corresponding Society'[759] a most important position since in 1795 tens of thousands of LCS supporter attended meetings in London. He gave information to the Home Office which enabled the authorities to arrest the whole of the LCS committee.[760] There seemed to be plenty of people who volunteered information, including of course magistrates, even though 'Home Secretary Portland was extremely wary of unsolicited information'.[761] Examples are legion. In September 1800 Portland wrote to an informant in Bishop's Stortford, thanking him for a copy of a letter, and saying that he would put a notice in the London Gazette offering a reward for information.[762]

A rare recorded example from Dyfed occurred in 1793. On 24 January of that year Henry Dundas, the Home Secretary, in 1805 to be impeached and acquitted of malpractice as treasurer of the navy, wrote to John Lloyd of Haverfordwest congratulating him on:

> detaining the seditious Publications mentioned in the Information which you transmitted to me… I am afraid that you will not be able to make out any connection between the Pamphlets and Mr. Rees, so as to render him an Offender; but it would be full as desirable if you

could bring home the other Charge of seditious Discourses in the Pulpit – I have within these few days heard thro' another Channel of the seditious conduct of Rees, and it would be extremely gratifying, if any Act could be fixed upon him, that would lay him fairly open to Prosecution, perhaps some Plans may be adopted by you, for watching over his Proceedings.

Dundas finished by consoling Lloyd with the compliment that the 'disposition to discourage seditious doctrines' shows 'The Loyalty and Attachment of the County of Pembroke to the King and Constitution'.[763]

Although this is a rare documented case, it is evidence that the spy network set up by Portland and his office to counter revolutionary activity spread its tentacles as far as the remotest parts of Wales. In March 1795 a report to the government from Lord Dynevor in March 1795 confirmed that seditious literature was circulating in Haverfordwest.[764]

Although from time to time sheriffs, and even the lords lieutenant, would be active if there was civil disturbance, the justices of the peace were the first line of defence against social unrest. The Tudors:

relied upon them as the principal upholders of good order in the countryside… (they) had given them ever increasing duties.

By the eighteenth century, because of the increase in the numbers, their ranks were increasingly filled by minor gentry.[765] The job involved hearing criminal cases, administering the poor law, controlling vagabonds, controlling disease in animals, and maintaining the highways. 'They were assisted either by a small number of constables or else by the "posse comitatus"'.[766]

The magistracy for hundreds of years were notoriously ludicrous, and comical indeed, had they not been so dangerous. Jenkins offers a summary:

Justices of the peace were a mixed group. Some suffered from poor health. Others were over-fond of tippling: the Glamorgan magistrates who tried Vavasor Powell in 1669 were as drunk as lords. Many were apathetic and bone idle.[767]

Despite the numbers appointed 'the real work of running county government was done by about a quarter of the whole bench'.[768] Such inactivity was due substantially to the fact that many – perhaps a third – although having property in the county, did not live there. But there was also 'apathy and a lack of public commitment – age and infirmity.' During the second half of the eighteenth century this was remedied by the appointment of clerics which 'was especially marked in Pembrokeshire'.[769] By 1832 more than one-fifth of magistrates were clergymen.[770] The harshness of the magistracy is legendary, and examples are not difficult to find:

> At the Pembrokeshire Epiphany Quarter Sessions of 1742 – Dorothy Rees and Mary David separately found guilty of stealing petticoats valued in both cases at under a shilling, were sentenced to transportation to America for seven years[771]

It is worth dwelling on the career of an especially notorious example of a bad Justice, since he also illustrates the worst flaws which were not uncommon in the gentry. After a very lawless career:

> It is not surprising to learn, therefore, that (Herbert) Lloyd was struck out of the Commission in 1755 'for some very illegal acts', one of which was his marching with a mob on the Esgair-y-Mwyn leadmines in 1753 and personally pointing a cocked pistol at Lewis Morris' head.[772]

As master of Peterwell (Cardiganshire), his name became a byword for: 'a petty tyrant: gambling losses forced him to mortgage most of his property.' He was described, admittedly by a rival candidate for election, as having 'principles so little fixed, and his character so unstable'. Although he became an MP 'there is no record of him having spoken in the House'. He committed suicide on 19 August 1769.[773]

When it came to the local constables, they were, like the magistrates they served, of dubious worth, largely, as we shall see in respect of the military, because they were sympathetic to their own people. In Bridgend, the authorities found it difficult to maintain order because 'those employed as Constables rather lean to the country people'.[774] Much later, in 1842, the situation was the same, as the Metropolitan Police Inspector sent to help to deal with the Rebecca riots wrote of the local constables:

> I am sorry to say that they are determined not to assist and... I feel sure that if the two men (officers he had brought from London) and

myself were to go out and come in contact with the mob that the specials would desert us and very likely assist the mob.[775]

And if they were not sympathetic, they were frightened. *The Times* wrote on 22 June 1843 that:

> The Welsh special constable is a timorous animal, more so it would appear than the Welsh rioters – and it has long been plain that the ordinary police force of the country was absolutely incompetent to deal with the skilful and daring 'Rebecca'.[776]

Yet occasionally at least they must have been of some use. On 17 April 1801 the Quarter Sessions held in Haverfordwest authorised payment to eight petty constables for two, three and four days' attendance at the Cornmarket for preventing disturbances there.[777]

The main agents of control were the several varieties of armed forces. These military and para military forces were vastly expanded because of the Napoleonic wars, and there was massive recruitment to the regular army and navy, the militia, the newly formed yeomanry, and the force of 'volunteers'. In December 1803, it was reported that the army had been doubled and now had almost 120,000 men. There were 84,000 militiamen, and there were 380,000 volunteers. The 'gross force of the United Kingdom might then be considered as 700,000 men in arms,' although as Fox went on to point out they were signally short of weapons, a matter of constant debate and anger.[778] The effect of this huge force on the ordinary lives of people was described by a contemporary:

> every town was, in fact, a sort of garrison – in one place you might hear the 'tattoo' of some youth learning to beat the drums, at another place some march or national air being practised upon the fife, and every morning at five o'clock the bugle horn would be sounded through the streets, to call the volunteers to a two hours' drill.[779]

Not only was this a strange state of affairs but as we have seen this meant that there was a plentiful supply of people to deal with troublemakers.

There was, of course, a regular standing army, but this was mostly unreliable and corroded by an accumulation of corruption and incompetence. It was a commonplace that the soldiery were regarded with contempt. In a letter of 1678 the opinion is expressed that 'the overflowing scum of our nation is enlisted'.[780] The military were also famously unreliable, an unreliability which was especially pronounced during the French Revolution. In 1797, and concomitant with the naval mutinies at the Nore and Spithead, a typical circular was sent to 'every barrack throughout England'. It contains statements such as:

> Are we not men? – Were not the sailors, like us mocked for want of thought, though not as much despised for poverty as we are? Have they not proved that they can think? – Why is every regiment harrassed (sic) with long marches, from one end of the country to another, but to keep them strangers to the people and to each other? – Don't they (officers) owe their promotions to their connections with placemen and pensioners, and a mock Parliament which pretends to represent the people? – THE POWER IS ALL OUR OWN – BE SOBER, BE READY.[781]

This immediately provoked several 'loyal' responses from units, notably signed by non commissioned officers. In the course of suppressing the mutiny at the Nore the other ranks of the Royal Welch Fusiliers sent a message to the king saying that despite the 'distribution of certain handbills – no atrocious villain has ever yet been daring enough to attempt – To seduce the Royal Welch Fuzileers from their hitherto unerring fidelity'.[782]

Most of the problems of the British Army would not be addressed until Edward Cardwell's reforms in the second half of the nineteenth century, against enormous resistance of the landed gentry; reforms which were, in their time radical, but which nevertheless preserved the essence of privilege for the ruling classes into the twentieth century. These reforms included the abolition of flogging in peacetime in 1868, although this went on during active service until 1880 and, against almost universal opposition, the cessation of the practice of the purchase of commissions in 1871. One of the most significant steps he took was to add to the plain numbering of regiments an association with locations, notably counties. By the time the army was being reformed the government had begun to use regular troops much more to control disturbances, as happened in the Rebecca riots. As the analysis in this book is of events in Wales, we can note, in passing the deployment of what came to be Welsh regiments, at the time of the events under discussion.

The position was that in 1797, those regiments which were later to have such strong Welsh association except for the Fusiliers and a recruitment base in Wales, did not have such an association. There were three such regiments. The 23rd were raised in 1689, and were designated the Royal Welch Fusiliers. The 24th Foot, raised in 1689, and first established in their barracks in Brecon in 1873, eventually became, in 1881, the South Wales Borderers, and the 41st was designated The Welch Regiment in 1831. Throughout the period we are discussing, all of these were a long way from Wales. In 1797 the 24th were in Canada, the 41st had just finished a tour in the West Indies, and the 23rd were in the East of England, helping to suppress the naval mutineers at the Nore. At the time of Rebecca the 24th were variously in Canada (1829–1841), Plymouth (1841–43) Glasgow (1843), and Ireland (1843–46). The 41st were in India fighting, *inter alia*, in the first Afghan War, while the 23rd were in Canada and the West Indies. At the end of the eighteenth century the authorities had, therefore to rely for armed control on the militia in its several forms, and later the Yeomanry.

There was, in any case reluctance to use soldiers. In February 1795 John Vaughan of Golden Grove wrote to Campbell (Cawdor) that 'Lord Dynevor's Troop of Yeomanry, 35 strong had gone to Aberystwyth "to quell some tumult among the miners occasioned by their stopping vessels freighted with corn… I hope the Magistrates wou'd interfere and put a stop to the exportation of Barley"'. And referring to a riot at Carmarthen in early 1795, he pronounced that 'in my opinion they (the magistrates) acted very rashly and hastily in sending for the cavalry'.[783] And not only were they often unwelcome, troops were expensive. Haverfordwest Common Council passed a resolution on 4 April 1751 'that an application be made to the government for the speedy removal of a troop of dragoons recently sent to the town to assist the magistrates in preventing and suppressing riots on the grounds that there had been no riots there for many years and that the dragoons 'were chargeable on many inhabitants'.[784] Almost 100 years later little had changed. When the Pembrokeshire Yeomanry, in the form of three officers and 26 troopers were called out in January 1843 to help put down the Rebecca riots and the Carmarthenshire magistrates realised they had to pay for them, they sent them home.[785]

Adequate local forces might have controlled disturbance but there had been a tradition of apprehension about the creation of all but a minimum force of armed men, an issue which had been a political flash point since the Civil Wars. The debate had been entangled with a variety of political issues and alliances, but the outbreak of war with France in 1756 modified the resistance. This was further reduced in 1795 because of fear of an invasion.[786] The upshot was that the 'conservative-minded gentry and clergy began to abate their traditional hostility to government'[787] especially with regard to the establishment of county forces of militia.

As a result of hostilities, in 1757 the Militia Act was passed, which established local regiments to which civilians were called. This was followed by Acts of 1762, 1769, and 1796. These were extremely unpopular and, sometimes, instead of preventing riots, the militia themselves rioted, protesting against service. Nor was this surprising, when it is remembered that the system had every ingredient which has made military service unpopular at all times and in all places. It was, for example, selective by ballot. And those selected could nominate substitutes, who were evidently people with little option. In 1770, following the 1769 Act which enabled rounding up defaulters, there was a riot in Chirk when a mob of some two to three hundred threatened to kill the magistrates if they proceeded with a ballot. There was another riot in the same county of Denbighshire in April 1795, against the new Navy Act, and against balloting. In the long account of this sent to the Duke of Portland, the magistrate John Lloyd communicates just how frightening a mob of '400 or 500 persons armed with bludgeons could be'. And also how determined the rioters were not to be enlisted.[788] And there were yet more disturbances, often serious, at the end of 1796 against militia service in Carmarthenshire, Merioneth Flintshire[789] and Montgomeryshire.[790]

Under the seminal 1757 Act the Lords Lieutenant of the counties had to raise and arm units. The purpose of these units was made clear in a response from the first regiment of Devon Militia 'promising to do their best when called upon to suppress the domestic enemies of king and constitution'.[791] From the subsequent behaviour of the Militia this was surely composed by the officers, since it was not a reliable or typical forecast of the behaviour of those called to arms. There was difficulty in recruiting, even when Lord Milford of Pembrokeshire, as a case in point, personally gave extra money.[792] But there were 'good' reports. Townsend was faced with a great many women supported by a number of other persons (who) had for some days past in the most riotous manner prevented the shipping of flour for the capital'. He and Rev. Mr. Hoste went there. 'I previously ordered a company of the Pembroke Militia – to Warham about a mile distant to wait for orders'. He twice read 'The Proclamation' and ordered the Militia to march. 'After driving the mob off with bayonets they secured and protected the flour and the ship'.[793]

Generally though the standard of discipline was as bad as it was in the regular army. 'Law breaking was rampant', 'men deserted in shoals', and there was a 'chronic state of insubordination'.[794] In April 1795 the Oxfordshire regiment of Militia went on the rampage in Newhaven and other places in Sussex and stole a considerable number of things: summed up as the 'outrageous behaviour of the Oxfordshire Regiment of Militia'.[795] Such behaviour was not simply the commonly alleged degenerate behaviour of a lawless peasantry. Weston describes how, at the beginning of the war against revolutionary France, it came to the notice of the Marquis of Buckingham that there was political agitation amongst the troops from the industrial areas. In the units from the West Riding, Nottinghamshire, Warwickshire and Westminster there was unrest, and the men were given 'little books'. In April 1795, the Oxfordshires mutinied in protest at the high price of corn, seizing grain, and selling it cheaply to the poor.[796] A letter from John Carne also dating from April 1795 noted that the Northampton Militia were to be sent to Falmouth. 'And having been informed that some of the privates were rather refractory a short time since at Plymouth' some Regulars should be sent. 'As 'tis likely from the great scarcity of corn or flour, that there may be some commotions in Cornwall and that the miners and others of the lower class may attempt to come into this and the neighbouring towns'.[797]

In Wells the 122nd regiment took butter and sold it at a reduced price, and in Chichester soldiers forced the mayor to become involved in fixing a fair price for bread. And there were many other occasions when soldiers intervened 'their officers looking steadfastly the other way'.[798] Crowd control was in any case very unpopular, being described by Viscount Barrington as 'a most odious service which nothing but necessity can justify'.[799] And soldiers whether regular, conscripts, or volunteers often agreed. There is a substantial amount of evidence which shows how they sided with the rioters.[800]

Nearer to the area with which this discussion is concerned, there was a local *cause célèbre* about collusion. It was alleged that the Fishguard Fencibles had helped protesters on 5 December 1795. Lady Milford sent a letter to Portland on 30 December 1795,[801] in which she reported, as has been mentioned earlier that:

Lord Milford communicated Your Grace's letter to the Commanding Officer of the Fishguard Fencibles and received from him the inclosed answer which he has the honor of transmitting to your Grace.

In this letter the commanding officer of the Fencibles, Thomas Knox, who it will be remembered attracted such opprobrium after the French invasion, strongly denied that his regiment had been involved, and on 29 December 1795 wrote to say:

that Fishguard and its neighbourhood are in a state of perfect tranquility and have been ever since the 5ᵗʰ Instant. The gross misinformation of the proceedings on that day contained in Mr. Bowen's letter to the Clerk of the Privy Council will, I trust be fully and satisfactorily contradicted by Right Honourable The Lord Milford and the two magistrates who were then present at Fishguard and whom I beg your Lordships permission to make acquaintance therewith, the rudder of the vessel was taken off at the recommendation of the Magistrates with the consent of the owners present and of the Master who even directed the people how to do it. The meeting on the 21ˢᵗ was called by Govr. Vaughan and myself of the neighbouring Justices and Gentlemen when a subscription was entered into to buy butter... to be retailed at... present market price, the rudder was carried to the quay on the 21ˢᵗ with its irons and now lies there, the Master refusing to take it back. I have seen no appearance of a riot. I was not at Fishguard on the 5ᵗʰ Instant but two of my officers who were there, have assured me, the men of the Corps who were then in Fishguard... behaved perfectly contrary to the Collector's statement. One man only of them assisted in taking off the rudder, but the Corps were not assembled that day, it was not a day of exercise, nor did the Magistrates apply for their assistance; nor have they since then called for it or wanted it, the vessel may sail whenever the owners think proper. I have the honour to be your Lordships most obedient humble Servant Thos. Knox.[802]

His denial was supported by an article in the *Cambrian Register* in 1795 where it was stated 'the commanding officer of the fencibles... attended most humanely on the occasion, from a wish to mediate between the parties, and satisfy both, with as little violence as possible to either'.[803] The writer was wrong in implying that Knox was there, but he no doubt meant the officer commanding. This is an important issue because the incident has tended to be given as an example of troops supporting rioters,[804] which the writer of the *Cambrian Register* seems to consider 'a charge of the foulest calumny'.

Even the regulars were suspect. A Rev. Robinson writing from Lichfield wrote to the Duke of Portland, Secretary of State for the Home Department, in October 1800 that colliers were:

making pikes and instruments to cut the bridles of the cavalry if they are sent for to disperse them – the military will, I am apprehensive,

reluctantly be prevailed on to act against them. It is said that the dragoons, who were asked to charge the rioters of Wolverhampton, bid
them get out of the way, telling them at the same time they liked a
large loaf as well as they did.

But unlike many of the clergy, Mr. Robinson did not only advocate repression: he went on to ask for a reduction in the price of corn.[805] His mistrust
was well placed. A note was circulating amongst the West London Militia in
October 1800 arranging a meeting of 'brother soldiers':

> for we had better dy by the sword than starve in the land of plenty
> & being shoor the petition will be of no use but that of flummery, as
> others have been before. Death or Plenty.[806]

Some however felt that even these troops were better than none. A Mr.
Lloyd wrote in the next month pleading that the Warwick Fencibles should
stay in Ruthin.[807] Although there were plenty of requests for the soldiers to
be removed because of bad behaviour.

In Dyfed the militia were duly raised as the Act required. In 1759 the
Carmarthenshires and the Pembrokeshires were established, followed in
1760 by the Cardiganshires. The association between the exercise of power,
and control through the military is easily demonstrated by the fact that in
the early days of the Pembrokeshires, the Colonel of the regiment was Sir
Hugh Owen of Orielton who was also Lord Lieutenant. On 18 August
1795 when the Hook miners rioted in Haverfordwest, the main body of
the Carmarthenshires were in Pembroke, with a detachment in Haverfordwest.[808] The Pembrokeshire militia were in East Anglia.[809] When the protesters arrived at the quay on the river Cleddau, they were confronted by 50 militiamen. As we have also seen the women tried to 'subvert' them, but they
loaded their guns and the protesters dispersed. The likely explanation for the
unusual harshness of the militia is that being from Carmarthen, they were
most unlikely to have had sympathy for the people of south Pembrokeshire,
commonly called by their Welsh speaking neighbours 'Pembrokeshire pigs'.
Not all were so reliable. In Merthyr the view was held that the Glamorgan
Militia 'would be of little service as there are a great many Merthyr people
amongst them'.[810]

The reliability of the militia being at least uncertain, the interest excited
amongst radicals by the French Revolution, and the onset of the war with
France which accelerated the movement of the bulk of the regular army

overseas, led to an important development in 1794. Ostensibly at the request of the king, Pitt made a speech in March in which he announced the augmentation of the military. His proposals included the expansion of the militia, but of the greatest significance was the proposal, in a plan sent to the Lords Lieutenant, to establish a local Cavalry to be made up of 'Gentlemen, Yeomen, Farmers and substantial Tradesmen'. The purpose was clear. Under section VI of the plan, this new force was to be called out 'for the suppression of riots or tumults within their own or adjacent counties, or – in case of invasion'.[811] The proposal became law in 1794, and within a year 48 yeomanry cavalry and 119 infantry units were established.[812] The fact that they had to provide their own horses was another indication of both their background and their targets. In the event it seems that they were rather more reliable than their more plebeian colleagues in the militia. The response from Pembrokeshire was immediate. Within weeks, on 19 April 1794, Lord Milford chaired a meeting in London at which it was decided to establish the 'Pembrokeshire Company of Gentlemen and Yeomanry Cavalry'. Indeed so swift was the response that when a Precedence List of the Yeomanry Regiments was ordered in 1919, the number one position was accorded to the Pembrokeshire (Castlemartin) Yeomanry Hussars.[813] Carmarthenshire was not far behind. Lord Dynevor and 'the gentlemen of the county' offered to raise two troops of Yeomanry Cavalry, and government approval was given on 27 September, 1794.[814] But in Cardiganshire, where there was not a strong magistracy, and where the gentry 'as a whole were not keen to be sworn in as special constables' no troop of Yeomanry was established.[815]

They were used principally for riot control, which was of course a paramount reason for their establishment. The new force seems to have worked quite well, at least from time to time. The Pembroke Fencibles, under Captain Ackland, and the Yeomanry paraded on market days to put down any riots.[816] On the other side of the country in a letter of 22 December 1795 Townsend wrote of Essex that 'in these parts where there is Yeomanry Corps they are quiet', but he goes on to plead for more troops 'if the Evil (sic) increases.' He hopes too that the Admiralty will 'correct the sailors who join in these commotions (sic) in the seaport towns'. He goes on to say that 'Mr. Hoste is arrived from Holkham, and 'I learn that Mr. Coke and the other magistrates have settled such allowances at Wells for the poor (which have been much neglected there) that all is quiet and the flour shipped; but it is doubtful whether the pilots will act'.[817] They were, it seems of help in Wales. 'In the strike of 1816 the Swansea, Cardiff, and Monmouthshire corps were on duty for long periods – Viscount Sidmouth wrote "There is no feature in your late Proceedings more satisfactory than the Conduct of the Yeomanry Cavalry'".[818]

As to the behaviour of the troops when dealing with disorder they would not collude with rioters as a rule, but as in Haverfordwest could be relied upon to 'do our duty'. When they did the degree of violence naturally varied enormously:

The ruling class commonly suppressed the crowd with a degree of sheer ferocity, using the army, death and transportation sentences, disturbances were usually controlled by a degree of temperance which staggered European observers – food riots, for example, may have ended in bloody affrays, and even executions – in Britain the sword was unleashed and the gallows deployed with *comparative* moderation' (his italics).[819] In Ireland where Cornwallis was to complain of the 'numberless murders that are hourly committed by our people without any process or examination whatever, the Yeomanry – now take the lead in rapine and murder.[820]

The final group to be discussed as part of the battery of repression are The Volunteers. They numbered 'in the war of 1793 at most a hundred thousand'.[821] The manifest idea was to create a body of trained men who could act as a reserve. But the formation of the Volunteers in 1794 had a much more sinister political purpose, so that it was, for example, 'an integral part of the Government's campaign to break up the Foxite opposition, form a national conservative coalition, and harass and discredit the Radicals by judicial persecution'.[822] At a more practical and immediate level they could be used to put down resistance. 'For the Government's military planners, the Volunteers were mainly an instrument of repression' and they were used to put down riots (as in Inverness), and generally keep order:[823]

The Volunteers were in fact the perfect cadres for political clubs. The brilliant uniforms they affected were a splendid piece of propaganda in themselves, impressive to the onlooker and tickling the vanity of the recruit. The parades and days of exercises were a perfect setting and pretext for patriotic speeches'.[824] Apart from the no doubt welcome festive occasions the Volunteers caused, there were distinct practical advantages in being a Volunteer. For example the poor were exempted then from the hated militia service.[825] The more prosperous, on the other hand, were worried that service might make 'people more politically conscious' with the result that the wealthy might be attacked.[826]

But the need to have a huge army proved to be paramount, and considerable pressure was exerted on people to 'volunteer'. Any who 'demurred were dismissed or evicted'.[827] The clergy, predictably, were to the fore in organizing the Volunteers, and there was one over-riding consideration:

In short (as one Armed Association noted) – the Volunteers 'encouraged and restored a due principal of subordination amongst the different classes of the people – induced the heedless to reflect openly upon the advantages they actually enjoy and the doubtful issue of innovation – rendered disloyalty unfashionable, sedition dangerous and insurrection almost impossible.[828]

These were the manifestly coercive ways in which discontent was controlled. But especially in respect of Wales there are other more subtle, not so obvious factors, which played their part in that process. One concerns the relationship of the powerful Welsh community in London and their organisations to Wales, and to the misery and political activity of those who still lived there. After the increasing settlement of Welsh people in London in the sixteenth century, they established a number of organisations, some of which turned their attention to Wales. One of these was The Welsh Trust, established in 1674 by a vicar, Thomas Gouge, an Englishman it may be noted, who was encouraged by Stephen Hughes, a native of Carmarthen. Hughes was involved in the publication of substantial amounts of religious literature, including the bible in 1678, and *Pilgrim's Progress* in 1688.[829] Gouge collected money from wealthy people, and used it in fact to make the Welsh more literate in *English*. This activity ended with the death of Gouge in 1681.

The next organisation to target Wales was The Society for the Propagation of Christian Knowledge. This was established in 1699 by Thomas Bray, another Englishman, but his two main supporters were local gentry Sir John Philipps of Picton in Pembrokeshire, and Sir Humphrey Mackworth of Neath. During its existence (it seems to have faded after the Hanoverian succession) it distributed many thousands of books, was responsible for sponsorship of two editions of the bible, and opened Charity schools, paying for teachers and books.

These two initiatives seem to have owed little to the interest or commitment of the London Welsh. It was, however, at the beginning of the eighteenth century that they began to organise, no doubt from an awareness of a need for social status. As part of the means of doing this there was created a myth of the noble antiquity of the Welsh, and their distinctive heritage. The creation of such myths, and the resurrection of the Arthur legend was encouraged by the 'discovery' in the 1570s by John Dee, a very distinguished figure, that Arthur had conquered Scandinavia, and much besides, which should be regarded as part of the British Empire. This notion of antiquity was brought into play with the establishment of The Honourable and Loyal

Society of Antient Britons, which was followed by a pamphlet in 1717 by a Thomas Jones entitled *The rise and progress of the most honourable and loyal society of antient Britons*. In 1717 there was established a charity school – the Welch School, which survived until recently, albeit in a different form, and which it may immediately be noted is almost the sole evidence of any help given to the poor, least of all in Wales, by the organisations of the London Welsh.

There was some hope that the Society would, in some way help Wales. A man called Moses Williams, whose 'heart bled for his country' addressed the Society in 1717, and he:

> urged exiled Welshmen to raise Wales from its provincial torpor and penury by investing huge capital sums to facilitate the building of universities, charity schools, workshops, almshouses, and hospitals. His blueprint was shrewd and full of common sense. But it fell on deaf ears.[830]

This is hardly surprising since the objectives of this Society and its several successors did not include, either in theory or in practice, concern about the people left behind, and not at all any engagement in pressure for change. Its stimulus, like that of similar groups was centred upon a culture of self preservation, and self promotion. And so the new Society, perhaps to distance it and its members from the taint of Jacobitism, which, as we have seen dogged the Welsh, asked Caroline, Princess of Wales, whose birthday was on 1 March, to become Patron, and the Prince of Wales became President. Both were at the St. David's day service in 1714. In September the cultivation of royalty continued with an address to the king by the stewards, and Thomas Jones, Secretary and Treasurer of the Society was 'immediately rewarded with a knighthood'.[831] It was to the Welsh landowners that the members looked for credibility, and so it was the Earl of Lisburne, 'a leading London Welshman', who asked the Princess to become Patron.[832] Such leadership could hardly be expected to lead any campaign to improve the lives of the poor, least of all those still surviving in the Principality.

In 1751 the first Cymmrodorion Society was founded, and in 1755 its 'Constitutions' were approved. In 1751 it set out some impressive intentions including 'the improvement of trade and manufacture in Wales'. A letter 30 years later to the Welsh magistrates promised, *inter alia*, to 'send models of every new or improved machine or implement of husbandry – at the expense of the Society', and 'to present gold medals or bounties for the improvement of agriculture, forestry, trade and commerce'.[833] But even sympathetic writers like Jenkins and Ramage are forced to conclude that 'little actually seems to have been done'.[834] And yet apologists write that ; 'we are in danger of forgetting the social and philanthropic motives which in the minds of the founders of the Society loomed fully as large as the intellectual'.[835] Or again: 'the Society counted. It had come to be regarded as a leader and organ of opinion in Welsh matters. Such things do not happen without some reason'.[836]

In 1771 another London Welsh Society was founded – the Gwyneddigion. Once again there is a welter of claims about the operation of this Society which have little basis in fact. Thus it is described by Gwyn A Williams as a 'new and radical society of the Gwyneddigion',[837] while Owain Myfyr, a famous figure in the organisation declared in 1789 that 'Liberty in Church and State is the aim of this Society'.[838] 'It seemed to him that the newly restored Eisteddfod should be a form of propaganda for political radicalism'.[839] Such claims abound in accounts of their activities. 'There was a conscious and deliberate effort to confer positive benefits upon Wales'.[840] Further:

in a consideration of the history of Welsh life in London, the opportunities afforded to the lower middle and even to the poorer Welshman loom even more large. The rank and file of the later Welsh Societies in London were composed of such folk, and their influence upon their home-keeping relations has from time to time been demonstrably important.[841]

However, neither in this account nor elsewhere are such claims demonstrated. There is no evidence, for example, that they took any interest in the well being of the desperately poor *merched y gerddi* (the garden girls) who, from about 1760, walked to London to work in the gardens and orchards of the capital. This sad phenomenon has even been described as offering 'these girls new opportunities which they were glad to accept'.[842] One summary of the work of the second Cymmrodorion was 'neither have we come across any reference to constant charitable work such as undertaken by the first Society' The only 'evidence' which is slender indeed is the gift of a pair of spectacles to a man in Anglesey in response to an appeal by him.[843] So what did these several Societies achieve?

It has to be conceded that the Societies were the focus of the resurrection of Welsh culture, some of it lost, some of it mythical, but nevertheless important to a Wales which was in a state of social decay. The Gwyneddigion, for example published the works of the medieval poet Dafydd ap Gwilym, and they established the Myvyrian Archaiology (sic) of Wales. The omni present Owain Myfyr (Jones) was the 'editor' although he 'probably did little more than paying for it'.[844] The second and third volumes however were tainted by the emerging tradition of forgery in this resurrection, since 'they were bedevilled by Iolo Morganwg's fabrications'.[845] Myfyr also claimed the editorship of manuscripts 'which were mostly copied for him, and edited for him by other men'. This piece of behaviour is justified by Jenkins and Ramage because it should 'be remembered that he was willing to pay large sums for the copying and printing'.[846] But their pursuit of the notion of the Welsh discovery of America excelled all their other fantasies.

Nothing illustrates the futility of much of the activity of the London Welsh societies at the end of the eighteenth century than the effort they put into arguments about the Welsh Indian tribes, supposedly the descendants of those who had been led there in the twelfth century by a Welsh Prince, Madoc. Books were published, including one by a 'Dr John Williams, a learned Welsh divine of Sydenham' in 1791 which purported to be 'An enquiry into the truth' about Madoc,[847] and 'Rhys published the *Cylchgrawn* so that its profits could be donated to the search for the Welsh Indians in order to introduce them to the Gospel.[848] In 1791 at the *Eisteddfod* at Llanrwst a manuscript was circulated which claimed that these Indians 'are at this time a free and distinct people, and have preserved their liberty, language and some traces of their religion to this day'.[849] It is almost beyond belief, even within the context of the time that so much could be written on this subject, to the exclusion of the urgent problems facing the Welsh people, and, at the same time as the world was electrified by the publication of books by Price, Burke and Paine.

The resurrection or creation of the institution of the *eisteddfod* is regarded as a most singular and valuable contribution made by the Societies. For our purpose the institution serves to illustrate again that whatever was commendable about it, it was of little relevance to the misery of Wales. The closeness of identity with the powers in England is nowhere more effectively illustrated than in an event at the first *Eisteddfod* held at Corwen in 1789, which was promoted by the London Gwyneddigion Society. A medal was offered 'for the best extempore verse on any of the following subjects':

1. The recent recovery of King George III.
2. Queen Charlotte.
3. The Prince of Wales.

4. Mr. William Pitt.
5. On the recovery of the Nannau Estates.
6. Corwen Bridge.
7. The Hare.
8. Dr. Willis, the King's Physician.[850]

A measure of what is at best ambivalence, or at worst posturing, can be seen from the fact that at the St Asaph *Eisteddfod* in 1790 the society chose as its theme Liberty. – 'the most precious treasure on the face of the earth'.[851] This was clearly a highly relevant, not to say controversial topic. But the prize was won by the ultra authoritarian, traditionalist Dafydd Ddu Eryri. And 'in Dafydd Ddu's ode, there is nothing to indicate sympathy with, or, indeed knowledge of the French Revolution'.[852] And the second prize essay by Walter Davies (Gwallter Mechain) was 'greatly discounted by his ever re-curring apology for the British Government, and his flattering descriptions of the favourable conditions under which Welshmen lived… He was almost blind – or appeared to be – to the grave injustices, religiously, socially and politically, which still had the sanctions of law in this country.'[853]

Small wonder then that when the 'national' *Eisteddfod* was proposed in the early nineteenth century, 'the nobility took a great delight and interest in this novelty'.[854] The total dynamic is a vivid example of how the gentry and the London Welsh formed an unholy alliance to protect their interests. This is reinforced by the fact that the great landowners, such as the Williams Wynns were closely involved. Around 1820, for example, the first President of the new Cymmrodorion was Sir Watkin, Member of Parliament for Denbighshire, Lord Lieutenant of that county, who raised a regiment in the Napoleonic war. He was supposedly reputed to be a 'clement' landlord, and 'the most liberal patron of agricultural improvement in Wales', although this is the kind of panegyric which is not easily validated.[855]

But nowhere can be found any evidence that such organisations were, as is commonly claimed, in the ranks of the radicals. Gwyn A Williams is an especially ardent advocate of that claim:

> These Druids were also Jacobins devoted to the principles of truth, liberty and natural law which the French Revolution, like the American revolution before it was trying to realise.

When the *Gorsedd* was launched 'they made liberty its motto',[856] 'for this new Jacobin nation was in the 1790s a pugnacious little minority'.[857] But such slogans are easily constructed. In this case they meant little. The only slight evidence that these fabricated Welsh cultural activities were of any interest or concern to the authorities was when, in '1798 the Cowbridge Volunteers dispersed a Gorsedd on Garth mountain the action was described as "democratic"'.[858]

The truth about the London Welsh and their organisations is that their first, and probably their only serious concern was with their own well being, and they cannot be blamed for that. After all, naturally 'the fruits of success went to those who aligned themselves with England and the English',[859] and 'in all probability the majority of these would not have cared whether they counted as Welsh or not'.[860] Even Jac Glan-y-gors secretary of the Gwyneddigion, and a founder of the Cymreigyddion, joked about the willingness to forget Wales and oddly enough their language, in their natural anxiety to advance their social status in London.[861]

The Welsh were not alone. The behaviour of emigrants has always tended to extremes of forgetfulness and nostalgia. In Scotland, Prebble describes how on 23 June 1815 it was reported that 'a number of Highland gentlemen had formed themselves into "a pure Highland Society in support of the Dress, Language, Music and Characteristics of our illustrious race in the Highlands and Isles of Scotland"'.[862] And this when the Highlanders had been reduced to emigration, starvation, and dispossession. Yet like the Welsh, the Scottish people who had been evicted continued to fabricate a mystical relationship. The Chisholm clan in Canada sent the 'Chief' 'an address of loyalty on his majority, acknowledging him as their chief and affirming their loyalty to him though they no longer lived in their homeland'.[863] In a world of cruel behaviour that particular chief was of the worst.

In the same way the emigrant Welsh, although at times more ambivalent, celebrated royal events and consoled the royal family when there were deaths.[864] In 1887 'throughout the United States the immigrants – except the Welsh – celebrated Victoria's Golden Jubilee';[865] but when the 1897 Jubilee came round 'the Welsh expressed their loyalty as they had not done ten years before'. And then in 1911 the crowning of the Prince of Wales 'fired their hearts'.[866]

The matter of language in Wales became of enormous debate, especially after the publication of the Blue Books. But the Blue Books merely raised the scale of a debate which was in evidence much earlier. Since the sixteenth century there has been considerable and heated debate about the Welsh language. There can be found, predictably, two broad views. The first is concern is that the disappearance of the language would seriously undermine, if not destroy those pillars which support Welsh culture in its many forms.

In the eighteenth century the Morris brothers expressed a very commonly held feeling that 'the old Wales of their boyhood was slipping away, and its language and literature with it'.[867] Not long afterwards the opposite view was expressed, admittedly in this case by an English visitor at the beginning of the nineteenth century:

> They who can talk only a local and obsolete dialect, must of necessity be confined to the spot where they were born; and in consequence contract notions as confined as their situation – they are cut off from every source of rational information[868]

The Blue Books report those who shared the same feelings as Morris such as a man from the Dissenting College, Brecknock:

> what then must the actual fact be to those who have worshipped and loved its accents from the earliest hours of child hood, and all whose fondest recollections and hopes are bound up in its existence.[869]

One of the reasons for the angry reactions to the Blue Books was because of their remarks about language. And some people *were* very angry at the 'Blue Books' comments on Welsh, including the one of the most offensive and patronising of all:

> The Welsh language is a vast drawback to Wales, and is a manifold barrier to the moral progress and commercial prosperity of its people. It is not easy to over-estimate its evil effects. It is the language of the Cymri, and anterior to that of the ancient Britons. It dissevers the people from intercourse which would help advance their civilisation, and bars the access of improving knowledge to their minds. As proof of this, there is no Welsh literature worthy of the name.[870]

But it should be remembered in their defence, that they were enjoined by Kay Shuttleworth that they should look 'especially into the means afforded to the labouring classes of acquiring a knowledge of the English language'.[871] They were, of course, as they generally were, merely repeating the evidence given to them, for example by the Dean of St. David's, who pointed out that the Welsh were 'very quick' and wanted to learn English 'thereby bettering their condition in life'. Or a Mr. Williams of Lampeter who said that 'no business can be done in the language' and that 'in agricultural life it is a great drawback not to know English. They cannot read the papers or know the prices'.[872] One vicar of Llan y Crwys in Carmarthenshire expressed the view that 'the exclusive prevalence of the Welsh language is a serious bar to improvement by impeding intercourse with England'.[873]

The problem for those who objected to the attack on Welsh, was that the Commission reported much evidence to show that ordinary people felt themselves to be at a disadvantage, if they were not conversant with English. A schoolmaster in Llandilofawr stated that:

> I have the elder children taught to read their bibles in Welsh (being their mother tongue), as well as in English. Parents, however, have objected that 'their children can learn Welsh at home'.[874]

This was a constant theme throughout the investigation, so much so that the summary was that although the social life into which the child is born is conducted in Welsh, 'you could not find in the purely Welsh parts a single parent, in whatever class, who would not have his child taught English at school'.[875] But there was a consolation since 'he possesses a mastery over his own language far beyond that which the Englishman of the same degree possesses over his'.[876] In a passing comment on the degree of literacy in Welsh the publisher of the Anglican *Yr Haul*, although described as 'the most unscrupulous of all the Welsh periodicals'[877] claimed that 'The Welsh peasantry are better able to read and write in their own language than the same classes in England'.[878] But this ability was limited since 'they have neither desire nor taste for reading any books or newspapers, excepting the bible or some Welsh religious publications'.[879] There were too practical disadvantages since:

> in the works the Welsh workman never finds his way into the office... his language keeps him under the hatches, being one in which he can neither acquire nor communicate the necessary information[880] – my district exhibits the phenomenon of a peculiar language isolating the mass from the upper portion of society.[881]

But although one reporter claims universal opinion on 'the manifold evils inseparable from an ignorance of English' he was even-handed enough to state that:

If interest pleads for English, affection leans to Welsh. The one is regarded as a new friend to be acquired for profit's sake; the other as an
old one to be cherished for himself, and especially not to be deserted
in his decline.[882]

This ambivalence, which is the most restrained word to describe it, was
the case throughout the nineteenth century. In the later nineteenth century
'most working-class Welsh people continued to see English as the language
of education, material advancement and social mobility, while Welsh remained the language of ignorance, poverty and social inferiority'. It is not
surprising therefore that all the late Victorian attempts by those who held
power, but who lived mostly outside Wales to persuade the less powerful
otherwise was doomed.[883]

A Mr. Williams in evidence to the 1896 Royal Commission on Land said
that poor farmers were trapped because they would: 'find it difficult to settle
in England or abroad. The style of farming, the language, customs, and religious worship would be different'. Of his father he said: 'He knew very little
English, and being at that time about 45 years of age, would have found it
extremely difficult to have settled down elsewhere'.[884] The landlords 'have
taken advantage of the tenants' ignorance of English, which has practically
bound them to the soil'.[885] A vivid example, independent of indignation, of
the disadvantage of not knowing English occurred in 1875 when the Duke
of Richmond's Agricultural Holdings Act was passed, which in part eroded
the sanctity of the contract between landlord and tenant. 'But it appears to
have had very little effect in Wales, few tenants in a largely monoglot Welsh
community appearing to appreciate its effects, and few landlords being anxious to explain them.' [886]

The general modern view of the historical situation is probably represented by MR Peate. She quotes Ieuan Gwynedd Jones who writes that 'the
pressing need to have a good command of English was felt at all levels of
Welsh society'. Peate goes on 'Remaining monolingual in the Welsh language was a mystic romantic vocation for the children of other people, rather than a "common sense" option for one's own'. The recognition of this fact
was deflected into blaming someone else for imposing it from outside: 'the
Commissioners and William Williams must be the culprits, the ones who
drove the wedge between the common people and their language'.[887] There
is also a cynical view that the exhortation to teach English to the 'labouring
classes' was economic as was education which Ieuan Gwynedd Jones ar-
gues 'was mainly a means of exerting control over the working class'.[888] The
same motive could, of course, as easily be ascribed to the Nonconformist

oligarchy with its insistence on the priority of Welsh. The debate has caused so much rancour, especially in respect of the role of the Blue Books in promoting it, that RA Butler saw fit to apologise for the attacks on Welsh in 1942. 'I wish today a hundred years later, on my own behalf and on behalf of the Government, to dissociate myself from that view, and indeed to work in the opposite direction'.[889]

The relevance of this to the discussion about the course of discontent, lies in the possibility that monolingualism inhibited the transmission of ideas and information, and that the Welsh people were, as a consequence, disadvantaged. This meant that those who were well versed in English were able to monitor and adjudicate on the flow of information, and so make language a vital tool for control. This reality was veiled by the dissemination of the belief that the issue was about the protection of the Welsh language, the attack upon which was just one way in which the English Establishment was a threat. Thus could social discontent be deflected into socially non threatening channels. It was manifestly a deeply conservative cause.

One of the indirect causes of the evaporation of social discontent was the substantial emigration which took place over a long period. The tradition of emigration from Wales was not new. After the Tudor take-over, there was a good deal of movement of Welsh men of talent to London and to the universities, especially Oxford, and notably Jesus College. One example for Wales of the devastating drift to London was James Howell, who was highly talented and politically eminent, ending a stunning career with his appointment as Historiographer Royal in 1661.[890] Another was Hugh Myddleton, one of three brothers from a family which originated in Denbighshire. One of Hugh's most famous achievements was the massive improvement to London's water supply, by building a 'new' river from Hertfordshire to north London. The new system was opened in 1613. Hugh was Welsh speaking, and kept a close watch on his Welsh property. But as became, and remained the tradition of the London Welsh:

> there is no doubt where their (the Myddleton brothers) world was centred. The main beneficiaries of their activities were London and themselves.[891]

The reasons for this movement varied from time to time, as, of course did the motivation of individuals. However the effect was to drain Wales of some of its most talented, and no doubt radical people.

As far back as the early eighteenth century emigration overseas was in full swing, and 'the effect of this emigration, in terms of quality as well as quantity upon the Baptist movement must have been crippling'.[892] As well as the fact that 'many of those who did emigrate (circa 1700–14) were men of experience and quality… the number must have been considerable'.[893] After the American Revolution, the movement of emigrants speeded up:

> There are abundant references also to emigrations in 1793, 1794 and 1795 from different places in Wales to America during this period. On account of the oppressive Acts people were encouraged by Morgan John Rhys, Dr. Samuel Jones, Dr. Wm. Richards, 'Siarl Marc' etc. to leave their native land and go to America, which was hailed as the land of Liberty and Peace. The records of the Baptist Churches in North-West Wales abound with references to the departure of members for the land of Liberty in the distant West.[894]

One of the interesting questions about the migrants concerns their background. HM Davies makes the point that 'the Welsh Quakers and Baptists who emigrated to America after 1680 were not desperate men "pushed" into the New World'.[895] Instead he shows that the typical emigrant was skilled and had some capital to keep him going until he could settle down:

> Emigrants were not mainly recruited from the lowest ranks of rural society: dependants on parish relief, widows, seasonal emigrants in search of work did not emigrate during the 1790s Welsh emigrants came chiefly from the middling sectors of society.[896]

The same point was made at the time. In a letter of May 1793 it was observed that 'the oppressed poor are too poor to pay their passage'.[897] The emigrants came from all over Wales, but one of 'the two main focuses of emigration to America during the 1790s were Pembrokeshire and Carmarthenshire'.[898] As one explanation, a Pembrokeshire man at the time wrote that the Baptist churches in West Wales were some of the:

> largest we have in Britain. That of Llanloffan (Llangloffan), in Pembrokeshire, which is the largest of all, consists of between eight hundred and nine hundred members.[899]

Gwyn A Williams also emphasises the scale and significance of emigration from Dyfed. 'The whole south west – was a stronghold not only of Welshness, of Methodism and of Dissent – but of emigration'.[900] And he goes on to elaborate the importance of these unusual links:

> The three counties was the region most intimately in contact with America, the source of some of the earliest migrations. Here, the Baptist trans-Atlantic international, focused on Pennsylvania and Rhode Island College, with its own small fleet of four or five favoured vessels, its endless flow of Jacobin letters between Wales's unofficial consul in the USA, Samuel Jones of Philadelphia, and his brethren back home found a firm and fecund anchorage.[901]

And not only were skills transported but so were political ideas:

> In central Wales in the late eighteenth century small commodity producers were turned into proletarians. The response was a distinctive and millenarian migration to the USA, highly Jacobin in temper, and the emergence of a rooted radicalism which was ultimately to debouch into Chartism.[902]

The question as to why people left Wales was debated then as it is now. In *Y Cronicl* in July 1852 a number of suppositions about emigration were enumerated, since the reasons for people wanting to leave were a matter of great interest. Most of the agricultural districts of Wales:

> have suffered much, both of insult and injury… over 70 persons, mostly young people, in the prime of life, left Llanbrynmair (Montgomery) this morning for America… there are similar parties leaving other districts – The constant decrease in the population of an agricultural district – is a sure sign of some terrible injustice on the part of landowners and their agents – (These are) the best class of tenants.[903]

George Lewis, the Independent minister at Carnarfon wrote of the reasons in 1793. These were the political situation of the dissenters, high rents, heavy taxes, and heavy tithes. He went on:

Is it to be wondered at that many wish to emigrate and spend the remainder of their days in America which we consider as the land of plenty and the land of liberty.[904]

There is no doubt that the disadvantages under which dissenters suffered was a major contributor A Welshman wrote to the Rev. William. Rogers in Philadelphia in 1793:

> Spurning the yoke of spiritual tyranny they tore themselves from their native land, and fled to the wildness of America! It hath long been the asylum of the persecuted. Your countrymen know the value of freedom: they purchased it with their blood.[905]

John Evans of Bala advocated emigration for the familiar anti Catholic reasons which were a linch pin in Nonconformist belief:

> America was historically free from the taint of the popish beast, whereas Britain was one of the ten horns which had been responsible for the persecution of the saints.[906]

In another familiar area of belief some Dissenters drew:

> correlations between contemporary events and prophecy which made them anxious about their future in a land which they perceived to be both corrupt and oppressive.[907]

In the August 1793 edition of the *Cylchgrawn*, Rhys published a series of articles which praised America, which included 'the text of the Virginian Declaration of Religious Freedom'.[908]

One central advocate of emigration was Morgan John Rhys. It will be remembered that he emigrated to America in 1794. Before his departure he published a pamphlet, in Welsh, which sought to convince his countrymen of the virtues of that country: *Y Drefn o gynnal crefydd yn Unol-Daleithiau America:Ynghyd a Darluniad Byr o Kentucky A Rhesymau digonol i gyfiawnhau'r cyfryw sy'n myned o'r Wlad hon i America, a Chyngor i'r Cymry (The Way that Religion is celebrated in the United States of America, with a short sketch of Kentucky, and adequate reasons to justify those who are leaving this country for America)*. He defined emigration as:

akin to the flight of the Children of Israel from the tyranny of the Pharaohs. – Babylon was gaining force, persecution was the inevitable result.

He wrote that: 'The second woe has passed by, the third is hastening upon us; perhaps it has already started'. He wanted the Welsh to consider the 'signs' and to act upon them by emigrating.[909] As early as 1797 there was published '*Can newydd o America*' (New Song from America) describing the journey to New York the city of liberty:

> a refuge where there is no hatred, or bloated oppressors, or yet a scant-ily clad beggar; and adding that if the poor of Wales could but cross the billowy Ocean, they would by honest toil live happily in a peaceful land and a region free from all fear.[910]

Not everybody including Nonconformists were as enthusiastic. Rather, there was furious opposition. There was disapproval notably from the ministers of the dissenting community. In a history of Welsh Baptists in 1812 the author, who was a minister, said that emigration was sinful and the same as 'schism, immorality, and backbiting'. Rhys was a special target. He was condemned by no less a person than Christmas Evans 'for his ingratitude to the state by criticising a government which had protected their liberties. The *Cylchgrawn* was a political enterprise, unworthy of a Gospel preacher.'[911]

A Welsh settler in America was another critic of Rhys. 'True Briton' wrote from New York state in April 1800 that 'Rhys had enticed the Welsh... to line his own pocket'. America 'was not a land for families nor was it a land for the poor – the only way to find happiness in a world of woe was to obey the Gospel at home in Wales'.[912] The Reverend Benjamin Evans of Drewen, Cardiganshire, said that 'it was an abnegation of responsibility to the church at home',[913] and in writing to an emigrating Pembrokeshire preacher admonished that:

> If you abscond, why not abscond alone?
> Why urge the flight of other lab'ring men,
> And leave the vineyard void of all its hands[914]

Another wrote that he:

> acknowledged that God's judgement was abroad in the land, but it

was the sinner not the state that had incurred the judgement of God – Emigration was a quest for worldly enhancement which implied a lack of trust in God's Providence as it applied in his native land.[915]

Yet another was addressed to those were convinced by the Madoc myth. They should remember that 'their religion was pagan or at best (or worst) papist'.[916]

The authorities throughout Britain were very worried about the scale of emigration, and this was especially true of Wales:

> In April 1729 so many people had left west Wales for America, leading to labour shortages that the Grand Jury in Pembrokeshire petitioned about this 'very pernicious practice that for several years been carried on by wicked and designing persons in this county in deluding great numbers of Ignorant Inhabitants and Labouring people.[917]

Two letters from Brecon and Crickhowell both written in April 1801 to the Home Office express concern about migration The first, dated the 7 April deplores the numbers leaving 'from every part of south Wales to America'. These 'lower orders' were 'too lazy to provide subsistence by their labour, or too restless to be satisfied with settle and regular government'.[918] The second writer, whose letter is dated 12 April wants more action. 'Emigration' he points out 'from these parts has been very considerable lately' because of agents from America and a pamphlet published in Welsh. Recently the parish lost a blacksmith and two carpenters, and he wants the ship stopped in Bristol.[919] The national government too was worried at the scale of emigration:

> Pitt's government, indeed, was afraid that the country was losing men with much-needed skills through emigration, and enacted legislation specifically against the emigration of artisans.[920]

This ban, which was probably not effective, was repealed in 1825.[921] It has been noted that the scale of emigration from Wales was considerable in the eighteenth century, and these increased during the nineteenth century:

> In 1857 a foreman in a south Wales ironworks told an American traveller that within the decade a score of men out of the mill's two

hundred – 'the pick of the workmen' – had left for the States; he himself expected to join them in the spring.[922] – immigrants ran half the collieries in Washington state in 1894.[923]

Despite the many exhortations not to emigrate, migration continued, from the countryside to south east Wales and from Wales to other countries. Giving evidence to the Royal Commission of 1896, a Pembrokeshire farmer said that there had been a lot of emigration to England and Glamorgan:[924]

> During the last decade of the nineteenth century emigration from South West Cardiganshire was heavier than usual. Between 1891 and 1901 the population of the parish of Troedyraur fell by eight per cent, and after 1901 it continued to fall though at a slower rate.[925]

Some idea of the effect this movement must have had on Wales can be seen from the fact that census figures for 'foreign – born Welsh' in the US in 1880 were 83,302.[926] This would have been almost the equivalent of the entire population of a small Welsh county such as Pembrokeshire, the population of which was 94,140 in 1851.

There was one further measure of control which was so omni present that it deserves consideration in a separate chapter. This was the power of religion, and most especially the power of the Nonconformist religions. But all of the measures discussed, while they were effective at some times and in some places, did not immediately nor *entirely* destroy protest in Wales, as we shall go on to see in the Epilogue.

6

TOWARDS A THEOCRATIC WALES

I do not allow that any Methodist or any Bigot deserves the epithet of
Reformer. He is mentally corrupt and ought first to reform himself.[927]

There is no debate about the fact that Wales, in the eighteenth and nineteenth centuries was in the grip of an intense religious fervour. In fact an
enormous amount of received Welsh history centres upon that fervour. A
seemingly trivial, but significant example, is the fact that until the 1950s the
syllabus of Welsh history 'A' levels was dominated by topics about the heroes
of Nonconformity. The purpose of this chapter is to discuss that fervour,
and most important, to analyse its relationship to the demands for change
which were expressed, as we have seen, often violently.

Watts' analysis shows that in the religious census of 1851, west Wales
rates as part of a group of three areas that 'stand out as having a level of
religious observance well above the national average... but the highest estimated percentages of all were recorded in certain Welsh districts'. These
included Aberystwyth 78.6, Aberayron 72.3 and Cardigan 71.4. The Independents were especially strong in south Wales. In Carmarthenshire 20 per
cent of the population, and in Cardiganshire over 15 per cent were Independents, and in these and some other Welsh counties they outnumbered
Anglicans.[928]

The Baptists too were a large force. They comprised more than 10 per
cent of worshippers in Carmarthenshire, Pembrokeshire and Cardiganshire,
as well as in some other Welsh counties:[929]

It has been estimated that in 1800 the Baptists had some nine thousand members in Wales and more than a hundred thousand by the
end of the nineteenth century... Radical tendencies as in the preach-

ing of Morgan John Rhys, were also to be found among them and, although less revolutionary in character, these also lay behind the denomination's later support for political Liberalism.[930]

When it comes to the smaller groups, the Religious Census of 1851 reveals that there were 27 Unitarian congregations and eight Quaker meetings in Wales.[931] In respect of Roman Catholics:

> In 1773 Mgr Charles Walmesley, Vicar Apostolic of the Western District, reported to Rome that there were only 750 Catholics in the whole of Wales. By 1839, on the eve of the establishment of the Welsh District, the number of Catholics had reached 6,269, an increase of 735 per cent. This increase had occurred before the great influx of Irish famine refugees in the late 1840s.[932]

There has been much controversy about the validity of the Census: indeed before it had even been taken there was 'what came to be called "the arithmetic war"', but the view of a foremost Welsh historian is that as least as far as south Wales is concerned in important respects:

> It is reasonable to conclude, therefore, that the system devised by Mann (the official in charge of the operation) though far from perfect, achieved a fair degree of accuracy so far as the actual counting and recording of places of worship were concerned, their denominational allegiances, and the sitting accommodation they provided. There were anomalies certainly, and some of these can be corrected.[933]

But in Wales, even more than in England, 'nothing has been more difficult than to obtain an accurate estimate of their (dissenters) churches, and members, and congregations, and ministers'.[934] As Watts also points out it is difficult to make absolute distinctions between the several denominations when it comes to attitudes to political and social questions. One example he gives is that:

> The Unitarians conviction that politics were a legitimate field of Christian endeavour was often shared by Calvinists among the Old Dissenters, no matter how much they might detest the Unitarians' theology.[935]

And at an individual level, naturally people differed in their opinions about the relationship between religious beliefs and political action. There were, however, broad distinctions between denominations on these issues. It is also the case that in the general picture of the rejection of political radicalism by the Nonconformist oligarchy, there are individual exceptions. Some of these have been discussed in earlier chapters, but one rather less well known later example is William Rees (Gwilym Hiraethog 1802–83). He was the founder and successful editor of *Yr Amserau*, and remarkably took an interest in political affairs outside of Britain, to the degree that he 'met and corresponded with Garibaldi'.[936]

It is also the case that there were some major issues in which some Nonconformists sided with those who opposed injustice, even if they were often ambivalent. It is easy to find, for example, their commitment to the abolition of slavery, which, it should not be forgotten, was not a popular cause before its final abolition. A book by Benjamin Evans, published in 1789, 'wrote of "the sufferings of thousands of God's people in Jamaica and other places, submitted for the serious consideration of amiable Welshmen, in order to induce them to leave Sugar, Treacle, Rum"'.[937] And Gwallter Mechain in his famous prize essay at the 1790 St. Asaph Eisteddfod, in which he offers an apologia for the behaviour of the government, manages to fulminate against the slave trade.[938] Even then there was a hint of ambivalence. When, for example a society was formed in 1832 it was 'A Society for the abolition of the slave trade and for maintaining the political and religious rights of Nonconformists'.[939] They were also universally in favour of the repeal of the Corn Laws. Conferences were organised to coordinate campaigns, such as one in Carnarvon in 1841, when it was resolved:

> That the present Corn Law is a public evil, and essentially contradictory to the statutes of the divine writing, opposed to the moral and physical well being of the people, and injurious to the piety of the population in general.[940]

The question of Catholic Emancipation for obvious reasons presented a real problem, and opinion, predictably was divided. These ranged from the kind of view expressed at a meeting of Independents in Solva, Pembrokeshire in 1829 that all emancipation should be supported, including that of Catholics, to the exhortation to Protestants in *Seren Gomer* in May 1819 to petition against 'the family of Rome'.[941] As Hugh delicately puts it 'the attitude of the Baptists to the emancipation of Catholics was less clearly defined'.[942]

When it came to the question of the Age, that of Electoral Reform, the overall position can only be described as conservative and muddled. *Seren Gomer* of course was obliged to support the idea, but its achievement and implementation had to be 'moderate'. In an edition of 1820 it was pointed out that 'we support moderate reform – moderation in everything is beneficial and praiseworthy'. The policies advocated by radicals such as Cobbett would give power to 'uneducated, ignorant and dispossessed men'.[943] A representative sermon was preached by a Baptist minister in 1839 when he denounced the paying of members of Parliament, since this would allow into Parliament 'every kind of prater: tinkers, cobblers, chimney sweeps etc'.[944] Naturally, all in the several denominational hierarchies had views about Chartism. The Church of England Rector of Dowlais preached a famous sermon:

> showing that rebellion is inconsistent with the teaching of the church catechism – that a doctrine of equality was unscriptural and that God is alike the author of poverty and riches – that universal suffrage (one of the demands of the Chartists) would only lead to universal confusion.[945]

Generally the Nonconformist ministry agreed. One Principal of a Baptist college in Pontypool wrote an article which sought to distance Nonconformists from agitation of the kind that had erupted into violence in Monmouthshire in 1839. He claimed that 'thousands had been deterred from participation in the rising through the influence of Nonconformity'.[946] Such rioting led the editor of *Seren Gomer* to deplore 'bloody revolutions' while the editor of *Y Diwygwr* thought the riots 'sorrowful, lamentable and disgraceful'.[947] And the same views were commonplace when the Rebecca riots erupted shortly afterwards.

Of the welter of denominations, the Church of England clergy were unequivocal in their support of government and opposition to reform, never mind revolution. There were exceptions where there was mild flirtation with new ideas by people such as Bishop Watson, of which far too much has been made, as we shall go on to see. Much more typical was the parallel behaviour by the Welsh clergy to that of the Rev. Robert Wright of Itchen Abbas, Hampshire, who in a dispute, supposedly centred upon the evil effects of beerhouses, sent rioters to transportation or the gallows in 1830.[948]

The point has been made already that the Welsh clergy were prominent amongst the rank of the Justices, and since that meant ordering the removal of paupers, whipping, and so on, they were not likely to be popular. Now is the time to look at just one vivid example of their identification with the authorities, and the enthusiasm they brought to the task of control. One excellent case study is that of the Reverend William Powell of Abergavenny. He organised a network of informers and spies and so was a valuable source of information for the Home Department about potential trouble, for instance before the South Wales strike of 1816. When trouble came, as it did for example in 1816 he demanded that troops be sent, including cavalry, then organised troops and police, on one occasion personally directing the Scots Greys, and read the Riot Act. He was also 'the moving spirit' behind demands for a permanent police force in the mining districts.[949] He may have been more physical in his disapproval than most clergymen in the Church, but there can be no doubt where their loyalties lay.

Even Bishop Watson, who as we have seen was in some ways sympathetic to the French Revolution, in fact expressed the gravest doubts about it. He was one who 'expressed in their publications the dangers of acceding to all the demands for Reform – believing as he did that the constitution with all its defects was better than a republic; he was emphatic in his condemnation of democracy'.[950] David Davies is another to remind us that although Bishop Watson has been categorised by many as a reformer, and was tolerant towards Nonconformists, he wrote a pamphlet in 1798 entitled 'An address to the people of Great Britain' which 'went through many editions'.[951] And in his 'Charge' he reports:

Hearing, as he tells us, on every hand that there were loud murmurings, and seditious tendencies, in his diocese, he dealt with the same subject – (namely, the mistaken conceptions of Liberty which had spread in this country, as the aftermath of the French Revolution).[952]

He was, he stated:

sincerely of opinion, that few of us will live to see such a system established in France as will procure to its inhabitants half the blessings which our ancestors have enjoyed, which we do enjoy, and which it is our interest to take care that our prosperity shall enjoy, under the constitution of Great Britain.[953]

For their part after 1714 the Dissenters were solidly Hanoverian: not surprising with the lingering memories of the Stuarts and their popery. But after the restoration Welsh clergymen on the anniversary of the King's execution:

> dwelt on the themes of blood-guiltiness and humiliation, and the sinfulness of resistance to the Lord's anointed. Bitter denunciations were made of that devilish and 'bloody villainy' that had cast a blot over the nation.[954]

Of course it is to be expected that the Church of England would support governments with every means at its disposal, but there has been insufficient recognition or discussion about the role of Nonconformists and their support of governments, especially at the end of the eighteenth century. There is little doubt that the support given to the Parliament, by Welsh ministers before and during the British civil wars was considerable. Out of these years came a pantheon of Puritans whose opposition to the church, and especially Laud's doctrines was resolute. These included William Wroth – 'the Apostle of Wales' – the rector of Llanfaches in Monmouthshire – locus of the heart of the resistance, in a congregation which was established in 1638 or 1639. Then there was one of the best known, Vavasor Powell, who even opposed Cromwell, and ended his days in the Fleet prison in 1670.[955]

The hatred of the Established Church had been a cornerstone of Nonconformist belief since the seventeenth century, and this was to continue. The middle years of the nineteenth century saw 'a gradual renaissance on the part of the Church', which 'intensified and embittered Nonconformity now in its most active phase of expansion'.[956] But they were never, even in their earliest manifestation a radical social group. For in the period after 1660 'socially, the Dissenters were drawn from the ranks of the minor gentry'.[957] And in that fact lies an important source of the ancestry of that collusion between Nonconformity and gentry which led to the dispersal of putative radicalism, especially at the end of the eighteenth century. Nor should we be surprised that:

> Austerity and moral rectitude were the hall-marks of the Puritan, expected in their schoolmasters as much as in their ministers. There are also indications that they used their schools to uphold the social order as well as to promote spiritual welfare.[958]

Perhaps it was this brief manifestly anti authority tradition which has led to an automatic conferring of the title of radicalism on later dissenters. The

association of dissent with radicalism is an *idée fixe* in Welsh history and
to challenge it is to run the risk of unseating one of Wales' most cherished
myths, which is that Nonconformity in the period we are discussing was a
force for radicalism. Typical of this seemingly unchallengeable assumption
is such a claim that 'the Independents were prominent in the development
of radicalism in Wales'.[959] The claim has even been made that there was a
golden age of Welsh radicalism.[960] And apologists for the condemnation of
social agitation go on to make the contradictory claim that Nonconformists
were effective in causing social change:

> In Wales, for instance, alongside the mass demonstrations and vio-
> lent outbursts which culminated in the Chartist and Rebecca Riots,
> there developed *more responsible forms of agitation* through the pulpit
> oratory of Nonconformist ministers, the use of the printed word in
> periodical literature, particularly the magazines of the various religious
> denominations. (my italics)[961]

Quite how this myth came to be generated, and to be so uncritically accepted, especially by some historians of Wales is puzzling, since the evidence is
so slight. Especially is this the case if the meaning of radical, especially in the
political sense, and even in the restrained definition common to dictionaries
is considered. For a radical belief is one which seeks fundamental change, a
rejection of the entire *status quo*, and its replacement by something totally
different. The most casual perusal of the behaviour of the Nonconformist
denominations in Wales in the eighteenth and nineteenth centuries must
lead to the conclusion that to apply such an epithet to those denominations
would be a grave distortion of historical reality. Occasionally there is an
implication that the claim to radicalism must be restrained. Thus of Thomas
Gee, a hero to many, it has been written that:

> His Radicalism hardly touched the industrial areas of south Wales but
> his press played a vital role in shaping and leading public opinion in
> the rural parts for more than half a century.[962]

The explanation may be that he had no message for the industrial areas. Yet
the attempt persists to link Nonconformity to radical political causes. It is
true that during the French Revolution Dissenters remained generally loyalist: that great preachers of the early nineteenth century like John Elias and
Christmas Evans were strong Tories in politics; and that the predestinarian-

ism of the Calvinists, and of the Methodist branch in particular, smothered stirrings towards reform.

Then Carwardine goes on to draw attention to the fact that Joseph Harries, editor of *Seren Gomer* 'was a moderate reformer', and that Samuel Roberts 'SR' 'advocated franchise extension, Catholic emancipation, the abolition of religious tests and church rates, and the improvement of tenant conditions'. Leaving aside that church rates was a parochial not a radical issue, and that a cause like Catholic emancipation was *opposed* by most Nonconformists the few examples which can be quoted hardly justifies his conclusion:

> Despite the coolness and opposition of much of articulate Nonconformity to disruptive egalitarianism or levelling causes like Chartism or Rebecca, the links between Nonconformity and these movements were undeniable.[963]

He is nearer the political facts when he writes:

> The doctrines of election and reprobation, the total depravity of man, and his complete inability to do anything towards his salvation, were widely held in the three major Calvinist denominations, and in particular amongst Calvinistic Methodists.[964]

The truth of the matter is well summed up by Evans:

> the doctrine of Election and predestination had its political results: it was an age of complacency, and it was a Christian duty to be submissive to authority. In 1817 the Baptists declared in their conference that politics were incompatible with religious orthodoxy; it was 'not the province of Christians to debate and discuss politics but to behave humbly towards their superiors'.[965]

Evans illustrates the point by a quotation from the *North Wales Chronicle* when 'it deemed it necessary to warn its readers against the demands for a fuller representation of the people in parliament because it "confides the executive to too many hands who eager for the superiority over each other, become as many tyrants", and the result would be licence and anarchy'.[966]

The North Wales Gazette in 23 July 1812 'congratulates its readers on their immunity from Luddite disorders'. The *Cambrian Quarterly Magazine* 16 years later, 'rejoices that the "morality of the Principality" has saved it from those "degrading scenes of brutalised anarchy which have lately disgraced some parts of the Empire"'.[967] The Reverend Thomas Jones of Denbigh at the time of the Napoleonic Wars was another who demanded submission from the Welsh. They should not:

> be misled by deceptive promises and highly fallacious theories. He urged them all to be loyal, and bade them remember (1) That it was impossible for all to be rich. (2) That industries, and, therefore, a means of livelihood to the generality of people, are possible only through the inheritances and the ampler means, of others. (3) That if the rich were spoiled, unemployment, disorder, and all their sad consequences, would overwhelm the nation with disaster. Let them consider their duty to their God and their country.[968]

This is especially important in Wales because Nonconformity, radical or otherwise, as we shall go on to see, has been central to social life and the exercise of political power in the country. In the twentieth century the most famous and most virulent critic of the Nonconformist oligarchy Caradoc Evans may not have been absolutely accurate, but he certainly captured the spirit when he wrote: The chapel 'guides us to the polling booth where we record our votes as the preacher has commanded us'. '(The chapels) stand for everything which signifies anything to the draper and the dairyman – home, religion, friendship, the language, music.' And Caradoc Evans points out that the chapel 'sanctifies' class divisions.[969]

Not only was their influence paramount, but they were deeply distrustful of the working classes as Kenneth O Morgan points out:

> Nonconformity, not industrialism, was to form the basis of Welsh social and political development. As the gentry withdrew from national life, Nonconformist ministers became indisputable popular leaders the democratic basis of Nonconformity has, no doubt, been exaggerated. Its articulate leaders tended to feel themselves segregated from *y dosbarth gweithiol* (the working class). Their attitude towards unions and other working class movements was uniformly hostile the only religious body to give support to Chartism in Wales was the Unitarian.[970]

Yet, as ET Davies points out:

> Nonconformity from its beginnings in this society was essentially
> working-class in character, and there was evidence before 1851 that
> the workers in the old iron industry were 'religious' in the sense that
> they had some connection with the chapel.[971]

But he goes on to remind us: 'By the end of the nineteenth century Welsh
Nonconformity was fast reverting to its middle-class character as a result of
economic and social changes.[972] It could also perhaps have been due to disil-
lusion with a situation where:

> from 1832 to 1900 the Monmouthshire Welsh Baptist Association
> did not once discuss the social conditions of industrial Monmouth-
> shire, with the exception of the problems of temperance and Sunday
> closing.[973]

Working class Nonconformity was not of course confined to Wales, a point
made by Watts: 'the Nonconformist chapel touched the lives of far more
working class people in the first half of the nineteenth century than did
either political radicalism or trade unionism.[974] But the size of the working
class congregations did not affect the traditional attitudes of the oligarchy.
At the time of the 'Scotch Cattle' in the early nineteenth century the Calvinistic Methodists supported the insistence that workmen sign a declaration
not only that they were not members of a secret society, but that they did
not belong to a trade union.[975] And at their Assembly in 1831 communi-
cants were forbidden to join trade unions.[976]

The Baptists too excluded trade unionists. It is difficult to overestimate
the power of the oligarchy in diminishing the wishes of the working class
to achieve some kind of justice. It even affected union leaders, as Morgan
points out in the case of one of the most famous in Welsh trade union
history:

> The dominant voice among the Welsh miners during this period
> (the 1890s) was that of William Abraham (Mabon), secretary of the
> Cambrian Miners Association. A characteristic product of industrial
> Nonconformity, deacon of Capel Nazareth, Pentre, – he believed that
> there was no essential conflict of interest between capital and labour,

and that mutual adjustment would secure an agreement satisfactory to both sides – to Mabon, strikes and lockouts were primitive and unnecessary.[977]

The dissatisfaction with the Nonconformist approach to industrial strife was expressed in a letter to the *Evening Express* in 1898, which gave a judgement on Mabon's role in the coal strike of 1898: 'had Mabon been at the head of the children of Israel in Egypt they would still be making bricks'.[978] Ben Tillett in an address to miners in Pontypridd in 1893 used even more provocative language:

> I am sorry that the body of Welshmen are a mere rabble… As Welshmen they had for 20 years fed on patriotism and cant, chiefly cant – If they were the chosen people, they had been 20 years in the wilderness without a Moses or an Aaron – I want you to pledge yourselves to organise – Mabon has been preaching the obsolete doctrine that prices must not rule wages.[979]

Not only were they hostile to workers' unions, but also to Benefit Societies which were important in working class life. This was in part because the members took an oath of secrecy, and in part because they met in public houses.[980]

The dominance of Nonconformity may have been a feature of both countries, but there were some important differences between England and Wales. The Nonconformist oligarchy in Wales were able to utilise to their advantage two particular features of Welsh society. There was first an especial dislike of the Established Church because of its association with a notoriously oppressive gentry. And secondly there was the peculiarity of language. It is a commonplace of Welsh religious history that the clergy, especially at the senior levels were unable to speak Welsh. This enabled the Nonconformist ministers to communicate fully, and, most important to represent to their congregations a world in which the church, gentry, and in some senses the English, were a considerable threat to their ancient culture, and indeed their very way of life.

Their manipulation of the language issue in the aftermath of 'The Blue Books' is a clear example of this. Two Bishops were conscious of this central power of language. Bishop Ollivant of Llandaff (d. 1882) believed that 'the Welsh attach themselves to that place of worship, whether church or sectarian, in which their language is alone used,' while Bishop Burgess (d. 1837) of St. David's noted that 'the Welsh language is with sectaries a powerful means of seduction from the church'.[981]

Another important difference between Wales and England is that substantial areas of Wales remained as rural and isolated communities, which was very fertile ground for the influence of the increasingly influential minister. Finally, when people moved from rural to the developing areas of Wales, they brought their Nonconformist traditions with them, and these could survive in the relatively small industrial towns in, for example the Rhondda, which were not swamped by the scale of alien influence which affected the huge conurbations of places like London, Manchester or Liverpool. Jones and Williams in their discussion of the 1851 Census noted the transfer of the 'old rural pattern of religious organisation to the new conditions of the coal-field'.[982]

During all times of unrest in Wales, with the notable exception of the Unitarians, the Nonconformists were vociferous in their condemnation of 'troublemakers'. The best known of the few radicals amongst the clergy at the end of the eighteenth and the beginning of the nineteenth centuries – Joseph Priestley and Richard Price being two outstanding examples – were Unitarians. And if some note is taken of the distinguishing tenets of the Unitarian faith, that is not surprising. Central to these was the dominance of reason, and the rejection of dogma. This, in the secular world, gave them an interest in science, and a refusal to admit of any conflict between their advocacy of science and their acceptance of the existence of God. Priestley, for example, discovered oxygen, and Price's contribution to economics has already been noted. If to these is added a concern for people and the real world in which people suffered, and the rejection of that most important Christian belief that misery, whether personal or social, is the result of sin, then it is not surprising that such men quickly saw that there were ways to improve society which were man made. Dr. Priestley in his funeral oration on Price said:

> Dr. Price was the first, the loudest, and the most incessant in his cries against the most cruel, unjust and impolitical war, with our brethren across the Atlantic, which terminated, as he foresaw, in their Liberty, and the doubling of our debt.[983]

For the Unitarians political activity was the corollary of their belief that human problems could be solved by the rational application of knowledge. John Edwards, who succeeded Priestley as minister of the Unitarian New

Meeting in Birmingham after the riots of 1791, argued that politics and religion were inextricably linked: it was as logical to protest against politics being introduced into the pulpit as it was to 'exclaim against a volume of sermons being introduced into a manufactory'.[984]

But these were highly exceptional people, which is why they are so often written about. And it is common to speculate on what Price's attitude would have become if he had lived to witness the Terror. It is unlikely he would have changed his mind about the importance of justice through change as some did. And in the nineteenth century it is a commonplace that the Unitarian influence and concomitant radicalism in Merthyr Tydfil, was to make that town a legend.

The bulk of the Nonconformist leaders, from the onset of the revolutionary ideas emanating from France violently disapproved, and did everything in their power to persuade their audiences and congregations that such ideas were satanic. This they continued to do, with, if anything increasing fervour throughout the nineteenth century. And so when it came to politics, the position of the Nonconformist oligarchy, especially the Methodists was clear. There was some support from Nonconformists for the American Revolution. However, supporting a distant war in America was one thing – even Burke did so – but enthusing about a Revolution and a war which was so near was something else:

> During the French Revolution the great mass of Welsh dissenters had remained loyalist and quiescent – The events which saw the formation of a coherent working-class movement in Wales from the Merthyr rising in 1831 down to the Chartist rising at Newport in 1839 encouraged the leaders of the main denominations, the Methodists in particular, to warn their flock of the dangers of subverting worldly authority – Even a politically conscious journal like the *Diwygiwr*, however devoted only a small portion of its space to political affairs.[985]

But as time went on, the pressure of democratic, and even revolutionary ideas prove irresistible, and 'it would be hard indeed for the heirs of the tradition of Thomas Charles, Henry Richard, and Thomas Gee to repel the surging forces of democracy'.[986]

'The independent *Diwygiwr* of February 1839 gave a general welcome to the Charter, but it opposed the threat of violence and disorder'.[987] The bulk of Nonconformists 'looked with grave suspicion upon the scepticism and irreligion which became growingly characteristic of the leaders of the French

Revolution', and they 'dreaded the spread of unbelief and disloyalty to God and the King in this country'.[988] The Methodists:

> were obsessed with the duty of Christian submission and patience, to the utter oversight of the more strenuous demand of the age upon Christian courage for conflict in all its forms, not least in social tyrannies and cruelties – they were induced to become unduly apologetic and docile, from a dread of being deemed disloyal.[989]

The Baptists were equally against upheaval. In March 1817 Christmas Evans and the Baptist ministers of Anglesey:

> drew up a declaration which they sent to a local magistrate in which they dissociated themselves from the agitation for parliamentary reform and promised to excommunicate any of their members who spoke disparagingly of the king and government.[990]

An admonition from a figure like Christmas Evans (1776–1838) was not to be taken lightly since he was one of the most powerful preachers of his day, and in addition wrote hymns and theological pamphlets.[991]

More puzzling is the enthusiasm of Morgan John Rees for the Authorities since he is often paraded as a radical. It is *possible* that he was being self protective, or sarcastic when he wrote in his *Cylchgrawn Cymraeg* Part III:

> May the King live, may his family be godly, may his counsellors be wise, may his senators be upright, may his judges be just; may the country be reformed, and may the world have peace.[992]

From the Independents comes the view of a one time minister David Williams whose work has been discussed earlier. 'No doubt inspired by the French Revolution, he denounces the governments of Europe in a much more violent tone than in earlier writings'.[993] Yet 'In both the political and religious dialogues, Williams is at pains to avoid a revolutionary stance. Although he admires the civil disobedience of the Dissenters, his own position is gradualist, preferring consensus to party strife, and depending on the transformation of public opinion'.[994] By 1797, significantly in an anonymous publication, he was:

repudiating such pro French sentiments as he had displayed at the beginning of the Revolution: 'The mild dawn of what was mistaken for Liberty in France has been succeeded by tempestuous horrors and complicated miseries... Britain now stands alone in Europe as an example of constitutional freedom, avoiding the anarchy of the Revolution and the military despotism of Napoleon.

He was anxious that large armies formed to meet invasion should not lead to anarchy. He proposed a highly localised form of defence. But 'what is noticeable here is that they are seen primarily as a defence against the unruly populace, ex-servants, criminals and other malcontents' (the breeding ground for Jacobinism in the author's view). The writer in the *Monthly Review* 'remarks that the system of registration proposed by Williams smacks of a 'combination of the affluent against the indigent'.[995] As late as 1802 after a three month visit to France his report 'is full of hatred and scorn for the Napoleonic regime'.[996]

The Methodists were especially important in the fight to keep radicalism at bay. Not that they did not have enough troubles keeping their movement in order after the death of Wesley. But to that was added the argument over the French Revolution which 'meant that for Wesleyans the 1790s were a decade of particular bitterness'.[997] Oddly enough, they were accused of sympathising with the revolutionaries, and as a consequence being disloyal to king and country, although it is evident that these allegations sprang not so much from evidence of disloyalty as from a seizing of the opportunity to attack dissenters. In August 1799 a correspondent in Denbigh wrote to *The Gentlemen's Magazine* to allege that the preachers of 'the sect of Methodists called Jumpers' were 'the instruments of Jacobinism, sent into this country to disseminate their doctrines, and to distribute the works of Tom Paine'.[998] Also in the 1790s a curate from Anglesey wrote to the king that 'north Wales was being "overrun" by "hordes of Methodists descanting on the Rights of Man"'. In Denbigh a rebellion was blamed on the Methodists.[999] On 6 April 1795 a magistrate in Mold wrote to Portland condemning the Methodists 'to whom I have been a constant and steady opposer... the leaders of the late disturbance were entirely of that Class'.[1000]

The Methodists had to defend themselves, and they did with vigour. The truth is, of course that no opportunity was missed by the Methodist ministers to defend themselves by insistent support for authority. When there were troublesome events they 'encouraged the leaders of the main denominations, the Methodists in particular, to warn their flocks of the dangers of subverting worldly authority'.[1001] Thomas Charles of Bala, who in 1811 was instrumental in establishing the breakaway Calvinistic Methodist Church wrote to *The Gentleman's Magazine* in 1799:

> Can any fact speak more avowedly and more forcibly in proof of the loyalty of the Welsh Methodists, than that on the anniversary of the reduction of the French invaders in South Wales the Methodists have a public day of thanksgiving for that mercy?... on diligent inquiry I cannot find one single tract of the enemy of all godliness, T. Paine, translated into the Welsh language; of consequence, your correspondent must have been misinformed when he asserts that they have been distributed by the Welsh Methodists. A small publication, (Davies notes *Seren Tan Gwmmwl*) indeed, of a similar tendency was published a few years back in the Welsh language; but both the author and distributors of it were decided enemies of the Methodists – the leaders of the Welsh Methodists, without any exception, detest the principles contained in it.[1002]

In addition *Gair yn ei Amser* (A Word in Season), reputedly by the Reverend Thomas Jones of Denbigh (another whose loyalty to the government knew no bounds), was distributed in thousands in Welsh and English, and:

> in which the baneful influence of the French principles, and the devastation they produce, are contrasted with the superior blessings which we enjoy in our highly favoured country.[1003]

And Charles spoke and wrote repeatedly in the same vein. As did other hugely influential Methodist leaders, such as Howell Harris (1714–73):

> Basically, Harris (Howell) was conservative on his outlook towards the existing order. His action in joining the Brecknockshire Militia as an officer in 1759 has been interpreted as a gesture to demonstrate the loyalty of the Methodists to the Crown which it might have been in part, but one also suspects an inclination towards social climbing.[1004]

Since the Methodist Revival there had been no doubt that their interests had been almost exclusively religious. Related to their religious beliefs was support for social and political tradition, and there was very little evidence that they would advocate reforms which would ameliorate the misery which was the hallmark of the lives of the bulk of the Welsh people. Any suggestion or accusation that they would was met with firm rebuttal. And there is overwhelming evidence that their protestations were justified. When the Revolution began:

> the Methodist leaders were not as ready to listen to the French propaganda of Justice and Liberty-even before the excesses which followed as were the already existing Nonconformist bodies viz., the Baptist and Congregationalists.[1005]

The Reverend Thomas Jones of Denbigh was convinced, as he shows in a pamphlet he wrote in 1797 or 1798 that the 'radical and chief cause of the war was sin', and he goes on to appeal to the Welsh:

> not to be misled by deceptive promises, and highly fallacious theories he urged them all to be loyal – that if the rich were spoiled, unemployment, disorder, and all their sad consequences, would overwhelm the nation with disaster.[1006]

In short:

> sermons were preached in every part of Wales, urging the people to quiet themselves, and be loyal to the King and the Government, and Acts were passed to meet the special condition of the country, as it then was. All disturbances, and contentious feeling, were condemned unsparingly.[1007]

A typical meeting of Nonconformists was held in Newcastle Emlyn in February 1793, at which one of the resolutions was:

> That we shall embrace every opportunity to impress on the minds of those connected with us loyalty to the King, and reverence for the laws; and to discountenance every tumult or sedition, should such evils spring up within the circle of our influence.[1008]

Such resolutions were commonplace, and ED Evans offers an explanation:

while the Methodists were suspected of political disloyalty to the State they found it necessary to assert their loyalty by such resolutions as that passed at the Bala Association in 1798 which declared that people who criticised the government were unfit to be elders or even members of their societies – and at several Welsh towns in 1790–1 when the non-conformists demanded more freedom they were quick to emphasise that they were 'true to the King and Constitution'.[1009]

Such determination was expressed at the most senior levels of the Methodist hierarchy. A warning was issued on 7 August 1819 by Jonathan Crowther and Jabez Bunting, as president and secretary of the Methodist Conference, against 'unreasonable and wicked men' who sought to use 'the privations of the poor' as 'instruments of their own designs against the peace and government of our beloved country'.[1010] The seniors in the Methodist church in Wales too joined in the campaign to stamp out radical tendencies, actual or potential. Probably the most notable was John Elias (1774–1841). He was the 'most famous preacher of his denomination in his day' and was called 'the Methodist Pope'. He 'opposed all political radicalism, as well as the idea that the voice of the people was the voice of God'.[1011] There is no dispute about his power and influence: 'By the 1820's Elias had come to occupy the dominant position amongst Welsh Methodists that Bunting had enjoyed among the Wesleyans'.[1012]

A quite extraordinary attempt to defend the Welsh against charges of disloyalty came from Henry Richard (1812–88), Congregational minister, Secretary of the Peace Society, and who, in 1868, was elected Liberal MP for Merthyr. It is so bizarre that it is worth quoting at length. There is first his assertion of the utter loyalty of Welsh people to the crown:

I doubt whether there is a population on the face of the earth more enlightened and moral, more loyal to the Throne, more obedient to the laws, more exemplary in all the relations of life, than the inhabitants of Wales[1013]– I venture to assert that there is not in the whole extent of the British Dominions, from the Hebrides to the Punjaub, (sic) a community more loyal to the throne of Queen Victoria than the inhabitants of Wales.[1014] During the civil wars they, for the most part, passionately espoused the cause of the King. For the last hundred years or so there is probably no part of the United Kingdom that has given the authorities so little trouble or anxiety. Anything like sedition, tumult, or riot is very rare in the Principality.

He excepts the Newport Chartists but this was an 'English inspiration', and took place amongst the:

> mixed and half-Anglicised population of Monmouthshire… The great bulk of the Welsh people had no share whatever in the movement, but looked upon it with undisguised repugnance and horror.

As for Rebecca 'They had no political significance whatever, and implied no disaffection to the Government'.[1015] He even deplores the establishment of police forces in Wales because there is nothing for them to do, 'not even an *emeute* of small boys'.[1016] The renewal of religious life caused the Welsh to choose:

> wisely. Spiritual life first, and political rights and privileges afterwards. I, for one, cannot, therefore, profess to grudge the time lost by the Welsh people as respects political action, when I know how that time was employed, in carrying light into the dark parts of the country, in gathering churches, building chapels, establishing and organising Sunday schools. (The) leaders of that movement had a strong repugnance to see their disciples mixing in the strife of politics having rescued many of these novices from a state of the lowest ignorance and degradation – if drawn into the vortex of electioneering excitement they might fall back into the evil habits from which they had with so much difficulty been reclaimed.[1017]

His writing has a further aim: to deflect the inevitable anger of the poor towards the Church and the Landowners, who were of course the symbol of the power of the Church. The 'caricature' of the Welsh portrayed in the Blue Books was due to 'some of the local clergy' who represented the people as 'grossly ignorant, depraved and brutal'.[1018] And he is vitriolic about the gentry who do not know the language, are churchmen, treat their tenants badly, and in all respects a disreputable group. He especially deplores the fact that there has never been a single Nonconformist Member of Parliament, especially since 'Dissenters are, and must be, from the nature of their principles and the necessity of their position, Liberal in politics'.[1019]

He then goes on to paint the most romantic and extraordinary picture of life in the Welsh countryside:

During harvest time especially the fields often ring with the sound of song and psalm, to which is sometimes added – a beautiful custom, to my feeling – the voice of prayer lifted in thanksgiving to the great Giver, while the workers stand or kneel amid the fragrant hay – swaths they have just cut, or under the golden sheaves of corn they have bound and stacked.[1020]

How much happier they were now, in contrast to the:

dark days that preceded that era (the rise of Methodism) the sweet sounds of the mountain harp had been far too much associated with scenes of profane and riotous mirth from which it became the aim, as it was the duty, of the religious reformers to wean the people.[1021]

Another famous (in his day) Welshman expressed similar views. In a volume designed to counter what he perceived to be the distortions in the Blue Books, Sir Thomas Philipps wrote:

In our new and neglected communities, Chartism is found in its worst manifestations – not as an adhesion to political dogmas, but as an indication of that class antagonism which proclaims the rejection of our common Christianity, by denying the brotherhood of Christians. This antagonism originated, as great social evils ever do, in the neglect of duty by the master, or ruling class.[1022]

It will be noticed that he too is critical of the Establishment. As to the Newport rising of 1839, which he had been instrumental in suppressing, and for which action he was knighted, he denied that the plot had been facilitated by the fact that that people were able to communicate 'with each other in a language not understood by the authorities'. Rather, even if the events were not 'concerted with Englishmen' they were 'known to some of the Chartist leaders in England and Scotland'.[1023]

With regard to Rebecca, it did not resemble 'the usual peaceable disposition of Welshmen', and in any case did not 'originate in political causes, nor did they manifest disaffection to English institutions or hostility to English laws'.[1024] He saw the potential antagonism between England and Wales as something to be avoided especially 'given the 1848 revolutions on the continent and nationalist agitation in Ireland': for him this was 'a period of the world's history when the process of decomposition is active amongst nations'.[1025]

Furthermore, the Welsh had been polluted by 'immigrants from England and Ireland' who had caused most of the social problems found in the industrial areas of Wales. They 'had been driven thither by crime or want' and were 'characterized by much that is lawless and unrestrained'.[1026] Davies sums up the position well:

> there was the more docile and submissive teaching of earnest men, chiefly of the Calvinistic Methodist persuasion, which at this time, was in the early stages of its emergence, when the more fervently spiritual aspects of religion were emphasised, but, too often, at the cost of ignoring the hard facts of unjust laws, which, in that period, pressed so heavily upon the life and liberties of the nation.[1027]

This assessment is confirmed by a contemporary observer:

> The credit for the peaceable and obedient nature of the Welsh country people must go to the strong hold exerted over them by their ministers and by their own devotion to the Bible, by which their lives were ruled in a form of religion rendered all the more powerful and exclusive by its adherence to the Welsh language and its hostility to the Established Church.[1028]

By 1860 a writer in Murray's *Handbook for Travellers in Wales* felt able to observe that 'Chartism, and the fearful riots to which it gave birth' were a thing of the past, and 'it must be confessed that Dissenters have been the principal agents in humanising and softening the mass'.[1029] So if the powerful Nonconformist oligarchy were not interested in radical change what were they interested in? To what was their energy directed? And were they concerned about the sense of grievance which was so surely expressed by the poor who made up the bulk of the population?

There is abundant evidence to show that they were dismissive of the efforts of the poor, and the expanding industrial working class to better themselves. It might be expected that they would have supported the nineteenth century attempts to expand education. Of some significance is the fact that it was 'not until the middle decades of the nineteenth century were the Nonconformist churches, so active elsewhere, roused from their hostility towards secular aid for education'.[1030]

Yet they *were* of course interested in politics, but where in fact did most of their effort lie for a very long time? The preliminary to an answer must be an understanding of interdenominational relationships. Everything was subordinate to interdenominational strife. The factionalism was breathtaking, and went some way to stultifying political action. Everything descended into factional squabbles. This can be illustrated – and these are only illustrations – on a national and a local scale. The siting of the university colleges, for example, was dominated by narrow sectarian interest. The selection in 1883 of Bangor was 'bitterly opposed by many Nonconformists as "the only Conservative town and the only Church City in North Wales"'.[1031] In 1906 a Royal Commission on the Church and other Religious Bodies in Wales began its work. Morgan quotes Sir Henry Jones, a member and a Nonconformist, as saying 'I learnt for the first time how much ill-feeling religious men can entertain towards one another. Such an atmosphere of distrust, suspicion and pious malice I never breathed before or since'.[1032]

At a humbler level it has been observed that: 'The harmonies and disunities which existed outside the places of worship were brought into them'.[1033] Jenkins' chapter on 'Religion' while it shows its importance, and its positive side, is a catalogue of the unhappiness which was a feature of chapel life, and how the relationships outside the chapel were reinforced by the chapel. For example on one occasion a cottager spoke at length in chapel on an issue. When he stopped, 'a farmer spoke, saying "now that you wheelbarrow men" (every cottager had a wheelbarrow for use in his garden) have had your say, perhaps we "cartmen" may have ours'. And Jenkins goes on to illustrate that 'this division was sometimes bitter'.[1034] The chapel might become the public arena of private quarrels. 'Not infrequently I heard it said regretfully that "one must take the quarrel to the chapel".[1035] In one case – the parties came to actual fist fighting before one party seceded to establish a separate congregation and a new chapel'.[1036] A commonly made observation as the grip of the chapels tightened is that:

> For the Welshman of the early nineteenth century the endless theological wrangles between the various sects, or the debates between Church and Chapel would have appeared more important than the Merthyr Rising or the Rebecca Riots.[1037]

There were too, other grievous effects of the Nonconformist determination to present the Welsh as a hyper-moral people. By 1900 the myth had to be sustained that 'rural Wales was 100 per cent pure'. In that year Rev. Thomas

Jones the President of the Welsh Independents proclaimed that:

the Welsh rural areas are still the location of '*Hen Wlad y Menyg Gwyn-ion*', (a land of pure morals); only the southern industrial valleys have been corrupted through the influence of English people and their vicious habits.[1038]

Another minister went further, asserting that as well as being possessed of any number of virtues, the Welsh were one of the most 'loyal, moral and religious nations on the face of the earth'. Russell Davies, in drawing attention to these statements goes on to describe how the determination to present such a public face led to the persecution, cruelty and injustice which was the commonplace experience of the Welsh unmarried mother.

The strength of the grip of the oligarchy was a matter of comment throughout the nineteenth century:

The landlords are most of them of the old Church and King school – the tenantry are almost all Dissenters, with a spice of the fanaticism of the Covenanters about them. Still there is – or had been – a sort of feudal deference existing between the parties – but I suspect it to be the result of habit, rather than of feeling resulting from conviction, and which may readily be put aside on a change of circumstances. There is moreover another class more powerful perhaps even than the Landlord – and this is the Preachers – and the great bulk of the population are as much in their hands as the Papists of Ireland in the hands of their priests.[1039]

The Blue Books too contain observations about the theocratic nature of Welsh society:

Most singular is the character which has been developed by this theological bent of minds isolated from nearly all sources, direct or indirect, of secular information. Poetical and enthusiastic warmth of religious feeling, careful attendance upon religious services, zealous interest in religious knowledge, the comparative absence of crime are found side by side with the most unreasoning prejudices or impulses: an utter want of method in thinking and acting.[1040]

And so here is the answer as to how the Nonconformist oligarchy controlled and dealt with the wretchedness of so many in Wales. It was to intertwine religious and secular life, so that 'the status a man occupies in the religious field corresponds to that he occupies outside the religious field',[1041] and to advance the familiar *apologia* for the misery of life on earth with the promise of a better life after death:

> Those, for instance, who are placed in the lowest class of life here, and groan under the hardship of poverty and want, cold and naked-ness, should comfort themselves with this consideration, that when they have ended the days of their pilgrimage here upon earth, and are returned to their Father's house, they shall hunger no more, neither thirst any more – and that God shall wipe away all tears for ever from their eyes.[1042]

But the case has been advanced that there was a brighter side to chapel life:

> The Methodists have been criticised as other worldly, alleging that they were more concerned with preparing people for the next world than with people's plight in this. No doubt, they were conservative in outlook and preached forbearance but Methodism was anything but negative.

Evans goes on to praise the activities they encouraged. These included the opportunities for 'leadership' and the 'visit of celebrated preachers who were masters of oratory and drama sometimes brought a touch of theatre into their lives'.[1043] Against these treats though must be set the losses. 'The stress on personal conduct led to censure of levity of any kind and innocent pleas-ures like the *noson lawen* (merry evening) consequently declined'.[1044]

Perhaps the only thing upon which they were united and agreed was an incessant hatred of the Catholic church and the Pope. Watts points out that there should be no surprise at this:

> Dissent had, after all, as one of its chief original motives the con-viction that the Elizabethan Church of England was insufficiently purged of the taint of Catholicism, and in some Dissenting chapels in the eighteenth century copies of Foxe's *Book of Martyrs* 'were laid on the sacrament table by the side of the Bible'.

And of the Nonconformist denominations 'the most substantial Nonconformist opposition to the Catholic claims came, however, from the Methodists, both Wesleyan and Calvinistic'.[1045] The fear of Rome was personified
by a Flintshire MP, Samuel Smith, 'whose entire political creed at this time
centred on apprehension at the growth of Roman Catholicism'.[1046] Pioneering educational effort too was dominated by the same attitudes. Writing of
the launching of the SPCK's educational scheme in March 1699 Jenkins
points out that a cardinal aim 'was to rescue the Welsh peasantry from the
clutches of Rome and the thraldom of ignorance',[1047] while Charity Schools
'were designed to be not only nurseries of piety, but also 'little garrisons
against popery'.[1048] We have seen how such approval as there was of the
French Revolution by Nonconformists was based, not upon the potential
for beneficial change, but from the hope that the Catholic church in France
was on the brink of destruction. Indeed it was argued by some that a critical
cause of the Revolution was the nature of the Catholic church:

> The present change in France, and the judgment which has fallen
> upon the Papists, brings to mind, indeed, the sufferings of the Wal
> denses, and the godly Protestants, and the cruel persecutions to which
> they were subjected in that country, when the Bishop of Rome led an
> army to town.[1049]

This writer, John Owen of Machynlleth as well as being heartily anti-Catholic was an ardent supporter of authority. In his 1797 work *Golygiadau ar
Achosion ac Eiffeithiau'r Cyfnewidiad yn Frainc* (Views on the Causes and
Effects of the Change in France), from which the previous quotation is
taken he lists as one of the causes as 'the godlessness of the priests'. He then
goes on:

> What kingdom is so full of privileges, and so abundant in mercies, as
> Great Britain? – Does not the goodness of God to us as a nation call
> for obedience and gratitude? Behold here a tender Government, and
> beneficent laws – and the light of the Gospel, instead of the darkness
> of Popery.[1050]

Thomas Jones,[1051] a prominent Calvinist, was one of many who lost interest
in the Revolution, explaining that 'they have, to the utmost of their power,
pulled down popery; but they have set up irreligion in its place, which is far
worse'.[1052] And there were other writers who variously expressed their hatred

of Rome, linked the attacks on it in France with biblical prophecy, and expressed disappointment when its destruction lost what they considered should be an absolute priority. John Elias was forthright in his opposition to the Papists, the '"chief agents" of Satan'.[1053] Even the sober scientist Joseph Priestley, much persecuted himself, saw the destruction of the temporal power of the Roman church in France as partial fulfilment of the destruction of 'the mystical Babylon' foretold in the Revelation of John,[1054] seeing 'in the French victories a Herald of the Apocalypse and the Triumph of right'.[1055]

Second only to their hatred of the idea of Rome was their more practical battle against the Established Church. There were many, and often justified reasons for the animosity which was the hallmark of Nonconformist attitudes. These included matters such as discrimination over burial rights, which collectively are the quintessence of Welsh religious history. But the most persistent was the issue of the payment of tithes. Put simply, this was a tax which had to be paid to the Church, and to which, for predictable reasons, Nonconformists took great exception. The ultimate dispute was the demand for Disestablishment of the Anglican Church in Wales.

The issue of the payment of tithes was not new. Thomas Roberts (1765/6–1841) who was, in fact a Quaker, and 'one of the founders of the Cymreigyddion and an active member of the Gwyneddigion' wrote a pamphlet *Cwyn yn erbyn Gorthrymder* (A Complaint against Oppression) in 1798. In this, 'under the influence of the French Revolution of 1789, he attacked the Established Church in Wales and its tithes, as well as lawyers, doctors and the Methodists'.[1056] In the same publication he also denounces war, and advocates liberty, and the use of the Welsh language in the courts. But above all he 'lashes the clergy, bishops, doctors, and attorneys, with a scourge of scorpions'.[1057] The resentment about tithes was one of the great flashpoints of Welsh history throughout the nineteenth century. On such issues, as usual, there was disagreement between the denominations: 'The Calvinistic Methodists who had only in 1811 formally severed their connection with the Church of England did not join in this disestablishment agitation, which was carried on chiefly by Baptists and Independents. At a General Assembly held at Bala in June 1834 the Methodists unanimously adopted a recommendation proposed by John Elias, urging an attitude of non-interference with political questions, and condemning the attempts which were then made to obtain the separation of Church and State, while at the same time he declared his 'fidelity to The Thirty Nine Articles of the Church of England'.[1058]

The protests against tithes were to continue until the outbreak of the
'Tithe War' which began in the 1880s, were to affect nearly every Welsh
county, were to see violence, and were predictably to divide Welsh opinion.
The Tithe Act of 1892 went some way to lessening the protest, but disturbances continued in Dyfed until some years after that.[1059]

The central political interest was disestablishment, described as 'another
concomitant of Welsh subnationality', and the same author claims that the
first pioneer of the movement was Morgan John Rhys.[1060] In the 1868 election twenty-two Welsh members were returned pledged to support Welsh
Disestablishment and Disendowment, *and ever since it has been the one great
vital, permanent question* (my italics).[1061] It certainly dominated political debate for many years, often pushing aside much more urgent issues: 'Important though they were to Welshmen, the questions of land and education
were secondary to the vital and far reaching issue of the "alien Church"'.[1062]

Not that there was any unity amongst even Welsh Liberals about the issue. When Watkin Willams, the Member for Denbigh District gave notice
in 1869 that he was going to call for a motion to end the establishment of
the Welsh church, there was uproar amongst his colleagues, notably, but not
only, because they thought it premature.[1063] The matter rumbled on until
finally The Welsh Church Act, introduced in 1912 became law in September 1914, but because of the war its implementation was postponed. On 31
March 1920 the Church in Wales finally became disestablished, and partly
disendowed. Morgan describes how 'on the eve of the First World War –
Welsh disestablishment was at last made an active reality, the culmination of
the efforts of Welsh radicalism'.[1064] Leaving aside, again, the overstretching
to the point of misuse of the word 'radicalism', the fact is that by 1920 the
matter was of little interest in general in Wales. This was no doubt substantially due to the return from the War of many thousands of Welsh people,
who at last were able to put into perspective those matters which were urgent, and those which were not. Since Disestablishment came into effect it
has been 'a dead issue'.[1065]

So what did they the Liberals/Nonconformists achieve. After all, it has
been claimed that after the election of 1885 and subsequently, there was a
significant shift of power:

democracy had now transferred political power for the first time to
the majority of the Welsh people, and their religious organisations
were henceforward to take the initiative with denominational rivalry
put aside.[1066]

Apart from their priorities which have been discussed, there was an important issue about land. We have seen how tenant farmers in Wales suffered several disadvantages, notably insecurity of tenure, the habit of some landlords to raise rents when the tenants had improved the property, and the social, religious, and linguistic divisions between them. These factors were exacerbated by the infamous evictions, following the elections of 1868, of those who had not voted at the behest on the landowners, and by agricultural depression in the 1880s. A Land Commission was set up and reported in 1896, but apart from providing the historian with invaluable information about rural life (to which we will return), its effects were limited. This was because the Liberal government lost power, there was ameliorating legislation, and there was something of an upturn in the farming business. 'Thus, the seven bulky volumes of the Land Commission lingered on the shelves of public libraries, unheeded and unread'.[1067] And, almost incredibly, the influence of the chapel meant that 'by the time the Liberals were returned to power in 1905 the question of Land Reform had been replaced in public interest by that of Disestablishment of the Anglican Church'.[1068]

This is evidence of Morgan's point, noted above, of the supremacy of the matter of Disestablishment. It is also evidence of the 'bitter words' written in 1903 by Artemus Jones, a Liberal lawyer that 'The main feature of Welsh politics today is its stagnation'.[1069] And so, when the priorities and achievements of the Nonconformist oligarchy, and the Welsh liberals are scrutinised one cannot but be amazed at the difficulty in trying to find success. Morgan notes that 'the Sunday Closing Act of 1881 had formed the first legislative recognition of Welsh nationality'.[1070] But it has to be said that this was intrinsically a rather limited achievement in the much more urgent context of the desperate need to lessen poverty in Wales.

How did the Nonconformist oligarchy manage to develop and tighten its grip on Welsh society? And, how were they able to deflect every question of importance from Land Reform or poverty back to the agenda set by them, notably the obsession with Disestablishment? Their skill at doing so has been discussed several time throughout this book. But what was central was the fact that they were able to establish themselves as the intermediaries between the Welsh people and the outside world. And so they were able to present matters to do with the culture of the English, or the injustices perpetrated by the Established Church, or the evil of social unrest, or the ungodliness of Rome, in a way which their audiences, for the most part, were unable to challenge. Thus they ensured that, in Gladstone's phrase 'the Nonconformists of Wales were the people of Wales'.[1071] This was, of course, because the monoglot Welsh people were effectively blocked from outside influence, and as long as this mono lingualism persisted, Nonconformist control was assured. This is why, despite the desire to protect Welsh culture when attacks were made on the Welsh language, which may have been genuine, a much more sinister motive lay in the understanding that with greater access to the outside world would come the collapse of Nonconformist hegemony.

One important factor in this wall of exclusion they created was their substantial control over literature, which in turn was possible because of the limitations imposed on monoglot people:

> By 1866 it was estimated that there were in Welsh five monthlies, and eight weeklies, with a combined circulation of 120,000. They were from the first overwhelmingly Nonconformist – the growth of the Welsh press and its early association with the outlook of Non-conformity was a fundamental factor in shaping the outlook and the sensibilities of people throughout Wales.[1072]

A publisher, a Mr. Rees described to the Education Commission how he had tried in 1834, in Carmarthen, to start a magazine '*Cylchgrawn*', 'on the same plan as the "*Penny Magazine*"'. The idea, he explained, was to set a balance against the existing periodicals where 'religious information pre-dominates, and there is much polemical discussion in them. They circulate extensively among the labouring men, mechanics, and small farmers. They are mostly sectarian, and not very temperately written'. His venture failed because 'it wanted religious information, and consequently excited but little interest'.[1073]

So it can be seen that the tyranny of the Established Church was re-placed by the tyranny of Nonconformist religion. Indeed the dynamics of the transfer of power in Wales from church to chapel is a replication of the transition of the rule of Charles I to that of the Commonwealth. It was not to be broken until the rise to power of Labour organisations, and the social-ist parties at the beginning of the twentieth century. As left wing parties be-gan to emerge, there was some attempt by the Nonconformist hierarchy to colonise them, but in the main their loyalties still lay with the Liberal party. And any attempt to claim consanguity with the Left for reasons already dis-cussed was intrinsically doomed to failure. As Liberalism began to falter in the face of the strengthening Left in the twentieth century, so too the power of Nonconformity began to weaken. By the end of that century, in the life of Wales it was an historical vestige.

EPILOGUE

The position of the Welsh squirearchy in the later nineteenth and early twentieth centuries was a mixture of the lucky, the pathetic, the shrewd and the rich. Cannadine marshals some very interesting evidence about land ownership in Wales during that period. Even though there was only a small number of local peers, most as we have seen of fairly recent creation, it appears that huge tracts of land were owned by peers who lived in England. Between 1894 and 1897 Lord Ancaster sold the Gwydir estate, and between 1898 and 1901 the Duke of Beaufort sold 26,000 acres in Monmouthshire, which included eight castles and Tintern Abbey. Between 1901 and 1910 there was sale of land by Lords Glausk, Ashburnham, Denbigh and Winchilsea.

The sales of land in the period 1910–14 is a revelation as to who owned land in Wales. Some of these lived in Wales, and some most decidedly did not. Between 1910 and 1914, amongst others the Duke of Westminster sold land in Flint, and the Marquess of Bute sold agricultural estates in Glamorgan and Monmouthshire. The big sellers, some ostensibly Welsh and some manifestly not, were Lord Powis, Lord Harlech, Lord Wimborne, The Duke of Westminster, and Williams Wynn. The Duke of Beaufort sold 5000 acres in Brecon in 1915, and in 1916 Lord Abergavenny sold the last of his Welsh properties in Monmouth.[1074] As late as 1930 The Marquess of Londonderry sold 9,000 acres in Merioneth.[1075]

When it came to local landowners, in 1872 'there were 571 squires or great landowners in Wales'. Between them they held 60 per cent of the land: 'half the land area of Carnarvonshire was owned by just five families'.[1076] 'One of the largest in acreage in was Earl (as he now was) Cawdor, with his seat at Stackpole. He had over 100,000 acres and a rental of £45,000. However only half of this land was in south west Wales, while the rest lay in northern Scotland'.[1077] Cawdor's Golden Grove estate alone consisted of 33,782 acres bringing in a rental of £20,780.[1078] In 1883 the Pembrokeshire Picton estate consisted of 23,084 acres in Pembrokeshire and Carmarthenshire, worth £23,815 a year.[1079] In 1873 Lisburne at Crosswood in Cardiganshire owned 42,666 acres with a rental of £10,579. Sir Pryse Pryse of Gogerddan in the same county had 28,684 acres worth a rental of £10,634.[1080]

It was though a time which saw the beginning of the selling of estates. This was caused by the fact that money had to be raised to pay debts, increasingly to the government:

> By 1891 the Liberal party was publicly committed to levies on mining royalties, to taxation of land values and ground rents, and to the imposition of death duties.[1081]

The ultimate, though not the immediate effect of Death Duties legislation, was further to take money away from the landed class. Under the Act of 1894 the rate was eight per cent on £1 million. By 1919 valuation was not based on rent, but on the sale value of the estate, and had increased to 40 per cent in £2 million. An example of a family in Wales which suffered a spectacular financial disaster, as well as especial family sadness, were the de Rutzens of Slebech in Pembrokeshire. Because of two wartime deaths, £100,000 had to be found on an estate which was worth £4,000 a year.[1082] But an equally important cause of the demise of the estates was the reality that, with the onset of industrialisation, land was not as profitable an investment as the new industries. There was a steady process of disposing of land so that capital could be raised to invest elsewhere.

This whole process of disposing of land accelerated after the first world war for very sound economic reasons. An illustration from the west can be seen in sales by Lord Kensington. Having 'sold his London ground rents for £86,500 which established "a record in the annals of the landmarket"' in 1902–03,[1083] after the war his holdings in Pembrokeshire – fetched £100,000'.[1084] Yet another effect of the First World War was a shortage of those reserves of manpower upon which estates relied, attended by further migration to the urban areas. And, it may also be noted that the casualties among those who were heirs to the estates were significant especially because they were so prominent in society. But although the deaths of the heirs to major landowners were individually so calamitous for their families 'it must be stressed that the overwhelming majority of those notables who served *actually returned home*' (Cannadine's italics).[1085] When it came to smaller estates David Jenkins lists some which were broken up and sold:

Whereas the gentry owned fifty properties in the parish of Troedyraur (south Cardiganshire) in 1910, at the end of 1921 they owned only eighteen.[1086]

An example was the fate of the mansion of Mount Gernos in the parish of Llangynllo. In 1884 the owner had to raise £20,000. In 1907 with £18,000 still outstanding It became necessary 'to sell the greater part of the estate which was thereafter reduced to the mansion, home farm, and two small holdings, totalling 192 acres, along with the woollen mill'. Then the mill was sold and the rest in 1918. A new buyer of the mansion and the home farm, spent a good deal of money on them, but in the post war slump they were sold again. A farmer bought the mansion, stripped it, and turned it into a piggery, and it remained such until 1960.[1087]

The twentieth century ushered in the final demise of many such estates, usually for less opprobrious reasons, with the continuing movement towards the end of the hegemony of the landlords. There were practical problems such as the repeal of the Corn Production Act of 1921 which had underwritten the price of corn.[1088] But there were other political reasons. Some of these are set out in Davies' magisterial analysis. Perhaps the two most important of these were the erosion of the power base of influence and patronage which was a substantial feature of political reform and concomitant legislation especially in the second half of the nineteenth century:

> legislation, beginning with the Agricultural Holdings Act of 1883, and culminating in the Act of 1948, robbed landlordism of much of its meaning.[1089]

But he exhorts caution about the supposed speed of change, since in some Welsh counties the process was hardly speedy. Cardiganshire is one county which showed an 'absolute fall in the proportion of freeholders between 1887 and 1909'.[1090] He also suggests that the later Disestablishment of the Church in Wales in 1920, undermined another area of patronage.[1091]

This change in the locus of power leads to the broader question of political change. We should begin by recalling briefly what the situation had been for some four hundred years:

> The story of Welsh politics in the century between the Glorious Revolution of 1688 and the French Revolution of 1789 is one of the

tightening grip on the electoral system of an ever smaller group of powerful landowners.[1092]

We have already seen examples of this. In addition there was the time when Walter Rice, the Member for Carmarthen in James I first parliament could distinguish 'himself by being fined double the usual amount for non-attendance'.[1093] Or later one of the Vaughan family of Golden Grove at the end of the seventeenth and the beginning of the eighteenth centuries could hold an uncontested seat for 42 years.[1094] Before 1886 'Welsh members had been notoriously unobtrusive and inarticulate. One keen observer noted how in 50 years they had never made a mark: 'the limit of their ambition seems to be County Court judgeships'.[1095] This was a notable Welsh parliamentary tradition. As early as Pitt's reform proposals of the 1780s 'of the Welsh MPs' only Lord Bulkeley (Anglesey) and John Parry (Caernarvonshire) had shown any genuine interest in reform'.[1096]A quite stunning example of lethargy was the sole Welsh Dissenter in Parliament who sat between 1852 and 1857 the member for Cardiff, Walter Coffin. During all his time he never once addressed the House.[1097]

All of this behaviour by Welsh MPs is by now familiar. And there was an ambivalent attitude to their nationality. A certain pride in being Welsh, members of an old, brave, independent race, was manifested from time to time – Welshmen in London celebrated St. David's Day and joined appropriate societies, notably the Cymmrodorion after its foundation in 1751. Yet they would also refer to themselves as English in a way Scotsmen would never have done. Being Welsh was not part of their political culture, 'except on the rare occasions when it proved to be a useful propaganda weapon'.[1098]

This grip of the landlords was substantially maintained until the advent of reform agitation During the attempts to reform the parliamentary system Wales was active. In December 1830 John Frost organised the passing of a resolution which called for the extension of the franchise.[1099] The rejection of the second reform bill by the Lords in October 1831 led to a physical attack on Lord Hereford who lived near Abergavenny, a disturbance in Brecon, and exhortation to withhold tolls and taxes in Carmarthen and Monmouthshire.[1100] The famous riots in Carmarthen and Merthyr will be discussed briefly later in this chapter as evidence of the persistence of discontent in Wales.

But the political reforms of 1832 and 1867 may simply have altered and adapted the old rural, oligarchic and proprietary system. However:

the third Reform Act (1884–5) created a new and very different representational structure for the whole of Great Britain and Ireland, in which the cities and the suburbs were pre-eminent, and in which a working class electorate possessed the dominant voice.[1101]

Morgan believes that 'the Reform Acts of 1867 and 1884 followed by the Local Government Acts of 1888 and 1894, gave political power to the mass of the Welsh people'.[1102] The election which took place in 1868 especially was a turning point. To Lloyd George:

> it awoke the spirit of the mountains – The political power of landlordism was shattered as effectively as the power of the Druids.[1103]

It was a strange analogy when power passed to a kind of reincarnation of the Druid tradition in the shape of the Nonconformist clergy. The Reform and Redistribution Acts of 1884–85 also had a major effect enfranchising thousands of rural and industrial workers. In the election of 1885 'the Conservative party was swept out almost completely, retaining only four of the thirty four Welsh seats'.[1104] Although there was some rejection of the landlords they still occasionally dominated, for example Cawdor who stayed in Carmarthen: 'Only in counties like Cardigan, where there were no resident grandees, was Conservative organisation virtually non-existent'.[1105]

But the Welsh members were scarcely more energetic than their forebears. In a discussion of a proposal to have a Standing Committee to consider all bills relating to Wales in 1888, it failed, 'only eleven Welshmen troubling to vote for it, as against forty one Irish'.[1106] There were some brighter moments. The:

> evidence from Wales to the Report of the Select Committee on Parliamentary and municipal elections 1869 played an important part in the successful attainment of a secret ballot.[1107]

There were county council elections for the first time in January 1889 in which Liberals were victorious in every county except Brecknockshire 'The first elections to the new councils in January 1889 created a profound social and political revolution throughout Wales.'[1108] These elections also 'created a social transformation (where) the age-long ascendancy of landowners on the magistrates bench, self perpetuating governors of the country-side was abruptly terminated'.[1109]

It had not been long before that any challenge to the hegemony of the landlords would prove to be disastrous. In Merioneth in 1859 a challenge to the Wynn candidate, although unsuccessful, led to evictions on the Rhiwlas estate of those who had voted for the opposition.[1110] One specific case exemplifies the tyranny of landlords. It concerns the Zoar Calvinistic Methodist chapel near Llanfair Caereinion in Montgomeryshire. When the chapel was built 'more than 20 years ago – the late Sir Watkin (Wynn) had always an objection' to leases. In 1862 there was a by-election in Montgomeryshire and two of the deacons voted for the candidate opposing the Wynn candidate. The congregation was given notice to quit the chapel 'by way of revenging the election'. It was said by his lawyers that Sir Watkin knew nothing about it and that it had nothing to do with the election, although it was claimed that a solicitor said:

> Your party have acted shamefully by opposing his interests in the last election, considering all the chapel sites he has granted you. Mr. Jones, no more favours will be granted you by Sir Watkin.

The writer accepted that he probably did not give the order himself, but it 'was a black spot on Wynn of Wynnstay'.[1111] Such victimisation was to be a feature of the new electoral arrangements. The elections of 1859 and 1868 for example led to a series of notorious evictions, especially in Cardiganshire and Carmarthenshire because tenants voted Liberal.[1112]

Tom Ellis wrote in 1894 that 'The political subjection of Wales was complete – it had no voice in Parliament – no one to meet enemies at the gates'. Morgan adds that 'many of these later charges were much exaggerated'.[1113] Like the Nonconformists, the Welsh Liberals:

> suffered from the disunion of their own supporters over such issues as the Education and Licensing Acts, and from the revived cohesion of their Conservative opponents.[1114]

Even though later they were somewhat more organised, their history is one of splits and bitter disputes, 'malice, pettiness and mutual hostility' so that 'the degree of unity attained by the Welsh members was never very pronounced'.[1115] And as Morgan points out, when it came to the question of a Land Commission the Welsh party showed a 'fatal weakness – that lack of cohesion which was preventing them from using their opportunities in a manner comparable to the Irish. When the testing time came, they split in all directions'.[1116]

One exemplary victim was, of all people, Henry Richard. This great advocate of arbitration did not intervene in a strike in Merthyr, his constituency, which led the *Western Mail* to observe:

> Gorged with dinners and flattery in half the capitals of Europe, the fortunate ex-preacher brings to his disappointed constituents at Merthyr a list of the bills of fare with which he was regaled.

In a speech he had dealt at length with the enthusiasm with which he was greeted on his continental tour.[1117]

Eventually there was, however, one issue in which the Welsh Liberal Members were interested, and at which, at least some of them, worked very hard: land reform. The pulpits and the press maintained an incessant attack on what was summed up as 'being the one great cause of all the ills in contemporary rural society'. In *The Banner* Thomas Gee denounced the landowners as 'cruel, unreasonable, unfeeling and unpitying men' who were 'devourers of the marrow of their tenants' bones'. It was Thomas Gee who set up the Welsh Land League in 1886 'explicitly modelled on its Irish counterpart'.[1118] This followed meetings between Michael Davitt and Welsh land reformers and a lecture tour by Davitt.[1119]

It should be noted that this pressure group, like most in Wales sought to further the interests of farmers, not of poor labourers. But much as Lloyd George is supposed to have hated landlords, he drew back from wholesale change in land ownership. Morgan offers a curious explanation for this; 'Perhaps he felt at times that an expropriation of the Welsh landlords on similar lines to that proposed for Ireland would deprive the fragmented Welsh people of their traditional leadership.'[1120]

As part of this agitation in 1892 Tom Ellis introduced a Tenure of Land Bill, 'which would have given security of tenure, fair rents, and a land court, on the Irish model'. Gladstone's response was to appoint a Royal Commission to look at the question of land in Wales promising 'a thorough, searching, impartial and dispassionate inquiry'.[1121] This revealed a lot about the condition of the Welsh. Perhaps one unexpected result was that much evidence was submitted about the rural poor, and this will be discussed later. Even after the great victory of 1906:

The conduct of the Welsh members of Parliament is instructive here. They represented the new Welsh bourgeoisie of the later nineteenth century, the professional and business classes. Their fire was still directed at the unholy alliance of 'Beer and the Bible': one searches in vain, even among the speeches of Lloyd George, for reference to the basic issues of unemployment, depressed wages, and inadequate housing in the industrial South. The great coal stoppage of 1898 evoked little interest from the members from South Wales.[1122]

This conservatism found many expressions. For example, like many Nonconformist MPs Ellis 'had been an admirer of Cecil Rhodes' and 'strongly supported the imperial cause'.[1123] Above all, like the Welsh Liberals, Nonconformist ministers at the beginning of the twentieth century 'inveighed against the materialism and atheism of Socialist propaganda'.[1124] In the early 1900s 'the main opposition to the miners' demands came from the Liberals themselves'.[1125]

And there continued to be some remarkable examples of people who could not seemingly be shifted, and who help to lessen the surprise that Liberal Members did not fight for better conditions for labourers and the poor. One was Mathew Vaughan Davies who represented Cardiganshire between 1892 and 1921:

> he was an unlettered, uncultured squire, who was master of the local foxhounds; he had contested the same constituency unsuccessfully as a Conservative in 1885; and he ran the local Liberal constituency organisation virtually as an extension of his own estate.[1126]

But the behaviour of many Welsh MPs continued to be dismal. In the war years 1914–18 'The compliance of the Welsh Party was apparently won over all too easily by political honours and appointments, with the massive expansion of bureaucracy during the coalition government'.[1127]

The twentieth century ushered in the final demise of many estates, with the continuing movement towards the end of the hegemony of the landlords. But there is still argument about the wealth and power which they have retained. After all, were aristocrats to be bankrupt, they would still be aristocrats, with all the potential for recovery that embraces. Most 'Welsh' aristocratic titles are still held, and again examples may be drawn from Dyfed. As we have seen Milford and Cawdor are two of them. But the Milford title and the Picton estate are now separate, and Cawdor's Stackpole

Court was torn down in the mid twentieth century. Cawdor retreated to his Scottish estates. The historic seat of the Vaughans, and latterly owned by the Cawdors, Golden Grove, was until recently an agricultural college. There is still a Baron Dynevor, who lives in Worcestershire. The first Baron Kensington (1776) in the Irish peerage had been a William Edwardes, who was an MP for Haverfordwest. He inherited the estates of Rich through his mother on the death of his cousin the Earl of Warwick. The family represented the district for several generations, and then secured positions in Queen Victoria's household. In 1886, the Barony was transferred to the United Kingdom. After World War I the family home, Sealyham in Pembrokeshire was sold to the King Edward VII Welsh National Memorial Association, and became a Tubercolosis hospital. The present Baron Kensington lives in South Africa.

A typical example is the decline in the fortunes of the Pembrokeshire Meyrick family. Despite every effort to save the Bush House estate – for example the formation of a company in 1948 – the house became an educational institution. The family moved to Slebech. This house had been bought by Nathaniel Philips in about 1792, and his daughter Mary brought the estate to her husband Baron de Rutzen a member of the nobility of Courland in Russian Poland. It stayed with de Rutzen until 1944 when the last Baron was killed. It was empty until 1948 when Meyrick bought it. Then in 1959 he went to Gumfreston farm, and built a house in an adjoining field. This was renamed Bush House in 1985.[1128]

But despite these changes, there are still large tracts of land in Wales which are not owned by the people who work it. Davies points out statistics for 1970 which show that in that year '61.7 per cent of the land was owned by its cultivators'. But this means that over one third is still landlord owned. His conclusion is questionable therefore: that the ambition of 'destroying the grip of the great estate and of turning the mass of Welsh tenants into freeholders has largely been achieved'.[1129] A better premise is his observation that 'those who have held their land throughout all the vicissitudes of the twentieth century are still among the favoured of this earth.'[1130] And Harold Laski, in the interwar years, was expressing a political wish rather than a political fact, when he wrote:

The English aristocracy has long passed the zenith of its power. It no longer has a monopoly of those qualities which make for effective governance. It may even be said that the problems which confront civilisation today are of a kind which call less for the qualities of the aristocrat than almost any others that can be imagined.[1131]

In Wales, as in the rest of the country, the aristocracy adapted, and went for new positions of eminence. When universities were founded, Lord Aberdare was:

> President of the university colleges of Aberystwyth and Cardiff and became the first Chancellor of the federal university in 1895, while the fourth Lord Kenyon was later President of Bangor university college, and successively Senior Deputy Chancellor and Pro Chancellor of the university.[1132]

As to the peasantry there was no improvement in their condition in the nineteenth century. An important, though very controversial source about the state of the Welsh peasantry in the mid nineteenth century are what are commonly called The Blue Books, and to which reference has been made. These were the Reports of the Commissioners of Inquiry into the State of Education in Wales published in three substantial volumes in 1847. The Inquiry was advocated by the Welsh born member of Parliament for Coventry William Williams in Parliament in 1846. When the Reports were published 'his numerous detractors regarded him as the father of all the evils of the Blue Books',[1133] and he has 'come to be seen as a quisling motivated by hatred and contempt for the Welsh language, and by a love for all things English'.[1134] Nevertheless Peate goes on to write a balanced, but spirited account of his work and his care for things Welsh. But when the Reports were published Williams was the subject of immediate attack.[1135]

These ranged from the restrained and often scholarly to the excited and venomous. Owen Owen Roberts published an open letter in 1848 in which he stated that the attacks on the degenerate way Welsh domestic life was described 'should more properly be directed at the landlords, employers and clergy who were responsible'.[1136] He did not, of course, include the Nonconformist oligarchy in his blanket condemnation. This is not surprising as he goes on to describe the Anglican clergy in Wales as:

> a cringing, sneaking, low bred, mean, servile, back-biting set, who would make mischief between a Cow and a haystack.[1137]

Jane Williams (*Ysgafell*), on the other hand wrote a more scholarly reply in 1848, in which she demonstrated that the illegitimacy rates and crime levels were higher in parts of England than they were in Wales.[1138] Sir Thomas Philipps, and Evan Jones (Ieuan Gwynedd) made the same point extending the comparison to the continent.[1139] In an open letter to Williams in 1848 Ieuan Gwynedd wrote that he did not understand 'the state of feeling in Wales, and that he wished 'to annihilate the Welsh language by means of English schools'.[1140]

The very detailed account attracted enormous controversy and anger, so much so that it has taken its place in Welsh history as *Brad y Llyfrau Gleision* – 'The Treason of the Blue Books'. The claim was made at once that the Report painted an inaccurate and unfair picture of Wales. Objection was made to the attacks on the morality of the Welsh, especially the women, the demeaning of the Welsh language and the bias shown to the Church because, it was said Churchmen unduly influenced the Report. This is probably true, but it is also the case that Anglicans came in for their fair share of criticism, as when, for example they perverted the directions of trust funds and pocketed the proceeds.[1141] And there were objections to the description of education, which was deemed to be unfair. Worse, the Commissioners were English. The three barristers who sat on the Commission were later to be called 'libellous and mendacious foreigners' by an Anglican clergyman. Even the assistants were criticised. As Roberts points out 'none of the assistants made themselves popular in Wales'.[1142] In a sense this is irrelevant, since the issue to be addressed is whether or not they were accurate in what they reported, and of course in a Report of this length there is plenty of scope for debate.

A most serious complaint, made in 1848, was that one had deliberately 'mistranslated children's answers into English so as to make it appear that they had answered his questions incorrectly'.[1143] One historian goes so far as to write that folk memory was that 'the treachery' was the 'Glencoe and the Amritsar of Welsh history'.[1144] But as Ieuan Gwynedd Jones points out:

> the key to a critical understanding of the reports of the Commissioners is the oft-forgotten fact that, in essence, they were but the latest in a relatively long series of official papers designed to elicit information regarding the provision and quality of education of for the working classes and the poor in England and Wales.[1145]

One curious result was that the Nonconformists with their history of chronic bickering could join together in an attack upon a newly found common enemy.[1146]

It is inevitable that in such a vast report there will be contradictions, generalisations, and much parading of prejudice, which, it has to be said, is equally true of the plethora of response, consisting as it did of 'hundreds of letters and articles, many pamphlets, speeches and public meetings' which 'marked the furore'.[1147] It is certainly the case that certain parts of the Report, as we shall go on to see, portray a very degenerate people. And it is the case that some witnesses made absurd generalisations, such as the Rector of Begelly in Pembrokeshire who 'gave a deplorable account of this parish where the people were 'extremely cunning, but grossly ignorant'.[1148] And there are some snide remarks to which Nonconformists could reasonably have objected. In the area around Swansea, Llanelly and Neath for instance it was said that people attended public worship, almost all being Dissenters, but 'from their disregard of truth and laxity of morals, it is evident that their standard of morals is not what it ought to be'.[1149] And perhaps since the main purpose of education seems to have been to learn the bible, the Nonconformist ministry would object to the frequent reporting of occasions when children were unable to answer questions such as those asked at Llanwrda in Carmarthenshire. There 'not one of the class could tell me the meaning of "graven image" in the second commandment... the second class could hardly find the fifteenth chapter of Luke'.[1150] We shall see that there are many positive experiences which were set against these.

But what probably angered the powerful in Wales, which was, by this time the Nonconformist ministry, was *inter alia*, the continuing and utter wretchedness of the people, and the inevitable implication, not made in the Report but true, that if the country was in the grip of the Nonconformist establishment, then the latter must carry a large measure of responsibility. After all the people could not be blamed for the condition of their homes, the lack of school equipment and so on. We shall go on to see that the misery the Commissioners describe was both reported to them over and over, and was witnessed at first hand. Furthermore, credit was given to the chapels for some of the good features they describe, despite the Commissioners being in 'the hands of one class', by which Henry Richard means the Church. A cooler appraisal of the Report than that offered by Richard and others must show, not that they misrepresented the truth, but they reported it, and it was appalling. Sober reflection must ponder the truth of what they wrote.

Since it is difficult to make an intelligible summary of such a huge document, for the purpose of this discussion we will look at some of what they wrote about education in the three western counties. It should be said at once that the Reports are far from being totally condemnatory. Their remarks on the counties of Carmarthen, Glamorgan, and Pembroke they write of Llanelly:

The moral character of the place is much better than it used to be. Twenty years ago it was a frightful thing… on Sunday there was such open and indecent desecration of that day. The Dissenting Sunday Schools appear to have been mainly instrumental in effecting this happy change.[1151]

In the same way the Report states that in Brecknock, Cardigan and Radnor: 'the dissenting Sunday Schools are decidedly more effective for the purpose of religious instruction than those of the church'.[1152] Also in Carmarthenshire, they wrote of Llanfihangel ar Arth that:

The labourers are very ill off – their misery is extreme. As far as they can manage it they are anxious to send their children to school.[1153]

They also wrote favourably about Llangathen Court Henry Girls' School:

Reading is taught by this lady in a very superior manner, and all the questions which I asked on the chapter were answered with readiness and correctness.[1154]

Similarly in Llandilofawr Carmarthen Street Day School 'The five scholars whom I found present read with ease and answered the questions put to them in (sic) the New Testament correctly'.[1155]

In Lamphey in Pembrokeshire 'The reading on the whole was remarkably good', and the Schoolroom 'well supplied'. There were compliments in the visitors' books including some from Her Majesty's Inspectorate. Two boys were drawing maps which were 'remarkably well done' Senior class books were 'well written'.[1156] In the small village of Uzmaston although the school 'consisted only of a thatched mud hovel' there was a glowing report.[1157] Dewisland (Dewsland) Hundred, which is in the north west of Pembrokeshire was 'miserably provided with schools'. Out of 21 parishes no less than 12 had no school at all.[1158] It may be observed that although this is the kind of figure in the Report which angered Nonconformists and Anglicans alike, the Commissioners were merely reporting what they saw and what was reported to them. But even though the Hundred was 'miserably provided', in that Hundred at Brawdy, 'the master was a very intelligent person',[1159] and in one school in St. David's 'the schoolmaster appeared a superior man for a country Schoolmaster'.[1160] At another 'nine read with ease from the seventh chapter of St. Mark' and 'they parsed with readiness and accuracy'.[1161] At a third the children were 'reading even better than the adults'.[1162] And it was reported with pride that in the Hundred 'not a man of them had joined in the Rebecca riots'.[1163] These were some of the many complimentary remarks, which are not difficult to find, made about schoolmasters, the children and the standard of learning.

The Dissenting ministers themselves could be critical. 'The Reverend John Rees and other Dissenters at Tregaron said "The masters hereabouts are generally incompetent to teach properly"'.[1164] At the same time the Church does not escape the Commissioners' criticism. A schoolmaster in St. Clear's in Carmarthenshire gave evidence, which was duly recorded that:

> The endowed schools are almost all connected with the Established Church. In them the religious principles of the Church are taught, and attendance in church enforced; this is felt to be a hardship by the parents, and little pay schools are common even in the neighbourhood of endowed schools.[1165]

It is probably the case that they were rather more critical of Cardiganshire, although even there compliments were paid. In one Sunday School, an English Independent, 'Mr. Lloyd, who devotes much attention to this school; and his instruction to the class and the answers he elicited were very satisfactory'.[1166] But in another 'they all read in the most wretched manner'.[1167] In the Cardiganshire grammar schools:

> the future clergymen and the farmers were educated together. Cardiganshire (in which such schools were the most numerous and the most efficient) has been for more than a century quite a nursery of clergymen, ministers, and schoolmasters. The effects of these institutions are strongly impressed on the general education of the people around.[1168]

But, naturally they were critical too. 'I might quote endless instances to prove the miserable character and ill effects of the present school buildings in Carmarthenshire and Pembrokeshire. Indeed, Report after Report is too often only a wearisome repetition of such particulars'.[1169] In Wiston, in Pembrokeshire, the school was 'little better than a mud hovel' and here the master was 'thoroughly stupid and ignorant'.[1170] In Roose Hundred, in central Pembrokeshire, only five out of 27 parishes did not have a day school 'yet most of the schools in it are of an utterly inefficient character'.[1171] In Derllys Hundred in Carmarthenshire, out of 25 parishes, 12 had no school at all. 'For the quality of those schools which exist I must refer to the Reports, which, however, fail, in general, to convey the idea of the utter inefficiency which would be collected from a sight of the schools'.[1172] As far as many witnesses were concerned they were two persisting solutions: to send teachers to England, and to set up Normal Schools – that is teacher training colleges in Wales. This might improve the position of teachers as described by teachers themselves and summed up in Part I:

> No observations of mine could heighten the contrast – between the actual and the proper position of a teacher. I found this office almost everywhere one of the least esteemed and worst remunerated; one of those vocations which serve as the sinks of all others, and which might be described as guilds of refuge.[1173]

It was above all those parts of the Reports which dealt with everyday life in Wales which caused the greatest upset. And there were two main areas of report and subsequent complaint: living conditions and 'morals'. With regard to the first the evidence is overwhelming and beyond dispute that the lives of the west Wales peasants were as wretched as they had been at least since the eighteenth century. The Report positively bulges with such evidence, and again it must be emphasised that much, if not most, of it is gathered at first hand: 'I have myself visited many of the dwellings of the poor'.[1174] As we shall go on to see, the observations made in the Reports are commonly made in other books, and indeed in official reports. In Tregaron, Cardiganshire:

> dung heaps abound in the lanes and streets. There seemed seldom to be more than one room for living and sleeping in: generally in a state of indescribable disorder and dirty to an excess. The pigs and poultry form a usual part of the family.[1175]

In Cardiganshire in general the Commissioners opined, as had observers in the previous century that 'the Welsh cottages (were) very little, if at all, superior to the Irish huts in the country districts'.[1176] In Clarbeston (Pembrokeshire) 'the labourers in the parish were wretchedly poor'[1177] while in Marloes, which is not very far away, 'the houses were generally struggling and dilapidated, often partially unthatched: several are wholly in ruins and deserted'.[1178] The situation may be safely summed up as being that the observations of visitors in the 1790s were identical to those of the Commissioners in 1846, and would be repeated again in the Royal Commissions of 1867 and 1896.

Once again though it is essential to note that although people were poor, they were willing and anxious to educate their children and that this observation was repeated by others, including locals. In his report from the village of Camrose (Pembrokeshire) to the 1851 Religious Census the deacon of the Baptist chapel makes the point that:

> The weekly school has been tried by several schoolmasters since the erection of the Chapel but was given up for the want of scholars the schoolmaster could not find his own support by the number of scholars attending. We live in an agriculture (sic) district, the poorer class being too poor to pay for the schooling of their children.[1179]

The Commissioners made the same point about the same small parish. And it was also reported that although they lived at subsistence level, and had a very poor diet, the people were very keen to educate their children.[1180] Yet 'they are economical, and more cleanly than a stranger might think'.[1181] The point about cleanliness, incidentally, is commonly made. In Carmarthenshire, for example, we are told that one witness gave evidence that 'the labourers are desirous of cleanliness'.[1182]

A curate in Llanelly, who seemed to be notably devoid of any understanding of the people amongst whom he lived, gave as his evidence that:

> their dwelling are almost universally destitute of those conveniences which are necessary to the health and comfort of mankind; and from the practice of the males stripping to wash themselves in the presence of the females, the usual barriers between the sexes are done away with.[1183]

This witness must have been aware that this was the only way that miners could wash off the grime after working in their pit, and that the practice was perfectly normal and certainly did not, of itself 'result – in the frequency of illicit intercourse'. It was the only way a miner could wash until well into the twentieth century.[1184] But they were not only short of washing facilities. Part one of the Report dealt with the 'painful subject' of privies. 52.6 per cent of schools were 'utterly unprovided with privies'. This was hardly remarkable when a whole row of houses in the village 'had not a single not even a common, privy'. 'Where there is such a thing, it is a mere hole in the ground, with no drainage'.[1185] Also 'the children frequently did not know their own ages, and of time, in general, had still vaguer notions'.[1186] In Llanelly workhouse there was 'itch' in the girls' ward, and the ward was itself too offensive to enter. The boys were in old rags and were dirty.[1187]

A prominent feature of the Report is the 'immorality' which seemed to the Commissioners to be widespread. Once again it should be noted that they reported what they were told. Take, for example, the hysterical claim by the chaplain to the bishop of Bangor: 'I assert with confidence, as an undeniable fact, that fornication is not regarded as a vice, scarcely as a frailty, by the common people in Wales'.[1188] What every impartial commentator must agree upon is that this 'issue' had nothing at all to do with the brief given to the Commissioners, and it is fair to object to their discussing a matter which was of no relevance to their Inquiry. Although the objectors to the Report, largely Nonconformists, objected to this, it should be pointed out that much of the reflection on such behaviour came from their ministers. 'The want of chastity results frequently from the practice of "bundling", or courtship on beds during the night – a practice still widely prevailing'.[1189] This is when the unmarried men 'range the country at night'.[1190] In Dewisland they 'heard anecdotes of the gross and almost bestial indelicacy with which sexual intercourse takes place on these occasions'.[1191] Paradoxically, in the same district the general character was good: 'I have several times been told – that it was very good – nor had they ever to be carried before a magistrate'.[1192] Immorality is also said to be 'much increased by night prayer-meetings, and the intercourse which ensues in returning home'.[1193]

This association of Nonconformist worship with immoral behaviour was emphasised by a prominent, no doubt bitter witness David Owen. Dismissed by one conformist body for attempting to obtain money by fraud, he famously wrote as 'Brutus' in the church magazine *Yr Haul* which became 'the cleverest of all the Welsh periodicals'.[1194] His evidence was that in Carmarthenshire there were 'the vices of lying and cheating and unchastity'. At Revivals:

> when such meetings occur, a great stimulus and opportunity for immorality is given; the parties attending them are under great excitement, and often do not separate until a late hour… no educated man joins in them; but something of the same results accompany the common prayer-meetings.[1195]

In the district of Llandilofawr a witness said 'unchastity is so prevalent that great numbers of the young women are in the family-way previous to marriage'. There was also:

> the revolting habit of herding married and unmarried people of both sexes, often unconnected by relationship, in the same sleeping rooms, and often in adjoining beds without partition or curtain.[1196]

Yet a magistrate in Carmarthenshire offers a defence:

> In cases where marriage would be out of the question, from the superior rank of the man, the woman would not listen to proposals of an immoral kind. The first breach of chastity with a woman in the lower class is almost under a promise of marriage.[1197]

An additional source of repression at the time was the operation of the new Poor Law of 1834. One of the witnesses giving evidence to a Commission of Inquiry for South Wales summed up the experience as follows; 'I know that the Poor Law has created more dissatisfaction and disaffection in this country (Wales) than any other law that has been enacted for this century'.[1198]

Since the subject of the behaviour of women is being discussed, it is worth noting the especial horrors faced by women who fell on hard times. In addition to the Poor Law they were subject to the Bastardy Laws. In an Amendment in 1834 it was decreed that:

> A bastard should be what Providence appears to have ordained that it should be, a burden on its mother and where she cannot maintain it, on her parents.[1199]

To this end, the mother's evidence had to be independently corroborated, parishes could no longer pursue defaulting men, and men could no longer be jailed for non payment of maintenance. Small wonder then that Hagen writes that:

> South-west Wales in the nineteenth century could be a terrifying place for a deserted wife, widow, single mother, elderly or an orphan, illegitimate or otherwise.[1200]

The question, as we have seen, which more critics might have asked were those presented in scholarly fashion by Jane Williams (*Ysgafell*) Sir Thomas Philipps and Evan Jones (Ieuan Gwynedd): how did the levels of 'promiscuity' and illegitimate births in Wales compare with England, and for that matter with other countries? After all if there is what the Commissioners call quaintly lack of chastity in a community, then there are other ways of indulgence than some purely local custom such as 'bundling' which was seized upon for certainly 100 years by astonished English travellers. On the other hand of Carew in Pembrokeshire, it was said that the 'moral character of the people here is good'.[1201] And if people were 'herded', whose fault was that? Surely not the poor, whose style of life was such that life expectation in a representative district, Narbeth in Pembrokeshire, was 'not above 33 years as appears from the register'.[1202] And what is to be made of the odd observation that 'the want of shoes and stockings' was 'no sign of poverty?'[1203]

But a lot of the superficial evidence appears, or at least would have appeared to the Commissioners, to be incontrovertible. In north Wales the vicar of Denio produced figures from the books of the relieving officer which showed that in one quarter out of 29 births, 12 were illegitimate. In his parish of Llanor there was a woman with five illegitimate children by different fathers. Her sister had four illegitimate children and another in the village had four, all by different fathers.[1204] In November 1843 it was reported that the workhouse in Haverfordwest held 80 children, 60 of whom were bastards, and one woman had just delivered her ninth illegitimate child.[1205] Yet a doctor in Tenby claimed that 'bastardy is less frequent here than elsewhere in Wales',[1206] and defends 'bundling' as proof of honesty since it would 'be discontinued if the visitors were dishonest',[1207] although there was a counter claim that 'Pembrokeshire was said to be the worst county in Wales for bastardy'.[1208] And even if all of this were true, what did this have to do with education?

But there were examples of personal and social dignity, and enthusiasm for education. Some of these have been mentioned already. In Gumfreston, in Pembrokeshire, the Rector said 'the people are not drunken, and upon the whole are moral and steady'.[1209] In St. Clear's in Carmarthenshire, a girl asked the vicar's wife to teach her to read and she would do anything. 'What would she do?' She answered, '*Work for you all the days of my life*' (original italics). In the same place in another cottage, 'I found a boy with a little class book in Welsh, from which he was learning to spell some words for the Sunday-school: his mother, who had not been married, had given it to him'.[1210] A schoolmaster in the same place stated that 'I find the common people, among the thoroughly Welsh, in all the parts where I have resided, anxious to educate their children':

> Each child brings his own books to school, just as his father got it for him… they bring only the common books which we had 20 years ago and longer… this, however, is more the effect of poverty than anything else, I never ask for other books where I know the parents' circumstances to be bad: I go on as well as I can according to the means.[1211]

There were, of course, exceptional places. Ffrwd Vale Academy in Carmarthenshire was 'not a school for the labouring classes, nor yet altogether removed from them' and there it is reported of a 14 or 15 year old: 'I heard him construe two passages which I gave him, in Homer and Virgil, into remarkably good English, and parse them soundly'. He had been in school for two and a half years and before that he knew very little English.[1212] In Redberth, near Narbeth, after he had seen 'a truly excellent school', one of the inspectorate went to a wedding 'a sober spree, a lovely wedding, smart and well behaved'.[1213] And the people 'always seemed to me better dressed on Sundays than the same classes in England.[1214]

Nothing however was to console the critics then or since. A representative Nonconformist view was given by a Congregationalist minister and future member of Parliament, Henry Richard:

> While groping about in the dark for some means of acquiring the information they were in search of, they fell into the hands of one class, who hoodwinked and misguided them in every way possible. It was a picture of the people, as respects their intelligence, morality, and religion, which was unhesitatingly, and with singular unanimity, pronounced by all who had any real acquaintance with the country to be a gross and hideous caricature.[1215]

The condition of the countryside did not improve as the nineteenth century went on. In Cardiganshire:

> the main diet (of the lead miners) from about 1850 onwards was tea and bread and butter, with Sunday as the only day when fresh meat might be seen on the table. Little use was made of gardens, and coun-

try produce such as milk, eggs, fruit, and vegetables, were rarely seen on the workman's table.[1216]

As late as the beginning of the twentieth century miners left home on Monday with their food, lived in barrack type rooms for the week, and went home on Saturday. 'They slept two or more to a bed... the bedclothes were rarely washed, and the men had usually to do their own cooking'.[1217] Because of the shifts, beds had to be shared. 'Home' consisted of one or two bedrooms in a mud or stone structure, with low ceilings and 'very small windows'. The cottages at Bagillt 'were said to be dirty, ill-ventilated, and overcrowded, and most of the Halkyn miners' houses were such that all the members of the family had to sleep in the same bedroom'.[1218] It may be observed that these were the conditions reported by observers 200 years before.

In evidence to the Royal Commission on Land, which reported in 1896, one witness described the long and heavy work on his father's farm. He went on to describe his meagre diet. After about 30 years, he was asked: 'Any improvement today?'. His reply was: 'I live the same yet except for wholemeal bread'.[1219] Such evidence which dominates the Report is complimented by the evidence of the tyranny which seems to have been as much a feature of country life as ever it had been. There was considerable hostility to the work of the Commission. Meyrick of Bush for example would not give evidence,[1220] and despite the fact that the Ground Game Act of 1880 allowed tenants to take rabbits, one landowner, Charles Mathias of Lamphey Court would not allow it, and confiscated a man's net.[1221]

One of the most impressive witnesses was a man called William Llewelyn Williams.[1222] He had been an exhibitioner at Brasenose College, Oxford, Powis Classical Exhibitioner, and winner of the Bridgman's Prize Essays. He had acted as honorary Secretary to the central committee of Carmarthenshire farmers for the organising of evidence to the Commission. His late father had been a tenant farmer. He began by illustrating that, despite assurances of legal protection farmers were terrified to give evidence. He submitted a letter from a tenant who was prepared to have his written evidence submitted, as long as his name was not attached. He explains that he had kept the fact that he was giving evidence secret, but some of his relations had heard of it, and he had to 'pledge' to his mother that he would not give evidence. 'She believes that she shall suffer because of my giving evidence'.[1223] This dread was because 'the landlords of the county view with coldness, if not with aversion, the visit of the Commissioners'. There were two exceptions, he noted, Mr Vaughan Pryse Rice and Lord Dynevor. He might have added Lord Cawdor, whose recently retired agent gave evidence, and incidentally claimed that relations with the tenants were 'excellent: could not be bettered'.[1224] As an indication of the hostility of the gentry, Williams handed in correspondence he had had with Lord Emlyn, the heir incidentally of Cawdor, but who seemed to be much more obstructive. Williams had written to Emlyn who was the Chairman of the Quarter Sessions, and chairman of the joint police committee for permission to use Carmarthen town hall for meetings of the farmers' committee so that evidence could be prepared for the Commission. Emlyn replied that he 'did not think that the meeting you mention is one for which I should be justified in granting the use of the Town Hall'. Williams wrote again, pointing out that 'the object of the meeting is neither sectarian nor political', but to aid the inquiry. He also pointed out in his evidence that 'the hall is used for concerts, and, I believe, political meetings, but its use was denied to the farmers'.[1225]

This was hardly surprising when, for all the landowners knew the Report might jeopardise their positions. They had plenty to lose. Examples of estate sizes were given in evidence; Orielton was 'about' 3,200 acres,[1226] and Picton was stated to be 22,500 acres.[1227] But the considered view of Cannadine is that 'the landlords and their agents made a much better showing than they had in Ireland or Scotland'.[1228] The Report made a number of recommendations including for example the fixing of rents by county courts, which was predictably opposed by landowners, especially the two who were on the Commission. But by the time the Report was presented there was a Conservative government, and very little was to change.

In any case the Welsh farmers were very traditionalist. Even after 1918 the conservatism of the farmers of the Welsh moors and mountains was source of bewilderment to observers. For example, although the seaside resorts in Wales were in need of fresh farm supplies, because the local farmers did not exploit the opportunity, these supplies had to be brought in from England. The local farmers insisted on 'clinging to patterns of production developed in the pre-railway age, when their chief source of income walked to market over the droveways.[1229] Nor was there much improvement in the state of the farms in the 1920s, even if the post-war slump is taken into account. Equipment was:

> poor in the extreme: byres were dark, badly ventilated, with earth or cobbled floors, often covered with leaking thatch: calves and pigs were reared in filthy hovels. Few of the hill farms had a piped supply of water to the house or steading, in spite of a rainfall of fifty or sixty inches a year: water was carried from well or spring by the womenfolk of the farm families.[1230]

There was, naturally, a parallel degenerate picture in the cottages of the labourers.[1231] Even during the political advances of the late nineteenth century 'it should be noted that the conditions of farm labourers seldom complicates discussion' of land issues.[1232]

Nor did the protests cease. Indeed they tended to be more organised, and prolonged in the mid and later nineteenth century. After the foundation of the Friendly Associated Coalminers' Union in Lancashire in 1830, very soon miners in Flintshire formed branches, and almost immediately there were strikes, and after the calling out of troops, and arrests, the miners gained some concessions. But the employers determined to break the union, and there followed a period of industrial strife. The area then displayed such sympathy for Chartism and the authorities were so alarmed that the Home Office was asked for help. After further trouble 32 Chartists were tried at Welshpool in July 1839. Three men were transported, and others imprisoned.[1233]

There was constant trouble in the coalfields of north Wales, for example in Mold in the 1860s.[1234] And in general throughout Wales the violence was even more pronounced than it had been earlier. Chartism brought serious trouble to Wales as it did to other parts of Britain, and perhaps its most notable expression was the great Merthyr Riot of 1831. Again, in 1839 there were serious disturbances in east Wales, and one historian defines the 'struggle of 1839 (as) a class struggle'.[1235] During the Reform Crisis, Carmarthen, once again, was the scene of considerable and prolonged violence about political issues, but there were more basic and more traditional reasons. The Mayor and magistrates in June 1831 reported that of a population of about 12,000 'the great majority… are in indigent circumstances'.

In the Rebecca Riots in Pembrokeshire and Carmathenshire, not only was considerable damage done, but it took a long time for the situation to be brought under control. These began with the famous Efailwen meeting on 13 May 1839, and the story has often been told[1236] about the skill and organisation of the rioters which created such havoc. For example they invaded Lord Cawdor's Rhandir Mwyn lead mines 'and terrorised his imported Cornish miners'.[1237] The officer sent to try to subdue the rioters was Colonel James Love. He had had a distinguished career during the Napoleonic wars and went on to become a general, having *inter alia* confronted Chartist rioters, and 'saved Bristol during the terrible reform riots of 1831'.[1238] Yet he found it impossible to find, never mind confront Rebecca. Foster of *The Times* wrote that 'the government are pouring in troops' but 'they laugh at the display of power by the government'.[1239] This led to the Home Secretary James Graham writing to Peel suggesting Love should be replaced by a

general who had '1800 men including a regiment of cavalry and a demi brigade of guns' He sent troops too late and 'the troops are constantly paraded
before the people with apparent impotence'.[1240] Nor did the ever critical
Foster have much good to say about the behaviour of the squires in these
events. Towards the end he reported that 'where the gentry have forsaken
their sulky exclusiveness and come forward and met the people, the most
satisfying results have followed'.[1241]

The Poor Laws were one of the symbolic targets, and so they attacked
workhouses. Foster reported a comment showing the fear and loathing
the workhouse inspired: 'Do you, sir, think that because we are poor they
should take our children from their mother and me from my wife if I was
compelled to go in there?'.[1242] *The Times* reported further that 'the whole
country is suffering from the effects of the new Poor Law, against which
there appear to be universal feelings of detestation.[1243]

The 'Tithe Wars' of the late 1880s have been mentioned, but the unrest
in the countryside can be illustrated by the fact that there continued to be
disturbances in Cardiganshire and Pembrokeshire until the turn of the century.[1244] There was disorder at tithe sales in southern Cardiganshire as late as
1894 and 1895.[1245]

The response of the Liberals and the Nonconformist oligarchy to such
events has already been described. Sir Thomas Philipps being an example
when he denies that proper Welshmen had nothing to do with the Merthyr
riots or with Chartism. The technique used was to allege that that the roots
of Welsh misery lay in the dominance of Anglican landlords, their indifference or hostility to the Welsh language, and by extension to the people
themselves. The solution, which would result in greater happiness was the
disestablishment of the Welsh church.

There must be a final note on the 'vital permanent question' which was
mentioned in the last chapter. We have seen that there is evidence of some
interest in the matter in the late eighteenth century. The 1840s saw a more
systematic interest including the enthusiastic Henry Richard and Thomas
Gee but a motion in the House of Commons in 1870 attracted only 47
votes. 'During the election campaign of 1885, a lengthy exchange took
place between the Earl of Selborne and Mr. Gladstone in the correspondence columns of *The Times*, disputing the rights and wrongs of church disestablishment in England and Wales'[1246] and 'from the late 1880s onwards,
the popular crusade for disestablishment became the strongest, most deeply
rooted, and most irresistible of Welsh demands'.[1247] There were further in-
consequential discussions in 1886, 1891 and 1892.

When the Liberals won in 1892, they were obliged to take action and several disestablishment measures were brought before the House, but the opposition, notably from the Lords, stopped them, although a bill was introduced in 1894. By now Lloyd George had seen the political advantages of using this cause as a platform, and the bill received a second reading in 1895. The matter went on and was debated again in 1912, a debate of which *The Times* commented that 'it would be an exaggeration to describe the attitude of the country towards the Welsh Church Bill as one of interest, or even of concern'.[1248] The debate, and attempts to pass legislation, continued until in May 1914 a law was passed, with Keir Hardie begging that the matter be closed so that more important matters could be dealt with. When Disestablishment came, finally, in June 1920 it was 'to most people – not even a cause worth fighting for. The final debates of 1912–14 took place in a general atmosphere of widespread indifference'.[1249] 'The culminating achievement of Welsh Nonconformist radicalism was thus carried out in an atmosphere of profound anticlimax, in an empty Commons.'[1250]

By now a political awakening was taking place, and it had become clear that the issue had deflected the energy of the peasantry and the emerging working classes away from attacking the real causes of their misery. As the nineteenth century went on a signal shift in the population was from the rural to the urban areas, which led to the emergence and then the consolidation of a new industrial working class. 'by 1911 fewer than 20 per cent of the Welsh people occupied the countryside'.[1251] This new urban population was radical, even though much of that radicalism was for some time siphoned into the political wasteland of Disestablishment, a process carefully nurtured by the Nonconformist conservative clergy. Eventually, but only after a hard struggle, the true interests of the people at the lower end of society were recognised, helped by the policies of Lloyd George, who tried to stem the flow by initiating reforming legislation, and the inevitable and inherent inability of the chapel to understand the nature of the industrial worker. The emerging, more sophisticated public realised where the sympathies of *all* religious groups had lain, and so, inevitably there began the long process of the demise of Christian belief and practice, even though the *power* of the Established Church of England remains untouched. And so the disorganised, incoherent demands of the rioters and protesters of the end of the eighteenth and early nineteenth centuries, began, at last, to be met.

NOTES

Introduction

1 Dyfed comprises the three counties of Carmarthenshire, Cardiganshire and Pembrokeshire. the present title of the administrative district, and which will be the term used in this book to delineate the area.

2 Jenkins, Geraint H, *The foundations of modern Wales 1642–1780* (Cardiff, 1987), p88.

3 Howell, DW, *Land and people in 19th century Wales* (London, 1978), p.xi. But elsewhere Howell advises caution in estimating population numbers. See his Prologue to Howell, DW, *The rural poor in eighteenth century Wales* (Cardiff, 2000).

4 Malkin, Benjamin Heath, *The scenery, antiquities and biography of South Wales* (London, 1804) republished SR Publishers (1970), p.432.

5 *The Reports of the Commissioners of Inquiry into the State of Education in Wales 1847 Part I* p.389. In this book these will be referred to in the familiar shorthand as the 'Blue Books'.

6 *Royal Commission on the employment of children, young persons and women in agriculture 1867*, p.36.

7 Williams, Gwyn A, *The Welsh in their history* (London, 1982), p.17.

8 Coupland, Reginald, *Welsh and Scottish Nationalism: A study* (London, 1954), p.43.

9 Chrimes, SB, *Henry VII* (London, 1972), p.3.

10 Chrimes: *Henry VII*, p.4.

11 Anglo, S, 'The British history in early Tudor propaganda' *Bulletin of John Rylands Library 1961*, p.17.

12 Anglo: 'The British History', pp.20–21.

13 Henken, Elissa R, *National Redeemer: Owain Glyndwr in Welsh Tradition* (Cardiff, 1996), pp.54–5.

14 Henken: *National Redeemer*, p.18.

15 Jenkins: *The foundations of modern Wales*, p.173.

16 Anglo: 'The British history', p.36.

17 Anglo: 'The British history', pp.29–30.

18 Anglo: 'The British history', p.26.

19 Davies, John, *Victoria and Victorian Wales in Politics and society in Wales 1840–1922* (ed.) Jenkins, GH, and Smith, JB (Cardiff, 1988), p.8.

20   Coupland: *Welsh and Scottish nationalism*, p.59.
21   Chrimes: *Henry VIII,* c. 26.
22   Herbert, T, and Jones, GE, *Tudor Wales* (Cardiff, 1988), pp.32–3.
23   Herbert and Jones: *Tudor Wales,* p.28.
24   Jenkins: *The foundations of modern Wales*, p.214.
25   Jenkins: *The foundations of modern Wales*, p.300.
26   Coupland, Reginald, *Welsh and Scottish Nationalism: A study* (London, 1954), pp. 50–1.
27   Lloyd, HA, *The gentry of south west Wales 1540–1640* (Cardiff, 1968), p.93.
28   Entry under Acts of Union in *The Oxford Companion to the Literature of Wales* (ed.) Stephens, Meic, (Oxford, 1986).
29   Thomas, JE: *Radical Adult Education: theory and practice* (Nottingham, 1982), Chapter 3.
30   Chrimes: *Henry VII,* p.247.
31   Davies: Victoria and Victorian Wales, p.13.
32   Davies: Victoria and Victorian Wales, p.11.
33   Davies: Victoria and Victorian Wales, p.23.
34   Davies: Victoria and Victorian Wales, p.11.

Chapter One

35   English purchaser of the Erthig estate in Denbighshire about 1720, quoted Thomas, Peter DG, *Politics in eighteenth century Wales* (Cardiff, 1998), p.4.
36   Jenkins, Philip, *A history of modern Wales 1536-1990* (London, 1992), p.26.
37   Howell, David W, *The rural poor in eighteenth century Wales* (Cardiff, 2000), p.105. His chapter five gives a detailed account of the poorest in the community.
38   Gilpin, William, *Observations on the River Wye London 1772,* p.35 quoted Jenkins, Geraint, H, *The foundations of modern Wales 1642–1780,* p.279.
39   Jenkins: *A history of modern Wales,* p.37 He describes the detail of early Welsh-society
40   Malloy, P, *And they blessed Rebecca* (Llandysul, 1983), p.192.
41   Lloyd, HA, *The gentry of south west Wales 1540–1640,*(Cardiff, 1968), p.16.
42   Thomas, Peter DG, *Politics in eighteenth century Wales* (Cardiff, 1998), p.1.
43   Jenkins, Geraint H. *The foundations of modern Wales 1642–1780* (Cardiff, 1987) p.265.
44   Lloyd: *The gentry of south west Wales,* pp.37–38, pp.113ff.
45   Lloyd: *The gentry of south west Wales,* p.175.
46   Jenkins, JP, 'Jacobites and Freemasons in eighteenth century Wales', *Welsh History Review* 9 (1978–9) p.392.
47   See under 'Gogerddan' in The *Oxford Companion to the Literature of Wales* (Oxford, 1986)
48   Jones, Francis, 'Owen of Orielton' in *The Pembrokeshire Historian* 5 (1974), p.11.
49   Jones: 'Owen of Orielton', p.12.
50   Jenkins: *The foundations of modern Wales,* p.241.
51   GEC, (editor) *Complete baronetage Vol. II 1625–1649* (Exeter, 1904), under Pryse of Gogerddan.

52 Burke, John, and Burke, John Bernard (eds). *The extinct and dormant baronet-cies of England*, second edition printed for Scott Webster and Geary (London 1841), under Pryse of Gogerddan.

53 GEC: *Complete baronetage*, under Philipps.

54 Jones, Stuart EH, describes his attempt and failure in *The last invasion of Britain* (Cardiff, 1950), p.254.

55 Anglo, S, 'The British history in early Tudor propaganda', *Bulletin of John Rylands Library* 44 (1961), p.21.

56 Cannadine, D, *The decline and fall of the British aristocracy* (Yale, 1990), p.309.

57 See *The Oxford Companion to the Literature of Wales* under 'surnames' for a detailed discussion.

58 Jenkins: *A history of modern Wales*, pp.39ff..

59 Evans, ED, *A history of Wales 1660–1815* (Cardiff, 1993), p.9.

60 Jenkins, Geraint H, *The foundations of modern Wales*, pp.92–3.

61 Lloyd, HA, *The gentry of south west Wales*, p.25.

62 Jones, Francis, 'Owen of Orielton', pp.15–16 sets out in detail the fortunes of the family at that time.

63 Lloyd: *The gentry of south west Wales*, p.18.

64 Jones, Francis, 'The Vaughans of Golden Grove, I The Earls of Carbery', *Transactions of the Honourable Society of Cymmrodorion*, 1963 pp.96–7.

65 Jones, Francis, 'Golden Grove' in *Ceredigion* 4 (1960–3), p.262.

66 Jenkins: *A history of modern Wales*, p.48.

67 Lloyd: *The gentry of south west Wales*, p.197.

68 Lloyd: *The gentry of south west Wales*, p.94.

69 So described in Burke, John, and Burke, John Bernard (eds), *The extinct and dormant baronetcies of England* second edition (London, 1841), under 'Pryse of Gogerddan'.

70 Jenkins: *The foundations of modern Wales*, p.266.

71 Burke and Burke: *The extinct and dormant baronetcies of England* under 'Stepney'.

72 The Campbell family were ennobled in 1796, and in this book will be referred to as Cawdor.

73 Jenkins: *A history of modern Wales*, p.43.

74 Lloyd: *The gentry of south west Wales*, p.206.

75 Lloyd: *The gentry of south west Wales*, pp.40–41.

76 Agricultural Returns 1887 quoted Davies, John, 'The end of the great estates and the rise of freehold farming' *Welsh History Review*. 7 (1974–5), pp.186–211.

77 Lloyd: *The gentry of south west Wales*, p.37ff.

78 Green, F, 'The Barlows of Slebech', *West Wales Historical Records* III (1912), p.120.

79 Williams, G, 'The reformation in Pembrokeshire down to 1553', *The Pembrokeshire Historian* No. 1 (1959), pp.7–8.

80 Green: 'The Barlows of Slebech', p.149.

81 Lloyd: *The gentry of south west Wales*, pp.76ff. discusses some of these.

82 Lloyd: *The gentry of south west Wales*, pp.76–7.

83   See the entry under 'enclosures' in *The Oxford companion to the literature of Wales*.

84   Hassall, Charles, *General view of the agriculture of the county of Pembroke etc.* (1794), pp.14–15.

85   Lloyd: *The gentry of south west Wales*, p.95.

86   Lloyd: *The gentry of south west Wales*, p.36.

87   Lloyd: *The gentry of south west Wales*, p.114.

88   Lloyd: *The gentry of south west Wales*, p.97.

89   Lloyd: *The gentry of south west Wales*, p.162.

90   Lloyd: *The gentry of south west Wales*, pp.161–7.

91   Lloyd: *The gentry of south west Wales*, pp.89ff.

92   Lloyd: *The gentry of south west Wales*, p.129 for details.

93   Lloyd: *The gentry of south west Wales*, p.107.

94   Quoted Jenkins: *The foundations of modern Wales*, p.147.

95   Ararat, Roger, *de Ruvigny and Raineval, Marquis of, The Jacobite peerage: Baronetage, Knightage and grants of honour:* a facsimile of the original edition of 1904 (London and Edinburgh, 1974), pp.ix–x of his Introduction.

96   Thomas, Peter DG, *Politics in eighteenth century Wales*, p.138.

97   Jenkins, JP, 'Jacobites and Freemasons in eighteenth century Wales' pp.393–4.

98   Jones, Francis, 'The Society of Sea Serjeants', *Transactions of the Honourable Society of Cymmrodorion,* Pt 1 (1967), p.57.

99   Jones: 'The Society of Sea Serjeants', pp.65–6.

100   Jones: 'The Society of Sea Serjeants', p.74.

101   Thomas: *Politics in eighteenth century Wales*, p.11.

102   Thomas: *Politics in eighteenth century Wales*, p.139.

103   Jones: 'The Society of Sea Serjeants', p.61.

104   Jones: 'The Society of Sea Serjeants', p.62.

105   Jones: 'The Society of Sea Serjeants', pp.71–2.

106   Jones: 'The Society of Sea Serjeants', p.66.

107   Jones: 'The Society of Sea Serjeants', p63.

108   Jones: 'The Society of Sea Serjeants'.

109   Thomas, Peter DG, 'Jacobitism in Wales', *Welsh History Review* 1 (1960–3) p.283.

110   Thomas: *Politics in eighteenth century Wales*, p.135.

111   Thomas: *Politics in eighteenth century Wales*, p.58.

112   Jones: 'The Society of Sea Serjeants', p.67.

113   Thomas: 'Jacobitism in Wales', p.283.

114   Thomas: *Politics in eighteenth century Wales*, p.135.

115   Jones: 'The Society of Sea Serjeants', p.59.

116   Jones: 'The Society of Sea Serjeants', p.66.

117   Thomas: *Politics in eighteenth century Wales*, pp.146–7.

118   Jenkins: *The foundations of modern Wales*, p.310.

119   Lloyd: *The gentry of south west Wales*, p.118.

120   Lloyd: *The gentry of south west Wales*, p.212.

121   See Lloyd: *The gentry of south west Wales*, Chapter 1 for a full account of their fraudulent activity.

122   Thomas: *Politics in eighteenth century Wales*, p.8.

123   Jones, Francis, 'The Vaughans of Golden Grove', I, p.97.

124 Hassall: on *Pembrokeshire*, p.231.
125 Thomas: *Politics in eighteenth century Wales*, p.8.
126 Jones, Francis, 'Owen of Orielton', p.27.
127 Colyer, Richard, 'The Pryse family of Gogerddan and the decline of a great estate', *Welsh History Review* 9 (1978–9), p.407.
128 Howell, David W, *Patriarchs and parasites: the gentry of south-west Wales in the eighteenth century* (Cardiff, 1986), p108, quoting Carmarthenshire Record Office, Cawdor MS box 3/68.
129 Jones: 'The Vaughans of Golden Grove', I, p.97.
130 Jenkins: *A history of modern Wales*, p.67.
131 Jones: 'The Vaughans of Golden Grove' I, p.97.
132 Lloyd: *The gentry of south west Wales*, pp.198–200.
133 Blue Books: Part I, *Carmarthen, Glamorgan, and Pembroke*, pp.226 and 401.
134 Blue Books: Part I, p.229.
135 Davies, E.T., *Religion in the industrial revolution in Wales* (Cardiff, 1965), p.81.
136 Howell, David, 'Landed Society in Pembrokeshire circa 1680–1830', *The Pembrokeshire Historian* 3 (1971), p.37.
137 Davies, John, 'The end of the great estates and the rise of freehold farming in Wales', *Welsh History Review* 7 (1974–5), p.201.
138 Moore-Colyer, RJ, 'Thomas Johnes of Hafod (1748-1816) Translator and Bibliophile', *Welsh History Review* 15 No. 3 (June 1991), p.399.
139 Moore-Colyer: 'Thomas Johnes', p.400.
140 Malkin, BH. (1804). *The scenery, antiquities and biography of south Wales* (London: republished SR Publishers 19700, p.322.
141 Jenkins: *A history of modern Wales*, p.40, quoting Francis Jones.
142 Lewis, SJ, 'Trasiedi' Canlyn Arthur (1938), quoted Davies, J, 'The end of the great estates', p.210.
143 Morgan, KO. *Wales in British Politics 1868–1922* (Cardiff: University of Wales Press, 1963), p.56.
144 Howell: *Patriarchs and parasites*, p.136.
145 Jenkins: *The foundations of modern Wales*, p.307.
146 Jenkins: *The foundations of modern Wales*, p.308.
147 Thomas: *Politics in eighteenth century Wales*, p.234.
148 Thomas: *Politics in eighteenth century Wales*, p.10.
149 Jenkins: *The foundations of modern Wales*, p.306.
150 Howell: *Patriarchs and parasites*, p.46.
151 Howell: *Patriarchs and parasites*, p.183.
152 Howell: *Patriarchs and parasites*, p.187.
153 Colyer, Richard, 'The Pryse family of Gogerddan', p.415.
154 Jenkins: *A history of modern Wales*, p.95.
155 Jenkins: *The foundations of modern Wales*, p.100.
156 Jenkins: *A history of modern Wales*, p.41.
157 Thomas: *Politics in eighteenth century Wales*, p.4.
158 Jones, David JV, *Before Rebecca: popular protests in Wales 1793–1835* (London, 1973), p.40, quoting newspapers of 1843, and reports by Lloyd Hall.
159 *Cenedl* (1893) quoted Jenkins: *A history of modern Wales*, p.286.
160 *Tratto di Sociologia Generale* (Mind and Society), Para 2052 tr. and ed.

Livinston (sic), Arthur (NewYork, 1935), discussed by Crawford, W Rex, in Barnes, HE, *An introduction to the history of sociology* (1958).

161   Jenkins: *The foundations of modern Wales*, p.94.

162   Jenkins: *A history of modern Wales*, pp.53ff.

163   Jones: 'Owen of Orielton', p.25.

164   Jones: 'Golden Grove', p.268.

165   Jones: 'Owen of Orielton', p.32.

166   Jones: 'Owen of Orielton', p.30.

167   Jones: *The last invasion of Britain*, p.254.

168   Duffy, M. (2000). *The Younger Pitt*, London: Longman. p.41

169   Howell, 'Landed society in Pembrokeshire', p.35.

170   NLW Picton Castle Mss. 30 (April, 1683).

171   These details of this family are taken from Colyer: 'The Pryse family of Gogerddan', pp.407–25.

172   Becket, JV, 'The peasant in England: a case of terminological confusion?', *Agricultural History Review* 32 (1984).

Chapter Two

173   This remark is in a letter to the Home Office written in 1795 by Sheriff Foley PRO HO 42/35

174   Thomas Johnes' obituary in the *Cambrian Register*, 1818.

175   Malkin, BH. *The scenery, antiquities and biography of south Wales* (1804) (London: republished SR Publishers 1970), p.349.

176   Rutland, Duke of, *Journal of a Journey through north and south Wales, the Isle of Man &c &c* (London, 1805), p.125.

177   Rutland: *Journal,* pp.168–9.

178   Phillips, JR, *The history of Cilgerran* (London, 1867), pp.141–2.

179   Davies, Walter, (Gwallter Mechain), *General view of the agriculture and domestic economy of south Wales; containing the counties of Brecon, Caermarthen, Cardigan, Glamorgan, Pembroke, Radnor* (London, 1814) 2 Volumes, Volume 1, p.123.

180   Davies: *General view,* Volume 1, p.165.

181   Davies: *General view*, Volume 2, p.466.

182   Davies: *General view*, Volume 2, pp.283–4.

183   Davies: *General view*, Volume 1, p.134.

184   Davies: *General view*, Volume 1, p.135.

185   Davies: *General view*, Volume 1, p.132.

186   Thomas, David, *Agriculture in Wales during the Napoleonic Wars: a study in the interpretation of historical sources* (Cardiff, 1963). His Chapter 2 (pp. 33ff.) discusses evidence from several sources.

187   *The Oxford Companion to the Literature of Wales* (Oxford, 1986) under 'Tours'.

188   *Cambrian Register 1796,* pp.422–38. His reference is to Morgan, MA, *A tour to Milford Haven in the year 1791* (London 1795), and Warner, RA, *A Walk through Wales in August 1797.*

189   Rutland: *Journal,* pp.15–16.

190   Rutland: *Journal,* p.14.

191   Rutland: *Journal,* pp.158–9 and p.161.

192   Barber, JT, *A tour through Wales and Monmouthshire* (London, 1803), p.77.

193 Evans, J, *Letters written during a tour through South Wales in the year 1803 and at other times etc.* (London, 1804), p.279.
194 Rutland: *Journal*, p.192.
195 Rutland: *Journal*, p.190.
196 Rutland: *Journal*, p.107.
197 *Cambrian Register:* 1795, p.256.
198 Evans: *Letters*, p.305.
199 Evans: *Letters*, p.217.
200 Barber: *A Tour*, p.36.
201 Hoare, Sir Richard Colt, *Journals of tours in Wales* (London, 1796), section 19, p.477.
202 Hoare: *Journals of tours in Wales*, section xxiv, p.509.
203 Wigstead, H, *Remarks on a tour to north and south Wales in the year 1797* (London 1800), p.51.
204 Evans: *Letters*, p.217.
205 Evans: *Letters*, p.222.
206 Malkin: *The scenery*, p.578.
207 Malkin: *The scenery*, p.460.
208 Malkin: *The scenery*, p.564.
209 Malkin: *The scenery*, p.549.
210 Rutland: *Journal*, p.164.
211 Vaughan, HM, 'A synopsis of two tours made in Wales in 1775 and in 1811', *Y Cymmrodor* xxxviii, 1927, p.70.
212 Rutland: *Journal*, pp.192–3.
213 Hasssall: on Pembrokeshire, p.30.
214 Hoare: *Journals*, section 19, p.412.
215 Barber: *A tour*, pp.56–8.
216 Evans: *Letters*, p.278.
217 Phillips: *The history of Cilgerran*, p.26.
218 John, AH, *The industrial development of south Wales* (Cardiff, 1950), pp.24–5.
219 Jenkins, Geraint, *Literature, religion and society in Wales 1660–1730* (Cardiff, 1978) p.14.
220 Saunders, E, *View of the state of education in the diocese of St. Davids* (London, 1721), p.14.
221 Saunders: *View of the state of education*, p.24.
222 Saunders: *View of the state of education*, p.22.
223 Smith, Canon Gregory, 'The Right Reverend William Basil Jones' in Morgan, J Vyrnwy *Welsh Political and Educational Leaders in the Victorian Era* (London, 1908) p.150.
224 Davies, Leonard Twiston, and Edwards, Averyl, *Welsh life in the eighteenth century* (London, 1939), p.41.
225 Hassall: on Carmarthenshire, p.51.
226 Quoted Howell, DW, *The rural poor in eighteenth century Wales* (Cardiff, 2000), p.86.
227 For details of the small, but by local standards significant, quarrying industry see Roberts, Dafydd, 'Nhw oedd y chwarelwyr-arwyr y fro: The Pembrokesire slate quarrymen', *Llafur* Vol. 5, No. 1 (no date [1988?]). See also Phillips, *The history of Cilgerran*, p.167.

228   Lodwick, M and E, *The story of Carmarthen* (privately printed, 1954), p.79.
229   *Cambrian Register:* 1795, pp.254–5.
230   Wigstead: *Remarks on a tour,* p.54.
231   Phillips: *The history of Cilgerran,* pp.168–9.
232   Phillips: *The history of Cilgerran,* p.11.
233   Hoare: *Journals,* section 24, p.490.
234   Lewis, WJ, *Lead mining in Wales* (Cardiff, 1967), p.69.
235   Lewis: *Lead mining in Wales,* pp.250–1.
236   Jenkins, Geraint H. *The foundations of modern Wales 1642–1780* (Cardiff, 1987), pp.121–2.
237   Lewis: *Lead mining in Wales,* p.94.
238   Lewis: *Lead mining in Wales,* p.263. For a full account see pp.99ff.
239   *Cambrian Register:* 1796, p.495.
240   Jenkins, RT, and Ramage, Helen M, *A history of the Honourable Society of Cymmrodorion, and of the Gwyneddigion and Cymreigyddion Societies (1751–1951)* (London, 1951). This book has detailed biographies of the Lewis family.
241   Lewis: *Lead mining in Wales,* p.101.
242   For a full account see Lewis: *Lead mining in Wales,* pp.99ff..
243   Lewis, WJ, 'The Cwmsymlog mine in Cardigan', *Ceredigion* II/I (1952), pp. 27–38.
244   In *Ceredigion* IV/4 (1963), p.321.
245   Davies, Alun Eirug, 'Wages, prices and social improvements in Cardiganshire, 1750–1850', *Ceredigion* X/I (1984) pp.31–3.
246   Davies: 'Wages, prices and social improvements', p.34.
247   The double inverted commas are a quotation from Lewis: *Lead mining in Wales,* pp.267–8. Davies: 'Wages, prices and social improvements, pp.31–2.
248   Lewis: *Lead mining in Wales,* p.37.
249   Lewis: *Lead mining in Wales,* p.164.
250   Hassall: on Carmarthenshire, pp.50–1.
251   John: *Industrial development of south Wales,* p.8.
252   Jones, Francis, 'The Vaughans of Golden Grove' I, *Transactions of The Honourable Society of Cymmrodorion,* Part 1 (1963) pp.96–7.
253   Jones: 'The Vaughans of Golden Grove', p.207.
254   Hoare: *Journals,* Section 19, p.407.
255   Lewis: *Lead mining in Wales,* p.205.
256   Lewis: *Lead mining in Wales,* p.273.
257   Lewis: *Lead mining in Wales,* p.283.
258   Lewis: *Lead mining in Wales,* pp.283–4.
259   Lewis: *Lead mining in Wales,* p.284.
260   Warner, Reverend Richard, *A walk through Wales in August 1797* (London, 1798), p.65.
261   Malkin: *The scenery,* p.479.
262   Edwards, George, 'The coal industry in Pembrokeshire', *Field Studies* 1/5 (1963), p.1.
263   John: *The industrial development of south Wales,* p.2.
264   Howell: *The rural poor,* p.80.
265   Edwards: 'The coal industry in Pembrokeshire', p.13.

266 John: *The industrial development of south Wales*, pp.9–10.

267 Hassall: on Pembrokeshire, pp.58–9.

268 Hassall: on Carmarthenshire, pp.44–5.

269 Hassall: on Pembrokeshire, p.61.

270 Edwards: 'The coal industry in Pembrokeshire' p.13.

271 *The Cambrian Register*: 1817, pp.365–6.

272 Edwards: 'The coal industry in Pembrokeshire', p.13.

273 Bourne, MA, *A guide to Tenby* (1843), and Mackworth, H, *Reports of HM Inspectors of Coal Mines* (1854), quoted Edwards, 'The coal industry in Pembrokeshire' p.31.

274 Warner, Reverend Richard. *A second walk through Wales,* (London, 1799) p.338.

275 Lloyd and Turnor on Cardiganshire, p.17.

276 Phillips: *The history of Cilgerran,* p.167.

277 See Howell, David W. *Patriarchs and Parasites: The gentry of south-west Wales in the eighteenth century* (Cardiff, 1986) pp.109ff. for details.

278 Mavor, A, *A tour in Wales and through several counties of England* (London, 1806), p.63.

279 Jenkins: *The foundations of modern Wales,* p.287.

280 Jenkins: *The foundations of modern Wales,* p.298.

281 Jones, David JV. *Before Rebecca: popular protests in Wales 1793–1835* (London, 1972) p.1.

282 Davies, Leonard Twiston and Edwards, Averyl. *Welsh life in the eighteenth century* (London: Country Life, 1939) p.1.

283 Young, Arthur, *A six weeks tour through the counties of England and Wales (1768),* p.123.

284 Davies, Walter, *General view of the agricultural and domestic economy of south Wales,* volume 1, p.368.

285 *Cambrian Register:* 1818, p.177.

286 Hassall: on Pembrokeshire, Introductory Address.

287 Hassall: on Pembrokeshire, p.33.

288 For a full discussion of the complexities of tenure in Pembrokeshire see: Howell, David W, 'The economy of the landed estates of Pembrokeshire c1680–1830', *Welsh History Review* 3 (1966–7).

289 Hassall: on Pembrokeshire, p.34.

290 Hassall: on Carmarthenshire, p.31.

291 Hassall: on Pembrokeshire, p.37.

292 Hassall: on Pembrokeshire, p.31.

293 Hassall: on Pembrokeshire, p.47.

294 Hassall: on Pembrokeshire, p.49.

295 Jones, 'The Vaughans of Golden Grove, IV, Tory Coed-Shenfield-Golden Grove', *Transactions of the Honourable Society of Cymrrodorion'* (1966), p.159.

296 Hassall on Pembrokeshire, pp.16–17.

297 Hassall on Pembrokeshire, pp.12–13.

298 Hassall: on Carmarthenshire, p.30.

299 Hassall: on Carmarthenshire, p.39.

300 Hassall: on Carmarthenshire, p.47.

301 Hassall: on Carmarthenshire, p.50.

302 Hassall: on Pembrokeshire, p.17.
303 Hassall: on Carmarthenshire, p.39.
304 Hassall: on Pembrokeshire, p.37.
305 Hassall: on Pembrokeshire, p.18.
306 Lloyd and Turnor: on Cardiganshire, pp.10–11.
307 Lloyd and Turnor: on Cardiganshire, p.20.
308 Hassall: on Pembrokeshire, p.18.
309 Lloyd and Turnor: on Cardiganshire, p.12.
310 Davies: *General view of the agriculture etc.*, p.187.
311 Davies: *General view of the agriculture etc*, p.188.
312 Hassall: on Pembrokeshire, p.19.
313 Hassall: on Pembrokeshire, p.9.
314 Hassall: on Pembrokeshire, pp.19–20.
315 Hassall: on Carmarthenshire, p.48.
316 Lloyd and Turnor: on Cardiganshire, p.20.
317 Lloyd and Turnor: on Cardiganshire, p.28.
318 John: *The industrial development of south Wales*, p.5.
319 Lloyd and Turnor: on Cardiganshire, p.18.
320 Hassall: on Carmarthenshire, p.51.
321 Goddard, Nicholas, 'Agricultural literature and Societies' in *The Agrarian history of England and Wales*, p.375.
322 *Cambrian Register:* 1818, p.516.
323 Lloyd and Turnor: on Cardiganshire, p.9.
324 Warner: *A walk through Wales*, p.29.
325 Warner: *A walk through Wales*, p.31.
326 Hughes, PG, *Wales and the drovers; the historical background of an epoch* (Cardiff, 1943), p.11.
327 Howell: *Patriarchs and Parasites*, p.vii.
328 Skeel, Carol, 'The cattle trade between Wales and England from the 15th to the 19th centuries' *Transactions of the Royal Historical Society* Fourth series, IX (1926), p.136.
329 Skeel: 'The cattle trade', p.152.
330 Skeel: 'The cattle trade', p.151.
331 Davies and Edwards: *Welsh life in the eighteenth century*, p.vii.
332 Howell, DW, *Land and people in nineteenth century Wales* (London: Routledge and Kegan Paul, 1978) p.38.
333 Howell: *Land and people in nineteenth century Wales*, p.xiii.
334 Hobsbawm, EJ, and Rudé, G, *Captain Swing* (London, 1969), p.35.
335 Armstrong, WA, 'Food, shelter and selfhelp', *The agrarian history of England and Wales,* VI 1750–1850, p.743.
336 Hobsbawm and Rudé: *Captain Swing*, p.52.
337 Davies, Walter, *Agriculture of South Wales*, quoted Armstrong p.745.
338 Quoted Davies and Edwards: *Welsh life in the eighteenth century*, p.17.
339 Evans: *Letters*, pp.346–51.
340 Vaughan: *Synopses of two journeys*, p.49.
341 Davies and Edwards, *Welsh life in the eighteenth century*, pp.16–17, quoting Davies, Walter, *The Agricultural Survey.*

342 Peate, Iowerth C, *The Welsh House* (Liverpool, 1944), p.111.
343 Peate: *The Welsh House*, p.2.
344 Godwin, Fay, and Toulson, Shirley, *The drovers' roads of Wales* (London, 1977), p.25.
345 Howells, E, 'Pembrokeshire farming circa 1580–1620, *The National Libray of Wales Journal* IX (1955–6), pp.420–1.
346 Evans: *Letters*, p.327.
347 Quoted Malloy, Pat. *And they blessed Rebecca* (Llandysul: Gomer Press, 1983), p.16.
348 Peate: *The Welsh house*, p.59.
349 Rutland: *Journal*, p.193.
350 Howell, DW, 'The agricultural labourer in nineteenth century Wales', *Welsh History Review* 6 (1972–3), p.279.
351 Article on Gee in Morgan (ed.), *Welsh political and educational leaders*, p.535.
352 Thomas, Colin, 'Agricultural employment in nineteenth century Wales; a new approach', *Welsh History Review* 6 (1972–3), p.147.
353 Peate: *The Welsh House*, pp.68 and 71. See his Chapter IV for a detailed account.
354 From '*Welch Piety*', quoted Williams, Moses, *Selections from The Welch Piety* (Cardiff, 1938), p.121.
355 From '*Welch Piety*', quoted Williams, Moses, *Selections from The Welch Piety*, p.121.
356 Prize entry on 'The agriculture of north Wales', *Journal of the Royal Agricultural Society* vii (1846), p.572.
357 Howell: *The rural poor*, p.81.
358 Hassall: on Pembrokeshire, p.56.
359 Hassall: on Pembrokeshire, p.57.
360 Quoted Skeel: 'The cattle trade between Wales and England', pp.142–3.
361 Howell: 'The agricultural labourer etc', p.277.
362 Howell: 'The agricultural labourer etc'.
363 Lloyd and Turnor: on Cardiganshire, p.28.
364 Lloyd and Turnor: on Cardiganshire, p.31.
365 Lloyd and Turnor: on Cardiganshire, p.15.
366 Davies, Alun Eirug, 'Wages, prices and social improvements in Cardiganshire 1750–1850', *Ceredigion* xi (1984)', p.39.
367 Davies: 'Wages, prices and social improvements', p.41.
368 Davies: 'Wages, prices and social improvements', p.40.
369 Saunders: *View of the state of education*, pp.32–5.
370 Davies: 'Wages, prices and social improvements', p.43.

Chapter Three

371 John Jones (Jac Glan-y-gors), 'A Welsh hymn to be sung on the Fast day'. Printed in the *Chester Chronicle*, 4 March 1796 , quoted by Dodd, AH, *The industrial revolution in north Wales* (Cardiff, 1933), p.335. I am very grateful to Professor John Heywood Thomas who renders this difficult phrase as: 'Take bread as your mirror; you shall only look upon it'.
372 Peacock, AJ, 'Radicalism in East Anglia 1800–50', in Dunbabin, JPD (ed.), *Rural discontent in nineteenth century Britain* (London, 1974) p.27.

373   Peacock: 'Radicalism in East Anglia, p.39.

374   Peacock: 'Radicalism in East Anglia, p.29.

375   Beloff, M, *Public order and popular disturbances 1660–1714* (Oxford, 1938), p.56.

376   Howell, David W. *The rural poor in eighteenth century Wales* (Cardiff, 2000) p.178.

377   Roberts, GT, *The language of the Blue Books: the perfect instrument of empire* (Cardiff, 1998), p.218.

378   Roberts: *The language of the Blue Books*, p.218.

379   Howell: *The rural poor,* p.207.

380   For an account of piracy in earlier centuries see Lloyd, HA. *The gentry of south west Wales 1540–1640*, (Cardiff, 1968) pp.161 ff.

381   Hughes, Edward, *Studies in administration and finance* (Philadelphia, 1980), p.199.

382   Howells, BE, and KA (eds.) *Pembrokeshire Life 1572–1843* (Pembrokeshire Record Society, 1972), p.86.

383   Vaughan, HM, 'A synopsis of two tours made in Wales in 1775 and in 1811, *Y Cymmrodor* xxxviii 1927. p.72.

384   Evans, J. *Letters written during a tour through south Wales in the year 1803 and at other times etc.* (London, 1804), p.112.

385   Howell: *The rural poor,* p.192.

386   Winslow, C, 'Sussex smugglers' in Hay, D and Thompson, EP (eds.), *Albion's Fatal Tree* (London, 1975), p.121.

387   PRO, 6 February 1793, HO 42/24/373.

388   Evans, ED, *History of Wales 1660–1815* (Cardiff, 1993), p.195.

389   PRO, HO 42/52.

390   PRO, HO 42/61.

391   PRO, HO 42/61.

392   Jones Francis, 'Disaffection and dissent in Pembrokeshire', *Transactions of the Honourable Society of Cymmrodorion*, Sessions 1946–7, p.207.

393   Jones: 'Disaffection and dissent', pp.207–8.

394   Jones: 'Disaffection and dissent', p.219.

395   Jones, David JV. *Before Rebecca: popular protests in Wales 1793–1835* (London, 1972) p.4.

396   Thomas, David. *Agriculture in Wales during the Napoleonic Wars: a study in the interpretation of historical sources* (Cardiff, 1963) p.3.

397   Hobsbawm, EJ, and Rudé, G, *Captain Swing* (London, 1969) p.39.

398   Jones: *Before Rebecca,* p.7.

399   Williams, Glanmor, *The Welsh and their religion* (Cardiff, 1991) pp.118–9.

400   Jenkins, Geraint H. *The foundations of modern Wales 1642–1780* (Cardiff, 1987) p.117.

401   Jones, DJV. 'The Carmarthen riots of 1831', *Welsh History Review* 4 (1968–9), p.129.

402   Spurrell, W. *Carmarthen and its neighbourhood* (1879, reprinted Dyfed County Council, 1995), p.133.

403   Spurrell: *Carmarthen and its neighbourhood*, p.133.

404   *Carmarthen Antiquarian Society and Field Club Transactions* XXI, (1927), pp.68–9.

405   *Carmarthen Antiquarian Society and Field Club Transactions* LXX1V, 1933, p.2.
406   *Carmarthen Antiquarian Society and Field Club Transactions* LXX1V, 1933, p.2.
407   Thomas, Peter DG. *Politics in eighteenth-century Wales* (Cardiff, 1998), p.124.
408   Jones: *Before Rebecca*, p.121.
409   *Carmarthenshire Antiquarian Society and Field Transactions* XXIV (1933), pp.24–5.
410   *The Gentleman's Magazine 1755*, p.570.
411   *Carmarthenshire Transactions* XXIV, (1933), p.31.
412   Jones, Francis, 'The Vaughans of Golden Grove: I The Earls of Carbery', p.201.
413   Hoare, Sir Richard Colt. *Journals of tours in Wales* (London: 1796), xxiv, p.509.
414   Howell: *The rural poor*, pp.206–7.
415   Thomas: *Politics in eighteenth century Wales*, p.21.
416   Thomas: *Politics in eighteenth century Wales*, p.109.
417   Jones: *Before Rebecca*, p.45.
418   Howell, David W. *Patriarchs and parasites: The gentry of south-west Wales in the eighteenth century* (Cardiff, 1986), p.68.
419   Howell: *Patriarchs and parasites*, pp.67–8.
420   Evans, ED. *A history of Wales 1660–1815* (Cardiff, 1993) p.195.
421   Howell: *The rural poor*, p.9.
422   Howell: *Patriarchs and parasites*, p.68.
423   Howell: *Patriarchs and parasites*, p.69.
424   Jones, DJV, 'Distress and discontent in Cardiganshire 1814–1819', *Ceredigion* Volume 3 (1966), p.280.
425   Jones: 'Distress and discontent in Cardiganshire', p.280, quoting Williams, D, *A history of modern Wales*, p.83.
426   Jones: 'Distress and discontent in Cardiganshire', p.280.
427   See Jones: 'Distress and discontent in Cardiganshire', for details of these and similar incidents.
428   Jones: 'Distress and discontent in Cardiganshire', p.282.
429   Jones: 'Distress and discontent in Cardiganshire', p.284.
430   *Carmarthenshire Transactions*, XXVI p.25. The editor comments that this is the only contemporary reference to this disturbance.
431   Mayor of Pembroke to Newcastle, June 17, 1740, SP Dom. 36/50/1, and William Owen MP also to Newcastle, quoted Isaac,DG, 'A study of popular disturbances in Britain 1714–1795' (Edinburgh PhD, 1953). See also Ashton, TS, and Sykes, J, *The coal industry of the eighteenth century* (Manchester, 1964), p.119.
432   Howell: *The rural poor*, p.181.
433   Howell: *The rural poor*, p.186.
434   NLW archives, Eaton, Evans and Williams Schedule, p.410, Letter 719.
435   Spurrell: *Carmarthen and its neighbourhood*, p.124.
436   *Carmarthenshire Transactions* XXIV (1933), p.34.
437   *Carmarthenshire Transactions* XXIV (1933), p.591.
438   *Carmarthenshire Transactions* XXIV (1933), p.34.

439   *Cambrian Register*: 1795, p.454.
440   PRO HO 42/34.
441   PRO HO 42/34.
442   *Salopian Journal* 25 February 1795.
443   *Salopian Journal* 25 February 1795.
444   Howell: *The rural poor*, p.180.
445   *Salopian Journal* 4 March 1795.
446   *Shrewsbury Chronicle* 6 March 1795.
447   *Salopian Journal* 18 March 1795.
448   *Shrewbury Chronicle* 27 Febuary 1795.
449   *Salopian Journal* 4 March 1795.
450   This article by 'Gwinfardd Dyfed' entitled 'A statistical account of the Parish
       of Fishguard', is in the *Cambrian Register* (1795, published 1796), pp.240–
       64.
451   Thorne, R, and Howell, R, *Pembrokeshire in wartime 1793–1815* in How-
       ells, B (ed.), *Pembrokeshire County History*, Volume iii, (Aberystwyth, 1987),
       p.379.
452   PRO HO 42/35.
453   Edwards, George, 'The coal industry in Pembrokeshire', *Field Studies* 1/5.
       p.28
454   Vaughan: *A synopses of two tours*, p.75.
455   PRO HO 42/61.
456   NLW Great Sessions Records Pembrokershire 1801, 4/828.
457   NLW Great Sessions Records Pembrokershire 1801, 4/828.
458   Jones: *Before Rebecca*, p.28.
459   PRO HO 41/52.
460   *Carmarthenshire Transactions*, X (1914).
461   Jones: 'Distress and discontent in Cardiganshire', p.282.
462   Jones: 'Distress and discontent in Cardiganshire', p.282.
463   PRO HO 43/4.
464   PRO HO 30/8.
465   Rutland, Duke of: *Journal of a journey through north and south Wales, the Isle
       of Man &c &c* (London, 1805), p.159.
466   All the details of this episode are in NLW LLGC 21373.
467   The standard books on the invasion are Jones, Stuart EH, *The last invasion
       of Britain,* and Thomas, JE, *Britain's last invasion; Fishguard 1797* (Stroud,
       2007). The latter examines the astonishing mythology which has accumulated
       about this event.
468   Jones: *The last invasion,* p.56.
469   Wolfe, William Theobald (ed.) *Life and Adventures of Theobald Wolfe Tone.*
       Written by himself and extracted from his Journals (London, 1826), p.80.
470   Jones: *The last invasion,* p.45.
471   Jones: *The last invasion,* p.55.
472   Jones: *The last invasion,* p.54.
473   Jones: *The last invasion,* pp.104ff.
474   Jones: *The last invasion,* pp.116ff.
475   As is done by Williams, Gwyn A, 'Beginnings of radicalism' in Herbert, T,

and Jones, GE *The remaking of Wales in the eighteenth century*, (Cardiff, 1988), p.126.
476 Rutland: *Journal*, p.133.
477 Rutland: *Journal*, p.127.
478 Rutland: *Journal*, p.135.
479 Rutland: *Journal*, p.130.
480 Rutland: *Journal*, p.127.
481 Salmon, David, *The French invasion of Fishguard in 1797. Official documents, contemporary letters, and early narratives,* West Wales Historical Records xiv (Carmarthen, 1929), p.151.
482 Salmon: *The French invasion*, p.173.
483 Rutland: *Journal*, p.131.
484 Salmon: *The French invasion*, p.162.
485 Rutland: *Journal*, p.165.
486 Rutland: *Journal*, p.126.
487 Rutland: *Journal*, p.129.
488 Jones: *The last invasion*, p.72.
489 See Thomas, JE, *Britain's last invasion*, passim, for a discussion of this and other questionable stories.
490 Jones: *The last invasion*, p.87.
491 For details of the careers of father and son, see Jones: *The last invasion*, passim.
492 Rutland: *Journal*, p.161.
493 Rutland: *Journal*, p.162.
494 Rutland: *Journal,* pp.159-60.
495 An account of the trial of Thomas John and Samuel Griffith after the Fishguard invasion is given in 'Cwyn y cystuddiedig' (plaint of the afflicted), a leaflet probably by Dr.William Richards of Lynn, who was from Pembrokeshire. See Salmon, 'The French invasion of Fishguard', p.171. for a discussion of authorship. For full details of the trials, see Jones, *The last invasion*, Chapter vii.
496 Jones: *Before Rebecca*, p.27.
497 PRO HO 42/52.
498 Jones: *Before Rebecca*, pp.15–16.
499 PRO HO 34/37.
500 The debate is in *The Gentlemen's Magazine* July 1737.
501 This is reprinted in Foot, Michael, *The politics of paradise: a vindication of Byron* (London, 1988).
502 Pembrokeshire Record Office, Haverfordwest Records Folio 70, 1757, on the reverse of No.52.
503 PRO HO 42/35. Foley's letter is one of many from all over the country noting the seizing of corn.
504 PRO HO 42/35.
505 *Cambrian Register.* 1795, p.261.
506 Pembrokeshire Record Office, ROD/Lew/1/83.
507 Malkin, BH. *The scenery, antiquities and biography of south Wales* (London, 1804, republished SR Publishers 1970), p.430.
508 Malkin: *The scenery, antiquities etc*, p.526.
509 NLW ms. 1352 B.ff 310–14, quoted Howell, BE, and KA (eds). *Pembrokeshire*

Life 1572–1843 (Pembrokeshire Record Society, 1972). pp.112–14.

510 Jones: *The last invasion*, p.210.

511 NLW ms 1352 Howell: *Pembrokeshire Life* pp.112–14 , quoted Thorne, Roland, and Howell, Robert. (1987). 'Pembrokeshire in Wartime 1793–1815' in *Pembrokeshire County History* Volume III, Brian Howells (ed.), The Pembrokeshire Historical Society, Aberystwyth, The National Library of Wales. p.380.

512 NLW ms. 1352 B ff., 333–9, quoted Howell, BE and K, *Pembrokeshire Life*, p.83.

513 Carmarthen Record Office, Cawdor ms. 1/129.

514 Pembrokeshire Record Office, Haverfordwest Corporation Records, 1642 folio 2.

515 Howell: *The rural poor*, p.81.

516 Thorne and Howell: *Pembrokeshire in Wartime*, p.381.

517 Hassall: on Pembrokeshre, p.56.

518 Evans: *Letters written during a tour*, pp.280–4.

519 Hoare: *Journals of tours,* p.412.

520 Malkin: *The scenery, antiquities etc.* p.420.

521 Hassall: on Pembrokeshire, p.43.

522 PRO HO 43/7.

523 Wilkinson, David, *The Duke of Portland: Politics and Party in the Age of George I* (London, 2003), p.113.

524 PRO HO 43/7.

525 PRO HO 34/20.

526 Wilkinson: *The Duke of Portland*, p.115.

527 Wilkinson: *The Duke of Portland*, p.110.

528 Wilkinson: *The Duke of Portland*, p.114.

529 Pembrokeshire Record Office, PQ/C1/6.

530 Jones: 'Distress and discontent in Cardiganshire', p.282.

531 Dodd, AH. *The Industrial Revolution in north Wales*, (Cardiff, 1933), p.399.

532 Jones: 'Vaughans of Golden Grove' I, p.207.

533 John, Angela V, 'A miner struggle? Women's protests in Welsh mining history', *Llafur* Vol. 4, No. 1, (1984), p.72.

534 Thompson, Edward, 'The moral economy of the English crowd in the eighteenth century' in *Past and Present*. Volume 50 (1971), p.116.

535 Beloff: *Public order and popular disturbances*, p.64.

536 Beloff: *Public order and popular disturbances*, p.68.

537 Thompson: 'The moral economy', p.115.

538 Dunbabin: *Rural discontent*, p.24.

539 Howells: *Pembrokeshire life*, p.15.

540 Howell: *The rural poor*, p.186.

541 Jones: *Before Rebecca*, p.34.

542 Jones: *Before Rebecca*, p.34 quoting Hammond and Hammond: *The Village Labourer*, p.116.

543 NLW Great Sessions, Brecknock 1796, Gaol Flies Wales 4/389, quoted Jones: *Before Rebecca*, p.34.

544 NLW Nanteos mss. and Documents: undated letter from L Lewis to WW Powell, quoted Jones: 'Distress and discontent in in Cardiganshire', p.284.

545   NLW Bute L48/63.

Chapter Four

546   Morris, Lewis, *Tlysau yr hen Oesedd* (Holyhead, 1735), p.3.
547   The first is the view of the Webbs, S and B, quoted by Beloff, M. *Public order and popular disturbances 1660–1714* (Oxford, 1938) p.5.
548   Hobsbawm, EJ, and Rudé, G, *Captain Swing* (London,1969), p.66.
549   Wells, R, *Insurrection: the British experience* (London, 1983), p.20.
550   Wager, DA, 'Welsh politics and parliamentary reform 1780–1832, *Welsh History Review* 7/4/(1975), p.433.
551   Jones, DJV, 'The corn riots in Wales, 1793–1801, *Welsh History Review* 2 (1964–5), p.336.
552   Jones: 'The corn riots in Wales', pp.340 and 343.
553   Jones: 'The corn riots in Wales', p.341.
554   Evans, T, *The background of modern Welsh politics 1789–1846* (Cardiff, 1936), pp.28–9.
555   Davies, David, *The influence of the French Revolution on Welsh life and literature* (Carmarthen, 1926) p. 217.
556   Williams, Gwyn A. *Beginnings of radicalism*, in Herbert, T, and Jones, GE, *The remaking of Wales in the eighteenth century* (Cardiff, 1988) p.117.
557   Beloff: *Public order and popular disturbances*, p.30.
558   Howell, David W. *The rural poor in eighteenth century Wales* (Cardiff, 2000) p.188.
559   Wheeler, HFB, and Broadley, AM, *Napoleon and the invasion of England: the story of the Great Terror* (London, 1908) p.210.
560   Williams: *Beginnings of radicalism*, p.112.
561   Williams, Gwyn. *Locating a Welsh working class: the frontier years* in Smith David (ed.), *A people and a proletariat: essays in the history of Wales 1780–1980* (London, Pluto Press in association with *Llafur*, 1980), p.35.
562   Wager: 'Welsh politics and parliamentary reform', p.433.
563   Davies, Leonard Twiston and Edwards, Averyl, *Welsh life in the eighteenth century* (London: Country Life, 1939), p.40.
564   Jones, David JV, *Before Rebecca: popular protests in Wales 1793–1835* (London, 1972) p.27.
565   Wager: 'Welsh politics and parliamentary reform', p.431.
566   Cole, GDH, and Postgate, R, *The common people 1746–1938* (London, 1961), p.149.
567   Wager: 'Welsh politics and parliamentary reform', p.433.
568   Williams: *Locating a Welsh working class,* p.27.
569   Williams: *Locating a Welsh working class*, pp.18–19.
570   Williams: *Locating a Welsh working class*, p.16. It is one of the cases upon which he bases his argument.
571   Jones, David JV, 'More light on "Rhyfel y Sais Bach"' in *Ceredigion* v/i (1964), p.84. See also articles by Jenkins, David, in *Ceredigion* (1951), and Williams, David, in *Ceredigion* (1952).
572   Jones: 'More light on "Rhyfel y Sais Bach", p.84.
573   Rees, Eiluned, 'Developments in the book trade in eighteenth century Wales', *The Library* xxiv (1969) p.41.

574   Evans: *The background of modern Welsh politics*, pp.28–9.
575   Williams, Jac I, and Hughes, Gwilym Rees, *The history of education in Wales* (Swansea, 1978), p.30.
576   Jenkins, Geraint H, *The foundations of modern Wales 1642–1780*, (Cardiff, 1987) p.10.
577   Williams, Jac I, and Hughes, Gwylym Rees, *The history of education in Wales*, pp.51–3.
578   Jenkins: *The foundations of modern Wales*, p.240.
579   Jenkins: *The foundations of modern Wales*, p.253.
580   Jenkins: *The foundations of modern Wales*, p.245.
581   Jenkins: *The foundations of modern Wales*, p.248.
582   Jenkins: *The foundations of modern Wales*, p.207.
583   Jenkins: *The foundations of modern Wales*, p.206.
584   Jenkins: *The foundations of modern Wales*, p.207.
585   Jenkins: *The foundations of modern Wales*, p.209.
586   Jenkins: *The foundations of modern Wales*, p.207.
587   Williams, W Moses. *Selections from the Welch Piety* (Cardiff, 1938) p.6.
588   Williams: *Welch Piety*, p.114.
589   Williams: *Welch Piety*, p.118.
590   Williams: *Welch Piety*, p.114.
591   Williams, Glanmor, Entry under Griffith Jones in Thomas, JE, and Elsey, B, *International Biography of Adult Education* (Nottingham, 1985).
592   Williams: *Welch Piety*, p.10.
593   Jones, GE, and Roderick, GW, *A history of education in Wales* (Cardiff, 2003), pp.43–4.
594   Bell, the Reverend Andrew, quoted by Sutherland, O, 'Elementary education in the nineenth century' *Historical Association* (London, 1971), p.10.
595   Davies, BL, Entry under Thomas Charles in Thomas and Elsey, *International Biography of adult education*.
596   Davies, BL, Entry under Griffith Jones in Thomas and Elsey, *International Biography of adult education*.
597   Roberts, TR, *Eminent Welshmen ; a short biographical dictionary of Welshmen* (Cardiff and Merthyr Tydfil, 1908), p.35.
598   Entry in *The Oxford Companion to the Literature of Wales*.
599   Kelly, T, *A history of adult education in Great Britain* (Liverpool, 1962), p.67.
600   Phillips, Thomas, *Wales: The language, social conditions, moral character, and religious opinions of the people, considered in relation to education* (London, 1849), p.284.
601   Davies and Edwards: *Welsh life in the eighteenth century*, p.55.
602   Howell: *The rural poor,* p.137.
603   Griffith Jones in Thomas and Elsey: *International Biography of adult education*.
604   Thomas Charles in *International Biography of adult education*.
605   Williams: *Welch Piety*, p.113.
606   Richard, Henry, *Letters: Social and Political Condition of the Principality of Wales* (London, 1866), pp.10–11.
607   Jenkins, Geraint H, *Literature, religion and society in Wales 1660–1730* (Cardiff, 1978), p.19.
608   Beddoe, Deidre, *Welsh convict women* (Cardiff, 1979), p.26.

609 Blue Books: Part I, Appendix 235, Introduction, p.7.
610 Warner, Reverend Richard. *A walk through Wales in August 1797* (London, 1798), p.89.
611 Jenkins, RT, and Ramage, Helen M. (1951), *A history of the Honourable Society of Cymmrodorion and of the Gwyneddigion and Cymreigyddion Societies (1751–1951)* (London: Honourable Society of Cymmrodorion), pp.19–21.
612 Rees: *Developments in the book trade*, pp.37–8.
613 Rees: *Developments in the book trade*, p.38.
614 Jenkins: *The foundations of modern Wales*, p.216.
615 Spurrell, William. *Carmarthen and its neighbourhood 1879* (Carmarthen: reprinted by Dyfed County Council, 1995), p.120.
616 Rees: *Developments in the book trade*, p.35.
617 Rees: *Developments in the book trade*, p.41.
618 Rees: *Developments in the book trade*, p.42.
619 Rees: *Developments in the book trade*, p.40.
620 Lodwick, M and E. *The story of Carmarthen* (Carmarthen: privately printed, 1954) p.81.
621 Jenkins: *The foundations of modern Wales*, p.315.
622 Davies, HM, '"Very different springs of uneasiness": emigration from Wales to the United States of America during the 1790s', *Welsh History Review* 15/3 (1991), p.372.
623 See Thomas, DO, *Response to Revolution* (Cardiff, 1989), for succinct introductions to all the people discussed in this section.
624 Davies: *The influence of the French Revolution,* p.207.
625 Davies: *The influence of the French Revolution,* p.209.
626 Davies: *The influence of the French Revolution,* p.214.
627 For an assessment of the enormous impact these publications made see Thomas, DO, and Peach, B, (eds.) *The correspondence of Richard Price* (North Carolina and Cardiff, 1991).
628 Thomas and Peach: *The correspondence,* for additional observations etc., p.156.
629 Peach, B, *Richard Price and the ethical foundations of the American Revolution: selections from his pamphlets,* (North Carolina, 1979), p.284.
630 Peach: *Richard Price and the ethical foundations*, p.235.
631 Peach: *Richard Price and the ethical foundations*, p.183.
632 Peach: *Richard Price and the ethical foundations*, p.341.
633 Thomas, DO, *Richard Price and America* (Aberystwyth, 1975), p.23.
634 Thomas, Peter DG. *Politics in eighteenth-century Wales* (Cardiff, 1998) pp.220ff.
635 Thomas: *Richard Price and America,* p.41.
636 Paine, Thomas, *The Rights of Man; being an answer to Mr. Burke's attack on the French Revolution* (London, 1791), p.3.
637 Morgan is one of those described briefly in Thomas, *Response to Revolution*.
638 Williams: *Beginnings of radicalism*, p.117.
639 PRO HO 42/24.
640 Davies: *The influence of the French Revolution,* p.180. In pp.180ff. there is a long account of *Seren Tam Gwmmwl* in English.
641 Davies: *The influence of the French Revolution*, p.179.
642 Davies: *The influence of the French Revolution*, p.183.

643 Davies: *The influence of the French Revolution*, pp.183–4.
644 Davies: *The influence of the French Revolution*, p.185.
645 Davies: *The influence of the French Revolution*, p.188.
646 Davies: *The influence of the French Revolution*, p.18.
647 Williams: 'Locating a Welsh working class', pp.21–2.
648 Williams: 'Beginnings of radicalism', p.128.
649 Volney, Constantin Francois, *The ruins: or a survey of the Revolutions of Empire* (Washington, 2000) pp.4–5.
650 Blue Books: Part III, p.67.
651 Blue Books: Part III, p.67.
652 Blue Books: Part III, p.67.
653 Jones: *Before Rebecca*, pp.27–8.
654 Williams, David, 'The missions of David Williams and James Tilley Matthews to England 1793' *The English Historical Review* vol. 1. LIII (1938), p.653.
655 Williams: 'The missions', p.653.
656 Williams: 'The missions', p.653.
657 Thomas: *Response to Revolution*, pp.61–3.
658 Thomas: *Response to Revolution*, p.8.
659 Thomas: *Response to Revolution*, p.9.
660 Hugh, RL. 'The theological background of nonconformist social influence in Wales 1800–1850. (Doctoral dissertation, London, 1951), p82.
661 Thomas: *Response to Revolution*, p.19.
662 Thomas: *Response to Revolution*, p.89.
663 Davies: *The influence of the French Revolution*, p.60.
664 Davies: *The influence of the French Revolution*, pp.60–1.
665 Davies: *The influence of the French Revolution*, p.1–2.
666 Davies: *The influence of the French Revolution*, p.8.
667 Davies: *The influence of the French Revolution*, p.9.
668 Davies: *The influence of the French Revolution*, p5.
669 George, I, ' Tomos Glyn Cothi', *Journal of the Welsh Biographical Society* iv (1932), pp.106–7.
670 Davies: *The influence of the French Revolution*, pp.24–26.
671 Davies, Hywel M, 'Morgan John Rhys and James Bicheno' *The Bulletin of the Board of Celtic Studies* xxix part 1 (1980), p.111.
672 Davies: 'Morgan John Rhys and James Bicheno', p.111.
673 Davies: 'Morgan John Rhys and James Bicheno', p.112.
674 Davies: 'Morgan John Rhys and James Bicheno', p.113.
675 Davies: 'Morgan John Rhys and James Bicheno', p.113.
676 Davies: 'Morgan John Rhys and James Bicheno', p.120.
677 Davies: 'Morgan John Rhys and James Bicheno', p.122.
678 Davies: 'Morgan John Rhys and James Bicheno', p.123.
679 Davies: 'Morgan John Rhys and James Bicheno', p.124.
680 Williams: 'Beginnings of radicalism', pp. 133–4.
681 Williams: 'Beginnings of radicalism', p.136.
682 Quoted Davies: *The influence of the French Revolution*, p.31.
683 Davies: *The influence of the French Revolution*, p.43.
684 Williams, Gwyn A, 'Morgan John Rees and his Beulah', *Welsh History Review* 3 (1967), pp.42–3.

685 Davies: *The influence of the French Revolution*, pp.52–3. Although he writes on p.58 that 'Tomos' magazine predated it by 'some six months'.

686 See entry under 'Y Geirgrawn' in *The Oxford Companion to the Literature of Wales*.

687 Davies: *The influence of the French Revolution*, p.53.

688 Davies: *The influence of the French Revolution*, p.54.

689 Davies: *The influence of the French Revolution*, p.54.

690 See the entry under his name in *The Oxford Companion to the Literature of Wales*.

691 Davies: *The influence of the French Revolution*, p.129.

692 Davies: *The influence of the French Revolution*, p.156.

693 Davies: *The influence of the French Revolution*, p.156.

694 Davies: *The influence of the French Revolution*, pp.66–8.

695 Davies: *The influence of the French Revolution*, p.72.

696 Davies: *The influence of the French Revolution*, p.74.

697 Davies: *The influence of the French Revolution*, p.75.

698 Thomas: *Response to Revolution*, p.15.

699 Jones, David, *The Welsh Freeholder's vindication of his letter to the Right Reverend Samuel, Lord Bishop of St. David's, in reply to a clergyman of that diocese, together with strictures on the said letter* (London and Caermarthen, 1791).

700 Jones, David, *Strictures on a pamphlet entitled thought on the late riots at Birmingham* (1791).

701 Davies and Edwards: *Welsh life in the eighteenth century*, p.69.

702 Davies and Edwards: *Welsh life in the eighteenth century*, pp.143–4.

703 Davies and Edwards: *Welsh life in the eighteenth century*, p.147.

704 See the entry under 'Rhys Goch ap Rhiccert' in *The Oxford Companion to the Literature of Wales*.

705 Quoted by Thomas: *Response to Revolution*, p.81.

706 Thomas: *Response to Revolution*, pp.152–3.

707 Williams, Gwyn A, *The Welsh in their history*, (London, 1982), p.31.

708 Rees: 'Developments in the book trade', pp.33–4.

709 Pembrokeshire Record Office PQ/C/i/6.

710 Rees: 'Developments in the book trade', p.34.

711 Jones: *Before Rebecca*, p.165.

712 This is Appendix C, 'A memorandum on Welsh Agriculture and Land Tenure in Periodical Literature; to which is added a list of periodicals published in connection with Wales, and extracts from "*The Times*" relating to the state of South Wales in 1843'. Royal Commision 1896. Compiled by D Lleufer Thomas, Secretary.

713 Williams: 'Beginnings of radicalism', p.115.

714 Thomas: 'Memorandum', p.185.

715 Phillips, Thomas, *Wales: The language, social condition, moral character, and religious opinions of the people, considered in relation to education* (London: John W Parker, 1849) p.272.

716 Walters, G, 'The eighteenth century "Pembroke Society"', *Welsh History Review* 3 (1966–7), p.298.

717 Wheeler and Broadley: *Napoleon and the invasion of England*, Vol. 1, p.208.

718   Davies, JH, *A bibliography of Welsh ballads printed in the eighteenth century*, The Honourable Society of Cymmrodorion (London, 1911), Prefatory Note.

719   Davies: *A bibliography of Welsh ballads,* p.v.

720   Davies: *A bibliography of Welsh ballads,* p.xiv.

721   Rees: 'Developments in the book trade', pp.40–3.

722   Davies: '"Very different springs of uneasiness"', p.372.

723   Jenkins: *The foundations of modern Wales,* p.210.

724   Davies and Edwards: *Welsh life in the eighteenth century,* p.vii.

725   Colyer, Richard, *The Welsh Cattle Drovers; agriculture and the Welsh cattle trade before and during the nineteenth century* (Cardiff, 1976), p.45

Chapter Five

726   The response, during the Hook miners' riot, of a Carmarthen militiaman to a woman who pleaded with him not to shoot them. PRO HO 42/35.

727   Cole, GDH, and Postgate, Raymond, *The common people 1746–1938* (London: Methuen, 1961) p.113.

728   Wheeler, HFB, and Broadley, AM, *Napoleon and the invasion of England: the story of the Great Terror*, 2 Volumes (London, 1908), vol. 2, p.282.

729   Wheeler and Broadley: *Napoleon and the invasion of England*, vol. 2, p.247.

730   Wheeler and Broadley: *Napoleon and the invasion of England*, vol. 2, p.285.

731   Wheeler and Broadley: *Napoleon and the invasion of England*, vol. 2, p.249.

732   So curious in fact that its author merits an entry in *The Oxford Companion to the Literature of Wales*.

733   Poem by Holland Price (2nd edition, Wrexham), 1804.

734   Davies, David. *The influence of the French Revolution on Welsh life and literature* (Carmarthen: W Morgan Evans, 1926) p.151.

735   Wheeler and Broadley: *Napoleon and the invasion of England*, vol. 2, p.114.

736   Wheeler and Broadley: *Napoleon and the invasion of England*, vol. 2, pp.250–1.

737   Wheeler and Broadley: *Napoleon and the invasion of England*, vol. 2, p. 39.

738   Thomas, DO, *Response to Revolution: how the opening events of the French Revolution were perceived by some prominent Welshmen*, (Cardiff, 1989), p.89.

739   Beloff, M, *Public order and popular disturbances 1660–1714* (Oxford, 1938) p.65.

740   Duffy, M, *The Younger Pitt* (London, 2000), p.149.

741   Wells, R, *Insurrection: the British experience 1795–1803* (Stroud: Alan Sutton, 1983) p.23.

742   Duffy: *The Younger Pitt*, p.149.

743   Wilkinson, D, *The Duke of Portland; politics and party in the age of George III* (London: Palgrave Macmillan, 2003) p.135.

744   Wilkinson: *The Duke of Portland*, p.135.

745   Wilkinson: *The Duke of Portland*, p.135.

746   Duffy: *The Younger Pitt*, p.154.

747   Weston, JR, 'The volunteer Movement as an anti-revolutionary force 1793–1801', *The English Historical Review* 71 (1956), pp.603–14.

748   Duffy: *The Younger Pitt*, p.152.

749   For a full discussion of just how significant see Wells: *Insurrection*, chapter 2.

750   See Wilkinson: *The Duke of Portland* for a detailed account, pp.128ff.

751   Wheeler and Broadley: *Napoleon and the invasion of England*, vol.1, p.196.
752   Wilkinson: *The Duke of Portland*, p.134.
753   Wilkinson: *The Duke of Portland*, p.129.
754   Wilkinson: *The Duke of Portland*, p.125.
755   Wilkinson: *The Duke of Portland*, p.115.
756   Wilkinson: *The Duke of Portland*, p.114.
757   Wilkinson: *The Duke of Portland*, p.ix.
758   Wilkinson: *The Duke of Portland*, p.110.
759   Wilkinson: *The Duke of Portland*, p.126.
760   Wilkinson: *The Duke of Portland*, p.128.
761   Wells: *Insurrection*, p.39.
762   PRO HO 34/20.
763   PRO HO 43/4.
764   Thorne, Roland, and Howell, Robert. (1987). 'Pembrokeshire in Wartime 1793–1815' in *Pembrokeshire County History* Volume III, Brian Howells (ed.), The Pembrokeshire Historical Society, Aberystwyth, The National Library of Wales. p.379.
765   Howell, David W, *Patriarchs and Parasites: The gentry of south-west Wales in the eighteenth century* (Cardiff, 1986), pp.141–2.
766   Howell: *Patriarchs and parasites*, p.160.
767   Jenkins, Geraint H. *The foundations of modern Wales 1642–1780* (Cardiff, 1987), p.167.
768   Howell: *Patriarchs and parasites*, p.143.
769   Howell: *Patriarchs and parasites,* pp.144–5.
770   Jones, David JV, *Before Rebecca: popular protests in Wales 1793–1835* (London, 1972) p.166.
771   Howell: *Patriarchs and parasites*, pp.151–2.
772   Howell: *Patriarchs and parasites*, p.165.
773   Napier, L, and Brookes, J (eds), *The House of Commons 1754–1790* (London, 1964), entry under Herbert Lloyd.
774   PRO HO 42/34.
775   Malloy, Pat. *And they blessed Rebecca* (Llandysul: Gomer Press, 1983), p.42. See Jones: *Before Rebecca,* pp.172ff. for an account of the structure and uselessness of the then constabulary.
776   Malloy: *And they blessed Rebecca*, p.87.
777   NLW M300553005E.
778   Wheeler and Broadley: *Napoleon and the invasion of England,* vol. 2, pp.139–40.
779   Wheeler and Broadley: *Napoleon and the invasion of England*, vol. 2, pp.104–5, quoting George Cruikshank, the famous caricaturist and illustrator, who was the witness concerned.
780   Beloff: *Public order and public disturbances*, p.107.
781   Wheeler and Broadley: *Napoleon and the invasion of England*, vol. 1, pp.203–4.
782   Glover, Michael, *That astonishing infantry: three hundred years of the history of the Royal Welch Fusiliers 23rd Regiment of Foot* (London, 1989) p.36.
783   Jones: 'Golden Grove', *Ceredigion* 4 (1960–3), p.267.

784   Pembrokeshire Record Office, Haverfordwest Corporation Records, 2143 folio 44, p.161.

785   Malloy: *And they blessed Rebecca*, pp.44–5.

786   Western, JR, *The English Militia in the eighteenth century: the story of a political issue 1660*–1902 (London: Routledge and Kegan, 1965), p.127.

787   Western: *The English militia*, p.206.

788   PRO HO 42/34.

789   Howell, David W, *The rural poor in eighteenth century Wales* (Cardiff, 2000), pp.203–5.

790   Williams, Gwyn A, *Beginnings of radicalism*, in Herbert, T, and Jones, GE, *The remaking of Wales in the eighteenth century* (Cardiff, 1988), pp.122.

791   Western: *The English militia*, p.206.

792   Western: *The English militia*, p.269.

793   PRO HO 34/37.

794   Western: *The English militia*, pp.427-8.

795   PRO HO 42/35.

796   Western: *The English militia*, pp.427–8.

797   PRO HO 42/34,

798   Thompson, EP, 'The moral economy of the English crowd in the eighteenth century', *Past and Present* 50 (February 1971), pp.112–13.

799   Thompson: 'The moral economy', p.121.

800   See Wells: *Insurrection*, chapter 12 for a detailed account.

801   PRO HO 42/37.

802   PRO HO 42/37.

803   *Cambrian Register*: 1795, p.260.

804   See for example, Jones: *Before Rebecca*, p.30.

805   PRO HO 42/52.

806   PRO HO 42/52.

807   PRO HO 42/34.

808   Owen. B, *History of the Welsh militia and Volunteer Corps 1757–1908* (Wrexham, 1995), p.26.

809   Owen: *History of the Welsh militia*, p.73.

810   Jones: *Before Rebecca*, p.30.

811   Fellows, G, and Freeman, B, *Historical Records of the South Nottinghamshire Hussars Yeomanry 1794–1924* (Aldershot, 1928), p.2.

812   Duffy: *The Younger Pitt*, p.155.

813   Fellows and Freeman: *Historical Records*, p.325.

814   Glover, DG, '"Lord Dynevor's smart and efficient little corps": an historical account if the Carmarthenshire Yeomanry 1794–1815', *The Bulletin of the Military Historical Society* 44/176 (1994).

815   Jones, DJV, 'Distress and discontent in Cardiganshire 1814–1819', *Ceredigion* 3 (1966), p.286.

816   NLW ms. 1352B. Letter of 8 December 1795 to Campbell (Cawdor). Quoted in Howell, 'Pembrokeshire Life', p.112.

817   PRO HO 34/37.

818   Jones: *Before Rebecca*, p.184.

819   Wells: *Insurrection*, p.21.

820   Wells: *Insurrection*, p.163.

821 Western: 'The Volunteer Movement' p.612.
822 Western: 'The Volunteer Movement' p.605.
823 Western: 'The Volunteer Movement' pp.607–8.
824 Western: 'The Volunteer Movement' p.606.
825 Western: 'The Volunteer Movement' p.609.
826 Western: 'The Volunteer Movement' p.610.
827 Western: 'The Volunteer Movement' p.612.
828 Western: 'The Volunteer Movement' p.613.
829 There is an entry on Hughes in *The Oxford Companion to the Literature of Wales.*.
830 Jenkins, RT, and Ramage, Helen M, *A history of the Honourable Society of Cymmrodorion and of the Gwyneddigion and Cymreigyddion Societies (1751–1951)* (London: Honourable Society of Cymmrodorion, 1951), pp.248–9.
831 Jones, Emrys. *The Welsh in London 1500–2000* (Cardiff, 2001) p.62.
832 Jones: *The Welsh in London 1500–2000*, p.62.
833 Jenkins and Ramage: *A history*, p.86.
834 Jenkins and Ramage: *A history*, p.86.
835 Jenkins and Ramage: *A history*, p.89.
836 Jenkins and Ramage: *A history*, p.90.
837 Williams, Gwyn A. *Locating a Welsh working class: the frontier years* in Smith David (ed.), *A people and a proletariat: essays in the history of Wales 1780–1980* (London: Pluto Press in association with *Llafur,* 1980), p.30.
838 Jenkins and Ramage: *A history*, p.125.
839 Jenkins and Ramage: *A history*, p.3.
840 Jenkins and Ramage: *A history*, p.3.
841 Jenkins and Ramage: *A history*, p.4.
842 Jenkins: *The foundations of modern Wales*, p.277.
843 Jenkins and Ramage: *A history*, p.160.
844 Jenkins and Ramage: *A history*, p.120.
845 Jenkins and Ramage: *A history*, p.121.
846 Jenkins and Ramage: *A history*, p.97.
847 Williams, Gwyn A, *Madoc: the legend of the Welsh discovery of America* (Oxford, 1987), p.87.
848 Davies, HM, '"Very different springs of uneasiness": Emigration from Wales to the United States of America during the 1790s', *Welsh History Review* 15 (3 June 1991), p.393.
849 Williams: *Madoc*, p.89.
850 Davies, Leonard Twiston and Edwards, Averyl. (1939), *Welsh life in the eighteenth century*, (London: Country Life), p.161.
851 Davies: *The influence of the French Revolution,* p.195.
852 Davies: *The influence of the French Revolution,* p.198.
853 Davies: *The influence of the French Revolution,* p.199.
854 Jenkins and Ramage: *A history*, p.155.
855 Jenkins and Ramage: *A history,* p.151.
856 Williams: *Madoc,* p.103.
857 Williams: *Madoc,* p.111.
858 Williams: *Madoc,* pp.103–4.
859 Jones, Emrys (ed.), *The Welsh in London 1500–2000* (Cardiff, 2001), p.49.

860   Jones: *The Welsh in London,* p.55.
861   Jenkins and Ramage: *A history,* p.31.
862   Prebble, John, *The Highland Clearances* (London, 1969), p.142.
863   Prebble: *The Highland Clearances,* p.134.
864   Berthoff, RT, *British immigrants in industrial America 1790–1950* (Harvard, 1953), p.197.
865   Berthoff: *British immigrants,* p.202.
866   Berthoff: *British immigrants,* p.144.
867   Jenkins and Ramage: *A history,* p.19.
868   Mavor, William Fordyce, *A tour in Wales and through several counties of England including both the universities* (London, 1806), p.49.
869   Blue Books: part II, p.67.
870   Blue Books: part II, p.66.
871   Blue Books: part II, p.iii.
872   Blue Books: part II, p.67.
873   Blue Books: Part I, p.219.
874   Blue Books: Part I, pp.229.
875   Blue Books: Part I, p.6.
876   Blue Books: Part I, p.7.
877   Morgan, J Vyrnwy (ed.), *Welsh Political and Educational Leaders in the Victorian Era* (London: Nisbet, 1908), p.596.
878   Blue Books: Part I, p.235.
879   Blue Books: Part I, p.225.
880   Blue Books: Part I, p.3.
881   Blue Books: Part I, p2.
882   Blue Books: Part I, p.6.
883   Roberts, Gwyneth Tyson. *The language of the Blue Books: the perfect instrument of empire* (Cardiff, 1998) p.221.
884   Evidence to the Royal Commission, p.59.
885   Evidence to the Royal Commission, p.63.
886   Morgan, KO. *Wales in British Politics 1868–1922* (Cardiff, 1963) p.55.
887   Peate, MR, 'The Blue Books and after: William Williams and his legacy', *The Welsh Journal of Education* 5/2, (1996), p.102.
888   Peate: 'The Blue Books and after', p.98.
889   Ministry of Education pamphlet *Education in Wales,* (1948), p.24.
890   See his entry in *The Oxford Companion to the Literature of Wales.*
891   Jones: *The Welsh in London,* pp.48–9.
892   Morgan, DDJ, *The development of the Baptist movement in Wales between 1714 and 1815 with particular reference to the Evangelical Revival* (University of Oxford 1986), p.27
893   Morgan: 'The development of the Baptist movement', p.27.
894   Davies: *The influence of the French Revolution,* p.14
895   Davies: '"Very different springs of uneasiness"', p.371.
896   Davies:'"Very different springs of uneasiness"', p.383.
897   Davies:'"Very different springs of uneasiness"', p.381.
898   Davies:'"Very different springs of uneasiness"', p.384.
899   Davies:'"Very different springs of uneasiness"', p.386.
900   Williams: *Madoc,* p.96.

901 Williams: *Locating a Welsh working class*, p.20.
902 Williams: *Locating a Welsh working class*, p.19.
903 Thomas, D Lleufer, *Memorandum*, p.189.
904 Davies: "'Very different springs of uneasiness'", p.377.
905 Davies: "'Very different springs of uneasiness'", pp.375–6.
906 Davies: *The influence of the French Revolution*, p.15.
907 Davies: *The influence of the French Revolution*, p.373.
908 Davies: *The influence of the French Revolution*, p.374.
909 Davies, Hywel M, 'Morgan John Rhys, and James Bicheno Anti-Christ and the French Revolution in England and Wales', *Bulletin of the Board of Celtic Studies* xxix Part 1 (November 1980), p.126.
910 Davies: *The influence of the French Revolution*, p.167.
911 Davies: "'Very different springs of uneasiness'", p.387.
912 Davies: "'Very different springs of uneasiness'", p.396.
913 Davies: "'Very different springs of uneasiness'", p.388.
914 Davies: "'Very different springs of uneasiness'", p.389.
915 Davies: "'Very different springs of uneasiness'", p.390.
916 Davies: "'Very different springs of uneasiness'", p.392.
917 Jones, Francis, 'Disaffection and discontent in Pembrokeshire', *Transactions of The Honourable Society of Cymmrodorion 1946–7*, Sessions 1946–7, no volume number, p.222.
918 PRO HO 42/61.
919 PRO HO 41/61.
920 Davies: "'Very different springs of uneasiness'", p.379.
921 Berthoff, RT. *British immigrants in industrial America 1790–1950* (Harvard, 1953), p.31.
922 Berthoff: *British immigrants*, p.64.
923 Berthoff: *British immigrants*, p.54.
924 Royal Commission, 1896, Volume II, p.538.
925 Jenkins, David, *The agricultural community in south west Wales at the turn of the twentieth century* (Cardiff, 1971), p.263.
926 Williams, David, 'Some figures relating to emigration from Wales, *Bulletin of the Board of Celtic Studies*, vii (1935), p.407. For a further account of the extent of emigration in the nineteenth century , see Johnson, W Ross, 'The Welsh diaspora' in *Llafur*, Vol. 6, No. 2 (1993).

Chapter Six

927 Carlile, Richard, *Republican* 1 Feb 1822, quoted Williams, Gwyn A, 'Morgan John Rhys and Volney's "Ruins of Empires"', *The Bulletin of the Board of Celtic Studies* xx, p.58.
928 Watts, Michael R, *The dissenters: the expansion of evangelical nonconformity* (Oxford, 1995), Volume II, pp.36 and 39.
929 Watts: *The dissenters*, p.40.
930 Entry under 'Baptists' in *The Oxford Companion to the Literature of Wales*.
931 Watts: *The dissenters*, Volume II, p.81.
932 O'Leary, Paul, 'Irish immigration and the Catholic "Welsh district", 1840–1850' in Jenkins and Smith (eds), *Politics and society in Wales 1840–1922*, p.31.

933   Jones, Ieuan, and Williams, David, *The religious census of 1851: a calendar of the returns relating to Wales,* Volume One, South Wales (Cardiff, 1978), p.xxii.

934   Jones and Williams: *The religious census,* pp.xxiii–xxiv.

935   Watts: *The dissenters,* Volume II, p.166.

936   See his entry in *The Oxford Companion to the Literature of Wales.*

937   Davies, David, *The influence of the French Revolution on Welsh life and literature* (Carmarthen: W Morgan Evans, 1926) p.166.

938   Davies: *The influence of the French Revolution* pp.198–9.

939   Hugh, RL, *The theological background of nonconformist social influence in Wales 1800–1850* (University of London, 1951). p.204.

940   Hugh: *The theological background,* p.206.

941   Hugh: *The theological background,* p.221.

942   Hugh: *The theological background,* p.221.

943   Hugh: *The theological background,* p.213. See pp.210ff., for examples of both reform and restraint.

944   Hugh: *The theological background,* p.214.

945   Evans, ET, *Religion in the industrial revolution in south Wales* (Cardiff, 1965), p.81.

946   Evans: *Religion,* p.79.

947   Hugh: *The theological background,* pp.291–2.

948   Hobsbawm, EJ, and Rudé, G, *Captain Swing* (London, 1969), p.88.

949   See Jones, David JV, *Before Rebecca: popular protests in Wales 1793–1835* (London, 1972), passim, especially pp. 180–1.

950   Evans, T, *The background of modern Welsh politics 1789–1846* (Cardiff, 1936), pp.60–1.

951   Davies: *The influence of the French Revolution,* p.77.

952   Davies: *The influence of the French Revolution,* p.77.

953   Wheeler, HFB, and Broadley, AM, *Napoleon and the invasion of England: the story of the Great Terror,* 2 Volumes (London, 1908) Volume 2, p.116.

954   Jenkins, *Literature, religion and society in Wales 1660–1730* (Cardiff, 1978) p.19.

955   See Coupland, R, *Welsh and Scottish Nationalism: A study* (London: Collins, 1954), for a detailed discussion.

956   Morgan, KO, *Wales in British Politics 1868–1922* (Cardiff, 1963), p.18.

957   Evans, ED, *A history of Wales 1660–1815* (Cardiff, 1993), p.36.

958   Evans: *A history of Wales,* p.43.

959   Under 'Independents' in *The Oxford Companion to the Literature of Wales.*

960   Morgan, Prys, 'From Long knives to Blue Books' in Griffiths, Jones and Morgan (eds), *Welsh society and nationhood* (Cardiff, 1984), p.199.

961   Jones, Goronwy, *Wales and the quest for peace* (Cardiff, 1969), p.xv.

962   Entry in *The Oxford Companion to the Literature of Wales.*

963   Carwardine, Richard, 'The Welsh evangelical community' and "Finney's revival"', *Journal of Ecclesiastical History* 29 (1978), p.476.

964   Carwardine: 'The Welsh evangelical community', p.475.

965   Evans: *The background of modern Welsh politics,* p.198.

966   Evans: *The background of modern Welsh politics,* p.85.

967   Dodd, AH, *The Industrial Revolution in north Wales* (Cardiff, 1933), p.398.

968   Davies: *The influence of the French Revolution,* p.87.

969 Harris, John, '"Neighbours": Caradoc Evans, Lloyd George and the London Welsh', *Llafur* Vol. 5, No. 4 (1991), pp.92–3.
970 Morgan: *Wales in British politics*, p.13.
971 Davies: *Religion in the industrial revolution*, p.37.
972 Davies: *Religion in the industrial revolution*, p.148.
973 Davies: *Religion in the industrial revolution*, p.85.
974 Watts: *The dissenters*, Volume II, p.3.
975 Jones: *Before Rebecca*, p.111.
976 Dodd: *The industrial revolution in north Wales*, p.415.
977 Morgan: *Wales in British politics*, p.203.
978 Harvey, John, *Image of the invisible: the visualisation of religion in the Welsh nonconformist tradition* (Cardiff, 1999), p.114.
979 Stead, P, 'The Welsh working class' *Llafur* Vol. 1 (1972–5), p.90.
980 Evans: *Religion in the industrial revolution in south Wales*, p.76.
981 Jones, Ieuan Gwynedd, and Williams, David. (1978). *The religious census of 1851: a calendar of the returns relating to Wales Volume I South Wales with an introduction by Jones, Ieuan Gwynedd* (Cardiff: University of Wales Press), p.xxxiii.
982 Jones and Williams: *The Religious Census*, pp.xxxiv–v.
983 Davies: *The influence of the French Revolution*, p.215.
984 Watts: *The dissenters*, Volume II. p.347. These were the riots in which Priesley's house and equipment were destroyed. For a very readable account of Unitarianism, see Hostler, John, *Unitarianism* (London, 1981).
985 Morgan: *Wales in British Politics*, pp.14–15.
986 Morgan: *Wales in British Politics*, p.221.
987 Morgan: *Wales in British Politics*, p.13.
988 Morgan: *Wales in British Politics*, p.80.
989 Morgan: *Wales in British Politics*, p.81.
990 Watts: *The dissenters*, Volume II, p.399.
991 See his entry in *The Oxford Companion to the Literature of Wales*.
992 Davies: *The influence of the French Revolution*, p.32.
993 Williams, David, *Incidents in my own life which have been thought to have been of some importance*, edited with an account of his published writing by France, P (University of Sussex, 1980), p.117.
994 Williams: *Incidents in my own life*, p.91.
995 Williams: *Incidents in my own life*, pp.123–4.
996 Williams: *Incidents in my own life*, p.126.
997 Watts: *The dissenters, Volume II*, p.358.
998 Watts: *The dissenters, Volume II*, p.367.
999 Williams, Gwyn A. *Beginnings of radicalism*, in Herbert, T, and Jones, GE, *The remaking of Wales in the eighteenth century* (Cardiff, 1988), pp. 121–2.
1000 PRO HO 42/34.
1001 Morgan: *Wales in British politics*, pp.14–15.
1002 Davies: *The influence of the French Revolution*, pp.93–4.
1003 Davies: *The influence of the French Revolution*, pp.93–4.
1004 Evans: *A history of Wales*, p.82.
1005 Davies: *The influence of the French Revolution*, p.83.
1006 Davies: *The influence of the French Revolution*, pp.86–7.

1007 Davies: *The influence of the French Revolution*, pp.36–7.
1008 Davies: *The influence of the French Revolution*, p.116.
1009 Evans: *A history of Wales*, p.95.
1010 Watts: *The dissenters*, Volume II, p.403.
1011 See his entry in *The Oxford Companion to the Literature of Wales*.
1012 Watts: *The dissenters*, Volume II, p.421.
1013 Richard, Henry, *Letters on the social and political condition of Wales* (London, 1866), p.32.
1014 Richard: *Letters*, pp.41–2.
1015 Richard: *Letters*, p.72.
1016 Richard: *Letters*, p.73.
1017 Richard: *Letters*, p.81.
1018 Richard: *Letters*, p.32.
1019 Richard: *Letters*, pp.74–5.
1020 Richard: *Letters*, p.43.
1021 Richard: *Letters*, p.44.
1022 Phillips, Thomas, *Wales: The language, social condition, moral character, and religious opinions of the people, considered in relation to education* (London: John W Parker, 1849), p.50.
1023 Phillips: *The language, social conditions etc.*, p.53.
1024 Phillips: *The language, social conditions etc.*, p.53.
1025 Williams, Chris, 'Wales's "Unionist nationalist" Sir Thomas Phillips (1801–67)' *Llafur* Vol. 8, No. 4 (2003), pp.7ff.
1026 Phillips: *The language, social conditions etc*, p.14.
1027 Davies: *The influence of the French Revolution*, p.63.
1028 Malloy, Pat, *And they blessed Rebecca* (Llandysul: Gomer Press, 1983), p.15.
1029 Smith, David, 'Wales through the looking glass', in Smith, David (ed.), *A people and a proletariat: essays in the history of Wales 1780–1980* (Cardiff, 1980), p.217.
1030 Morgan: *Wales in British politics*, p.3.
1031 Morgan: *Wales in British politics*, p.50.
1032 Morgan: *Wales in British politics*, p.234.
1033 Jenkins, David, *The agricultural community in south-west Wales at the turn of the twentieth century* (Cardiff, 1971), p.194.
1034 Jenkins: *The agricultural community*, p.186.
1035 Jenkins: *The agricultural community*, p.187.
1036 Jenkins: *The agricultural community*, p.188.
1037 Morgan, Prys: *From long knives to Blue Books:* p.205.
1038 Davies, Russell, '"In a broken dream": some aspects of sexual behaviour and the dilemmas of the unmarried mother in south west Wales 1887–1914', *Llafur* Vol. 3, No. 4 (1983), pp.24–5.
1039 Howell, DW, *Land and people in nineteenth century Wales* (London, 1978) p.11.
1040 Blue Books: Part I, p.6.
1041 Jenkins, David, *The agricultural community in south-west Wales at the turn of the twentieth century* (Cardiff, 1971), p.193.
1042 Jenkins: *Literature, religion and society*, p.139.
1043 Evans: *A history of Wales*, pp.89ff.

1044 Evans: *A history of Wales*, p.89.
1045 Watts: *The dissenters*, Volume II, p.420.
1046 Morgan: *Wales in British politics*, p.172.
1047 Jenkins, Geraint H. *The foundations of modern Wales 1642–1780* (Cardiff, 1987), p.200.
1048 Jenkins: *The foundations of modern Wales*, p.201.
1049 Davies: *The influence of the French Revolution*, p.111. He is quoting John Owen of Machynlleth. See his entry in *The Oxford Companion to the Literature of Wales*.
1050 Davies: *The influence of the French Revolution,* p.107.
1051 See Thomas Jones' entry in *The Oxford Companion to the Literature of Wales*.
1052 Davies: *The influence of the French Revolution*, p.89.
1053 Watts: *The dissenters*, Volume II, p.421.
1054 Watts: *The dissenters*, Volume II, p.8.
1055 Williams: 'Morgan John Rees and Volney's *Ruins of empires*', p.61.
1056 See under his entry in *The Oxford Companion to the Literature of Wales*.
1057 Davies: *The influence of the French Revolution*, p.191.
1058 Morgan, J Vyrnwy, (editor). *Welsh Political and Educational Leaders in the Victorian Era* (London, 1908), pp.27–8, and Morgan, KO, *Wales in British Politics 1868–1922* (Cardiff, 1963), p.11.
1059 For a full discussion see Morgan: *Wales in British* politics, passim, and the entry on 'The Tithe War' in *The Oxford Companion to the Literature of Wales*.
1060 Morgan: *Welsh political and educational leaders*, p.27.
1061 Morgan: *Welsh political and educational leaders*, p.28.
1062 Morgan: *Wales in British politics*, p.133.
1063 Morgan: *Wales in British politics,* pp.30ff. for a discussion of reaction.
1064 Morgan: *Wales in British politics,* p.259.
1065 See entry under 'Disestablishment of the Anglican Church in Wales' in *The Oxford Companion to the Literature of Wales*.
1066 Morgan: *Wales in British Politics*, p.67.
1067 Morgan: *Wales in British politics,* p.177.
1068 See entry under 'Land Reform' in *The Oxford Companion to the Literature of Wales*.
1069 Morgan: *Wales in British Politics*, p.166.
1070 Morgan: *Wales in British politics*, p.242.
1071 Quoted Morgan: *Wales in British politics*, p.92.
1072 Morgan: *Wales in British politics,* p.9.
1073 The Blue Books: Part 1, p.7.

Epilogue

1074 Cannadine, D, *The decline and fall of the British aristocracy* (Yale, 1990) pp.106–7.
1075 Cannadine: *The decline and fall*, pp.106–7.
1076 Jenkins, Philip, *A history of modern Wales, 1536–1990* (London, 1992), p.278.
1077 Jenkins: *A history of modern Wales*, p.279.
1078 Jones, Francis, 'The old families of south west Wales', *Ceredigion* iv i (1960), p.14.
1079 GEC (ed.) (1904), *Complete Baronetage* (Creations by James I), p.178.

1080   Jones: 'The old families', p.13.
1081   Cannadine: *The decline and fall*, p.69.
1082   Cannadine: *The decline and fall*, p.197.
1083   Cannadine: *The decline and fall*, p.122.
1084   Cannadine: *The decline and fall*, p.107.
1085   Cannadine: *The decline and fall*, p.82.
1086   Jenkins, David, *The agricultural community in south west Wales at the turn of the twentieth century* (Cardiff, 1971), p.25.
1087   Jenkins: *The agricultural community*, p.25.
1088   Jenkins: *The agricultural community*, p.269.
1089   Davies, John, 'The end of the great estates and the rise of freehold farming in Wales', *Welsh History Review* 7 (1974–5) pp.186–211.
1090   Davies: 'The end of the great estates etc', p.189. He does however issue a caveat that these figures are problematic.
1091   Davies: 'The end of the great estates etc', p.209.
1092   Thomas, Peter DG, *Politics in eighteenth century Wales* (Cardiff, 1998), p.236.
1093   Lloyd, HA, *The gentry of south west Wales 1540–1640* (Cardiff, 1968), p.101.
1094   Jones, Francis, 'The Vaughans of Golden Grove, I The Earls of Carbery', *Transactions of the Honourable Society of Cymmrodorion* 1963, p.96.
1095   Morgan, KO, *Wales in British politics 1868–1922* (Cardiff, 1963), p.112.
1096   Wager, D, 'Welsh politics and parliamentary reform 1780–1832' *Welsh History Review* 7/4 (1975), p.431.
1097   Morgan: *Wales in British Politics*, p.18.
1098   Thomas: *Politics in eighteenth-century Wales*, p.13.
1099   Wager: 'Welsh politics', p.435.
1100   Wager: 'Welsh politics' p.44.
1101   Cannadine: *The decline and fall*, p.36.
1102   Morgan, KO, *David Lloyd George: Welsh radical as world statesman* (Cardiff, 1963), p.18.
1103   Quoted by Morgan: *Wales in British Politics*, p.22.
1104   Morgan: *Wales in British Politics* p.65.
1105   Cannadine: *The decline and fall*, p.144.
1106   Morgan: *Wales in British Politics*, p.108.
1107   Morgan: *Wales in British Politics*, p.28.
1108   Morgan: *Wales in British Politics*, p.107.
1109   Morgan: *Wales in British Politics,* p.107.
1110   Morgan: *Wales in British Politics*, p.20.
1111   Thomas, D Lleufer. *A memorandum on Welsh agriculture and land tenure in periodical literature to which is added a list of periodicals published in connection with Wales and extracts from the "Times" relating to the state of south Wales in 1843. Appendix C to the Royal Commission on Land in Wales and Monmouthshire* (London, 1896), pp.190–1.
1112   Morgan: *Wales in British Politics,* pp.25–7. See also Cannadine: *The decline and fall,* pp.59–60.
1113   Morgan: *Wales in British Politics*, pp.1–2.
1114   Morgan: *Wales in British Politics,* p.37.
1115   Cannadine: *The decline and fall*, p.116.
1116   Morgan: *Wales in British Politics*, p.126.

1117 Jones, GJ, *Wales and the quest for peace* (Cardiff, 1969), p.51.
1118 Cannadine: *The decline and fall*, p.60.
1119 Cannadine: *The decline and fall*, p.60
1120 Morgan: *Lloyd George*, p.19.
1121 Cannadine: *The decline and fall*, p.68.
1122 Morgan: *Wales in British Politics*, p.211.
1123 Morgan: *Wales in British Politics*, p.179.
1124 Morgan: *Wales in British Politics*, p.211.
1125 Morgan: *Wales in British Politics*, p.248.
1126 Cannadine: *The decline and fall*, p.147.
1127 Morgan: *Wales in British Politics*, p.281.
1128 McGarvie, Michael, *The Meyricks of Bush: the story of a Pembrokeshire family* (Glastonbury, 1988).
1129 Davies, John, 'The end of the great estates and the rise of freehold farming in Wales', *Welsh History Review* 7 (1974–5), p.186.
1130 Davies: 'The end of the great estates', p.195.
1131 Cannadine: *The decline and fall*, p.235.
1132 Cannadine: *The decline and fall*, p.575.
1133 Morgan, Prys, 'From Long knives to Blue Books' in Griffiths, Jones and Morgan (eds), *Welsh society and nationhood* (Cardiff, 1984), p.206. See pp.208ff., for details of the response.
1134 Peate, Mary Rose, 'The Blue Books and after: William Williams and his legacy', *The Welsh Journal of Education* 5/2 (1996), p.95.
1135 See Roberts, Gwyneth Tyson., *The language of the Blue Books: the perfect instrument of empire* (Cardiff, 1998), for a detailed account of the reactions.
1136 Roberts: *The language of the Blue Books:* p.210.
1137 Roberts: *The language of the Blue Books:* p.210.
1138 Roberts: *The language of the Blue Books:* p.311.
1139 Roberts: *The language of the Blue Books:* p.212.
1140 Quoted by Roberts: *The language of the Blue Books:* pp.214–5.
1141 The Blue Books Part II Appendix. 68, 74, 118, 159–60.
1142 Roberts: *The language of the Blue Books:* p.103.
1143 Roberts: *The language of the Blue Books:* pp.97–8.
1144 Morgan: *Wales in British Politics*, p.16.
1145 Peate: 'The Blue Books and after', p.96.
1146 Morgan: *Wales in British Politics*, pp.16–17.
1147 Morgan: 'From long knives to Blue Books', p.209.
1148 Blue Books: Part I, p.421.
1149 Blue Books: Part I, p.478.
1150 Blue Books: Part I, p.214.
1151 Blue Books: Part I, p.209.
1152 Blue Books: Part II, p.51.
1153 Blue Books: Part I, p. 220.
1154 Blue Books: Part I, p.222.
1155 Blue Books: Part I, p.223.
1156 Blue Books: Part I, p.391.
1157 Blue Books: Part I, p.404.
1158 Blue Books: Part I, p.394.

1159 Blue Books: Part I, p.396.
1160 Blue Books: Part I, p.395.
1161 Blue Books: Part I, p.395.
1162 Blue Books: Part I, p.399.
1163 Blue Books: Part I, p.399.
1164 Blue Books: Part II, p.31.
1165 Blue Books: Part I, p.245.
1166 Blue Books: Part II, p.146.
1167 Blue Books: Part II, p. 146.
1168 Introduction to the Blue Books: Part II, p.41.
1169 Blue Books: Part I, p.15.
1170 Blue Books: Part I, p.406.
1171 Blue Books: Part I, p.440.
1172 Blue Books: Part I, p.242.
1173 Blue Books: Part I, p.33.
1174 Blue Books: Part II, p.56.
1175 Blue Books: Part II, p.56.
1176 Blue Books: Part II, p.56.
1177 Blue Books: Part II, p.401.
1178 Blue Books: Part II, p.447.
1179 Jones, Ieuan, and Williams, David, *The religious census of 1851: a calendar of the returns relating to Wales*, Volume One, South Wales (Cardiff, 1978), p. 428.
1180 Blue Books: Part I, p.9.
1181 Blue Books: Part I, p.21.
1182 Blue Books: Part I, p.217.
1183 Blue Books: Part I, p.58.
1184 See Evans, Neil, and Jones, Dot, 'A blessing for the miner's wife: the campaign for pithead baths in the south Wales coalfield 1908–1950', *Llafur* Vol. 6, No. 3 (1994).
1185 Blue Books: Part I, p.17.
1186 Blue Books: Part I, p.20.
1187 Blue Books: Part I, pp.12–13.
1188 Blue Books: Part III (north Wales), p.68.
1189 Blue Books: Part I, p.57.
1190 Blue Books: Part I, p.394.
1191 Blue Books: Part I, p.394.
1192 Blue Books: Part I, p.394.
1193 Blue Books: Part II, p.57.
1194 Morgan, J Vyrnwy, *Welsh Political and Educational Leaders in the Victorian Era* (London, 1908), p.596.
1195 Blue Books: Part I, p.237.
1196 Blue Books: Part I, p.229.
1197 Blue Books: Part I, p.17.
1198 Hagen, G, 'Women and poverty in south-west Wales 1834–1914 *Llafur* Vol.7 Nos. 3/4 (1998–9) p.121.
1199 Hagen: 'Women and poverty', p.29.
1200 Hagen: 'Women and poverty', p.23.

1201 Blue Books: Part I, p.424.
1202 Blue Books: Part I, p.422.
1203 Blue Books: Part I, p.479.
1204 Blue Books: Part III, p.68.
1205 Hagen: 'Women and poverty', p.30.
1206 Blue Books: Part I, p.473.
1207 Blue Books: Part I, p.402.
1208 Blue Books: Part I, p.461.
1209 Blue Books: Part I, p.425.
1210 Blue Books: Part I, p.244.
1211 Blue Books: Part I, p.25.
1212 Blue Books: Part I, p.227.
1213 Blue Books: Part I, p.337.
1214 Blue Books: Part I, p.4.
1215 Richard, Henry, *Letters: Social and Political Condition of the Principality of Wales* (London, 1866), p.2.
1216 Lewis, WJ, *Lead mining in Wales* (Cardiff, 1967), p.285.
1217 Lewis: *Lead mining in Wales*, p.284.
1218 Lewis: *Lead mining in Wales*, p.285.
1219 Royal Commission on Land in Wales and Monmouthshire, 1895, Volume II p.567.
1220 Royal Commission: Volume II, p.578.
1221 Royal Commission: Volume II, p.585.
1222 Royal Commission: Volume III, pp.57ff.
1223 Royal Commission: Volume III, p.58.
1224 Royal Commission: Volume II, p.556.
1225 Royal Commission: Volume III, p.57.
1226 Royal Commission: Volume II, p.576.
1227 Royal Commission: Volume II, p.579.
1228 Cannadine: *The decline and fall*, p.67.
1229 Whetham, Edith H, *The agrarian history of England and Wales*, Volume viii 1914–1939 (Cambridge, 1978), p.34.
1230 Whetham: *The agrarian history*, p.197.
1231 Whetham: *The agrarian history*, pp.318 ff.
1232 Morgan: *Wales in British Politics*, pp.97–8.
1233 For an account of these events and other industrial unrest in north Wales, see Dodd, AH, *The industrial revolution in north Wales* (1933, Cardiff) pp.404–16.
1234 Burge, Alun, 'The Mold riots of 1869', *Llafur* Vol 3, No. 3 (1982).
1235 Wilkes, Ivor, South Wales and the rising of 1839. See also Jones: *Before Rebecca*, Chapters 5 and 6. See also Jones, DJV, 'The Carmarthen riots of 1831', *Welsh History Review* 4 (1968—9).
1236 See for example Williams, David. *The Rebecca riots: a study in agrarian discontent* (1955, Cardiff), and Malloy, Pat, *And they blessed Rebecca* (1983, Llandysul: Gomer Press)
1237 Malloy: *And they blessed Rebecca*, p.267.
1238 See his entry in *The Dictionary of National Biography*.
1239 Malloy: *And they blessed Rebecca*, p.140.

1240 Malloy: *And they blessed Rebecca*, p.247.

1241 Malloy: *And they blessed Rebecca*, p.277.

1242 Malloy: *And they blessed Rebecca*, p.148.

1243 Malloy: *And they blessed Rebecca*, p.102.

1244 See the entry under 'Tithe War' in *The Oxford Companion to the history of Wales*.

1245 Morgan: *Wales in British Politics* p.90.

1246 Cannadine: *The decline and fall*, p.487.

1247 Cannadine: *The decline and fall*, p.491.

1248 Quoted by Morgan: *Wales in British politics*, p.264.

1249 Cannadine: *The decline and fall*, p.493.

1250 Morgan: *Wales in British politics*, p.271.

1251 Howell, David W, 'The agricultural labourer in nineteenth century Wales', *Welsh History Review* 6 (1972–3), p.1

BIBLIOGRAPHY

Archive material from:

The National Library of Wales (NLW)
The Public Record Office (PRO) (National Archives)
Pembrokeshire Record Office (Pembs. RO)
Carmarthenshire Record Office (Carms. RO)

Newspapers

Cambrian Register
Salopian Journal
Shrewsbury Chronicle
The Gentleman's Magazine
The Times

Official reports

Reports of the Commissioners of Inquiry into the state of education in Wales, appointed by the Committee of Council on Education 1847: 'The Blue Books'.
Part I Carmarthen, Glamorgan, and Pembroke.
Part II Brecknock, Cardigan, and Radnor.
Part III Anglesey, Carnarvon, Denbigh, Flint, Merioneth, Montgomery.
Royal Commission on the employment of children, young persons and women in agriculture 1867.
Royal Commission on Land in Wales and Monmouthshire 1896.

Books

Ararat, R. (1974). *Introduction to The Jacobite Heritage: Baronetage,Knightage & Grants of Honour compiled and annotated by Melville Henry Massue, Marquis de Ruvigny & Raineval (1868–1921). Facsimile of the original edition of 1904,* London and Edinburgh: Charles Skilton.

Armstrong, WA, and Huzel JP. (1989). *Food shelter and self help, the Poor Law and the position of the labourer in rural society,* in *The agrarian history of England and Wales* Volume vi 1750–1850, Cambridge: University Press.

Ashton, TS, and Sykes, J. (1964). *The coal industry of the eighteenth century,* Manchester: University Press.

Barber, JT. (1803). *A tour throughout South Wales and Monmouthshire,* London: T Cadell and W Davies.

Barnes, HE. (1948). *An introduction to the history of sociology:* Tratto di Sociologia Generale (Mind and Society) tr. and ed. Arthur Livinston (sic) NY 1935, discussed by W Rex Crawford.

Beddoe, Deirdre. (1979). *Welsh Convict Women* Cardiff: Stewart Williams.

Beloff, M. (1938). *Public order and popular disturbances 1660–1714,* Oxford: University Press.

Berthoff, RT. (1953). *British immigrants in industrial America 1790–1950,* Harvard: University Press.

Burke, John, and Burke, John Bernard, (editors). (1841). *The extinct and dormant baronetcies of England* second edition, London: Scott Webster and Geary.

Cannadine, D. (1990). *The decline and fall of the British aristocracy,* Yale: University Press.

Chrimes, SB. (1972). *Henry VII,* London: Eyre Methuen.

Cole, GDH, and Postgate, Raymond. (1961). *The common people 1746–1938,* London: Methuen.

Colyer, Richard J. (1976). *The Welsh Cattle Drovers; agriculture and the Welsh cattle trade before and during the nineteenth century,* Cardiff: University of Wales Press.

Coupland, R. (1954). *Welsh and Scottish Nationalism: A study,* London: Collins.

Crawford, W Rex. See Pareto.

Davies, BL. *Thomas Charles* in *International Biography of Adult Education,* Thomas and Elsey. (editors). (1985). Nottingham: Department of Adult Education.

Davies, David. (1926). *The influence of the French Revolution on Welsh life and literature,* Carmarthen: W Morgan Evans.

Davies, ET. (1965). *Religion in the industrial revolution in south Wales,* Cardiff: University of Wales Press.

Davies, JH. (1911). *A bibliography of Welsh ballads printed in the eighteenth century,* London: The Honourable Society of Cymmrodorion.

Davies, John. (1988). *Victoria and Victorian Wales in Politics and society in Wales 1840–1922* Jenkins GH, and Smith JB.(editors). Cardiff: University of Wales Press.

Davies, Leonard Twiston and Edwards, Averyl. (1939). *Welsh life in the eighteenth century,* London: Country Life.

Davies, Walter, (Gwallter Mechain). (1814). *General view of the agriculture and domestic economy of south Wales; containing the counties of Brecon, Caermarthen, Cardigan, Glamorgan, Pembroke, Radnor.* 2 volumes, London: McMillan.

de Ruvigny see Ararat.

Dodd, AH. (1933). *The Industrial Revolution in north Wales*, Cardiff: University of Wales, Press.

Duffy, M. (2000). *The Younger Pitt*, London: Longman.

Dunbabin, JPD. (1974). *Rural discontent in nineteenth century Britain,* London: Faber and Faber.

Edwards, Averyl see Davies, Leonard Twiston.

Elsey, B. see Thomas JE.

Evans, ED. (1993). *A history of Wales 1660–1815*, Cardiff: University of Wales Press.

Evans, J. (1804). *Letters written during a tour through south Wales in the year 1803 and at other times etc.*, London.

Evans, ET. (1965). *Religion in the industrial revolution in south Wales*, Cardiff: University of Wales Press.

Evans, T. (1936). *The background of modern Welsh politics 1789–1846* Cardiff: University of Wales Press.

Fellows, G, and Freeman, B. (1928) *Historical Records of the South Nottinghamshire Hussars Yeomanry 1794–1924*, Aldershot: Gale and Polden.

Foot, Michael. (1988). *The Politics of Paradise: a vindication of Byron*, London: William Collins and Son.

France, P, (editor) (1980). *Williams David, Incidents in my own life which have been thought to have been of some importance*, University of Sussex Library.

GEC, (editor) (1904). *Complete baronetage Vol. II 1625–1649*, Exeter: Pollard.

Glover, Michael. (1989). *That astonishing infantry: three hundred years of the History of The Royal Welch Fusiliers (23rd Regiment of Foot) 1689–1989*, London: Leo Cooper.

Goddard, Nicholas. (1989). *Agricultural literature and Societies in The Agrarian history of England and Wales*, Volume VI 1750–1850, Cambridge University Press.

Godwin, Fay, and Toulson, Shirley. (1977). *The Drovers' Roads of Wales*. London: Wildwood House.

Harvey, John. (1999). *Image of the invisible: the visualisation of religion in the Welsh nonconformist tradition*, Cardiff: University of Wales Press.

Hassall, Charles. (1794). *General view of the Agriculture of the county of Carmarthen with observations on the means of its improvement*, London.

Hassall, Charles. (1794). *General view of the agriculture of the county of Pembroke with observations on the means of its improvement drawn up for the consideration of the board of agriculture and internal improvement*, London.

Henken, ER. (1996). *National Redeemer: Owain Glyndwr in Welsh Tradition*. Cardiff: University of Wales Press.

Herbert, T, and Jones GE. (1988). *Tudor Wales*, Cardiff: University of Wales Press.

Hoare, Sir Richard Colt. (1796). *Journals of tours in Wales*, London: 1796.

Hobsbawm, EJ, and Rudé, G. (1969) *Captain Swing*, London: Lawrence and Wishart.

Honourable Society of Cymmrodorion (1959). *The Dictionary of Welsh Biography down to 1940*, Oxford: Blackwell.

Hostler, John. (1981). *Unitarianism*, London: The Hibbert Trust.

Howell, DW. (1978). *Land and people in nineteenth century Wales*, London: Routledge and Kegan Paul.

Howell, David W. (1986). *Patriarchs and Parasites: The gentry of south-west Wales in the eighteenth century*, Cardiff: University of Wales Press.

Howell, David W. (2000). *The rural poor in eighteenth century Wales*, Cardiff: University of Wales Press.

Howell, Brian. (editor) (1987). *Pembrokeshire County History* Vol. 3, Aberystwyth: National Library of Wales.

Howell, R, see Thorne.

Howells, BE, and KA, (editors*)*.(1972). *Pembrokeshire Life 1572–1843* Pembrokeshire Record Society.

Hughes, Edward. (1980). *Studies in administration and finance 1558–1825 with special reference to the history of salt taxation in England,* Philadelphia: Porcupine Press.

Hughes, PG. (1943). *Wales and the Drovers: the historical background of an epoch,* London: Foyle's Welsh Co.

Jenkins, David. (1971). *The agricultural community in south-west Wales at the turn of the twentieth century,* Cardiff: University of Wales Press.

Jenkins, Geraint H. (1978). *Literature, religion and society in Wales 1660–1730,* Cardiff: University of Wales Press.

Jenkins, Geraint H. (1987). *The foundations of modern Wales 1642–1780,* Cardiff: University of Wales Press.

Jenkins, Philip. (1992) *A History of Modern Wales 1536–1990,* London: Longman.

Jenkins, RT, and Ramage, Helen M. (1951). *A history of the Honourable Society of Cymmrodorion and of the Gwyneddigion and Cymreigyddion Societies (1751–1951),* London: Honourable Society of Cymmrodorion.

John, AH. (1950). *The industrial development of south Wales,* Cardiff: University of Wales Press.

Jones, David. (1791). *The Welsh Freeholder's vindication of his letter to the Right Reverend Samuel, Lord Bishop of St. David's, in reply to a clergyman of that diocese, together with strictures on the said letter,* J John Johnson, London, and J Ross Carmarthen.

Jones, David JV. (1972). *Before Rebecca: popular protests in Wales 1793–1835,* London: Allen Lane.

Jones, Emrys. (2001). *The Welsh in London 1500–2000,* Cardiff: University of Wales Press.

Jones, GE, see Herbert, T.

Jones, GE, and Roderick, GW. (2003). *A history of education in Wales,* Cardiff: University of Wales Press.

Jones, Goronwy J. (1969). *Wales and the quest for peace,* Cardiff: University of Wales Press.

Jones, Ieuan Gwynedd, and Williams, David. (1978). *The religious census of 1851: a calendar of the returns relating to Wales Volume I South Wales with an introduction by Jones, Ieuan Gwynedd.* Cardiff: University of Wales Press.

Jones, Stuart EH. (1950). *The last invasion of Britain,* Cardiff: University of Wales Press.

Kelly, T. (1962). *A history of adult education in Great Britain,* Liverpool: University Press.

Knox, Thomas. (1800). *Some account of the proceedings that took place on the landing of the French near Fishguard, in Pembrokeshire, on 22nd February 1797; and of the inquiry held afterwards into Lieut.Col. Knox's conduct on that occasion by order of His Royal Highness the Commander in Chief,* London: A. Wilson.

Lewis, WJ. (1967). *Lead mining in Wales,* Cardiff: University of Wales Press.

Lloyd, HA. (1968). *The gentry of south west Wales 1540–1640,* Cardiff: University of Wales Press.

Lloyd, Thomas and Rev. Mr. Turnor. (1794). *General view of the Agriculture of the county of Cardigan with observations on the means of its improvement*, London: W. Smith.

Lodwick, M and E. (1954). *The story of Carmarthen*, Carmarthen: privately printed.

Malkin, BH. (1804). *The scenery, antiquities and biography of south Wales*, London: republished SR Publishers 1970.

Malloy, Pat. (1983). *And they blessed Rebecca*, Llandysul: Gomer Press.

Mavor, William Fordyce. (1806). *A tour in Wales and through several counties of England including both the universities*, London: Barnard: in Sir Richard Phillips *A collection of modern and contemporary voyages and travels*, Volume iv no. 3 1st series 1805–10, London.

Ministry of Education. (1948). *Pamphlet no. 2 Education in Wales*, London: HMSO.

McGarvie, M. (1988). *The Meyricks of Bush: the story of a Pembrokeshire family*, Glastonbury: Privately printed by Direct Offset.

Morgan, J Vyrnwy (editor). (1908). *Welsh Political and Educational Leaders in the Victorian Era*, London: Nisbet.

Morgan, KO. (1963). *Wales in British Politics 1868–1922*. Cardiff: University of Wales Press.

Morgan, KO. (1963). *David Lloyd George: Welsh radical as world statesman*, Cardiff: University of Wales Press.

Morgan, Prys. (1984). *From Long Knives to Blue Books* in *Welsh Society and Nationhood: Historical Essays presented to Glanmor Williams*, Davies, RR, Griffiths, RA, Jones, IG, and Morgan, KO. (editiors). Cardiff: University of Wales Press.

Namier, L, and Brooke. (editors). (1964). *The House of Commons 1754–1790* Volume 3, London: Published for the History of Parliament Trust by HMSO.

O'Leary, Paul. (1988). *Irish immigration and the Catholic 'Welsh District', 1840–1850* in *Politics and society in Wales 1840–1922 Essays in honour of Ieuan Gwynedd Jones*: Jenkins, Geraint H, and Smith, J Beverley, (editors), Cardiff: University of Wales Press.

Owen, B. (1995). *History of the Welsh Militia and Volunteer Corps 1757–1908: Carmarthenshire, Pembrokeshire and Cardiganshire (Part 1)*, Wrexham: Bridge Books.

Paine, Thomas. (1791). *The Rights of Man*, London.

Pareto, Vilfredo, Mind and society Tratto di sociologia generale translated and edited Arthur Livingston (sic) New York 1935, discussed by W Rex Crawford in Barnes, HE, *An introduction to the history of sociology* Chicago: University Press, 1958.

Peach, B. (1979). *Richard Price and the ethical foundations of the American Revolution. Selections from his pamphlets*, North Carolina: Duke University Press.

Peacock, AJ. (1974) *Radicalism in East Anglia 1800–50* in *Rural discontent in nineteenth century Britain*, Dunbabin JPD, (editor), London: Faber and Faber.

Peate, Iorwerth C. (1944). *The Welsh House*, Liverpool: The Brython Press.

Phillips, John Rowland. (1867). *The history of Cilgerran*, London: J Russell Smith.

Phillips, Thomas. (1849). *Wales: The language, social condition, moral character, and religious opinions of the people, considered in relation to education*, London: John W Parker.

Prebble, John. (1969). *The Highland Clearances*, London: Penguin.

Ramage, HM, see Jenkins, RT.

Richard, Henry. (1866). *Letters: Social and Political Condition of Wales*, London: Jackson, Walford and Hodder.

Roberts, Gwyneth Tyson. (1998). *The language of the Blue Books: the perfect instrument of empire*, Cardiff, University of Wales Press.

Roberts, TR. (1908). *Eminent Welshmen: a short biographical dictionary of Welshmen Volume I*, Cardiff and Merthyr Tydfil: The Educational Publishing Company.

Roderick, GW, see Jones, GE.

Rutland, Duke of: (1805). *Journal of a journey through north and south Wales, the Isle of Man &c &c*, London.

Ruvigny and Raineval, Marquis de, see Ararat, R.

Saunders, Erasmus. (1721). *View of the state of education in the diocese of St. Davids*, London.

Spurrell, William. (1995). *Carmarthen and its neighbourhood 1879*, Carmarthen; re-printed by Dyfed County Council.

Smith, David. (1980). *Wales through the looking glass* in Smith David (editor) *A people and a proletariat: essays in the history of Wales 1780–1980*, London: Pluto Press in association with *Llafur*.

Stephens, Meic. (editor) (1986). *The Oxford Companion to the Literature of Wales*, Oxford: University Press.

Thomas, D Lleufer. (1896). *A memorandum on Welsh agriculture and land tenure in periodical literature to which is added a list of periodicals published in connection with Wales and extracts from the "Times" relating to the state of south Wales in 1843. Appendix C to the Royal Commission on Land in Wales and Monmouthshire*, London.

Thomas, David. (1963). *Agriculture in Wales during the Napoleonic Wars: a study in the interpretation of historical sources*, Cardiff: University of Wales Press.

Thomas, DO. (1975). *Richard Price and America*, Aberystwyth.

Thomas, DO. (1989). *Response to Revolution: how the opening events of the French Revolution were perceived by some prominent Welshmen*, Cardiff: University of Wales Press.

Thomas, DO, and Peach, B (editors). (1983). *The correspondence of Richard Price*, North Carolina: Duke University, and Cardiff: University of Wales Press.

Thomas, JE. (1982). *Radical adult education: theory and practice*, Nottingham: University of Nottingham.

Thomas, JE. (2007). *Britain's last invasion; Fishguard 1797*, Stroud: Tempus Publishing.

Thomas, JE, and Elsey, B (1985). *International Biography of Adult Education*, Nottingham: University of Nottingham.

Thomas, Peter DG. (1998). *Politics in eighteenth-century Wales*, Cardiff: University of Wales Press.

Thorne, Roland, and Howell, Robert. (1987). 'Pembrokeshire in Wartime 1793–1815' in *Pembrokeshire County History* Volume III, Brian Howells (editor), The Pembrokeshire Historical Society, Aberystwyth, The National Library of Wales.

Tone, William Theobald Wolfe. (1826). *Life and adventures of Theobald Wolfe Tone. Written by himself and extracted from his journals*, London: Burns Oates and Washbourne.

Turnor, See Lloyd, Thomas

Volney, Constantin Francois. *The ruins: or a survey of the Revolutions of Empires* translated James Marshall (2000). Washington: Woodstock Books.

Warner, Reverend Richard. (1798). *A walk through Wales in August 1797*, London: Cruttwell.

Warner, Reverend Richard. (1799). *A second walk through Wales,* London, Cruttwell.

Watts, MR. (1995). *The dissenters: the expansion of evangelical nonconformity,* Oxford: University Press.

Wells, R. (1983). *Insurrection: the British experience 1795–1803,* Stroud: Alan Sutton..

Western, JR. (1965). *The English Militia in the eighteenth century: the story of a political issue 1660*-1902, London: Routledge and Kegan.

Wheeler, HFB, and Broadley, AM. (1908). *Napoleon and the invasion of England: the story of the Great Terror* 2 Volumes, London: John Lane.

Whetham, Edith H. (1978). *The agrarian history of England and Wales,* volume viii 1914–1939, Cambridge: University Press.

Wigstead, H. (1800). *Remarks on a tour to north and south Wales in the year 1797,* London.

Wilkes, Ivor. (1984). *South Wales and the rising of 1839: class struggle as armed struggle,* London and Sydney: Croom Helm.

Wilkinson, D. (2003). *The Duke of Portland; politics and party in the age of George III,* London: Palgrave Macmillan.

Williams, David. (1955). *The Rebecca riots: a study in agrarian discontent,* Cardiff: University of Wales Press.

Williams, Glanmor. (1991). *The Welsh and their religion: Historical Essays.* Cardiff: University of Wales Press.

Williams, Glanmor. (1985). 'Griffith Jones' in *International Biography of Adult Education,* Thomas and Elsey (editors). Nottingham: University.

Williams, Gwyn A. (1982). *The Welsh in their history,* London: Croom Helm.

Williams, Gwyn A. (1980). *Locating a Welsh working class: the frontier years* in Smith David (editor) *A people and a proletariat: essays in the history of Wales 1780–1980,* London, Pluto Press in association with *Llafur.*

Williams, Gwyn A. (1987). *Madoc: the legend of the Welsh discovery of America,* Oxford: University Press.

Williams, Gwyn A. (1988). *Beginnings of radicalism,* in Herbert, T, and Jones, GE, *The remaking of Wales in the eighteenth century,* Cardiff: University of Wales Press.

Williams, Jac I, and Hughes, Gwilym Rees. (1978).*The history of education in Wales,* Swansea: Christopher Davies.

Williams, W Moses. (1938). *Selections from the Welch Piety,* Cardiff: University of Wales Press.

Winslow, C. *Sussex smugglers* (1975), in Hay, D, Linebaugh, P, and Thompson, EP, (editors), *Albion's fatal tree: crime and society in eighteenth century England,* London: Allen Lane.

Young, Arthur: (1768). *A six weeks tour through the counties of England and Wales,* London.

Journal articles

Carmarthenshire Antiquarian and Field Club Transactions, various dates.

Anglo, S, 'The British history in early Tudor propaganda', *Bulletin of John Rylands Library* 44 (1961).

Beckett, JV, 'The peasant in England: a case of terminological confusion?' *The Agricultural History Review* 32 Part II (1984).

Beynon, Oswald, 'Lead mining at Esgair y Mwyn in the time of Lewis Morris (1752–55)', *Cardiganshire Antiquarian Society Transactions* XI (1936).

Burge, Alun, 'The Mold riots of 1869', *Llafur* Vol. 3, No. 3 (1982).

Carwardine, Richard, 'The Welsh evangelical community and "Finney's Revival"', *Journal of Ecclesiastical History* 29 (1978).

Colyer, Richard, 'The Pryse family of Gogerddan and the decline of a great estate', *Welsh History Review 9* (1978–9).

Davies, Alun Eirug, 'Wages, prices, and social improvements in Cardiganshire 1750–1850', *Ceredigion* xi (1984).

Davies, HM, '"Very different springs of uneasiness": Emigration from Wales to the United States of America during the 1790s', *Welsh History Review* 15 (3 June 1991).

Davies, Hywel M, Morgan, 'John Rhys, and James Bicheno Anti-Christ and the French Revolution in England and Wales', *Bulletin of the Board of Celtic Studies* xxix Part 1 November 1980.

Davies, John, 'The end of the great estates and the rise of freehold farming in Wales', *Welsh History Review* 7 (1974–5).

Davies, Russell, 'In a broken dream: some aspects of sexual behaviour and the dilemmas of the unmarried mother in south west Wales 1887–1914', *Llafur* Vol. 3, No. 4 (1983).

Edwards, George, 'The coal industry in Pembrokeshire', *Field Studies* 1/5.

Evans, Neil, and Jones, Dot, 'A blessing for the miner's wife: the campaign for pithead baths in the south Wales coalfield 1908–1950' *Llafur* Vol 6, No. 3 (1994).

George, I, 'Tomos Glyn Cothi' *Journal of the Welsh Biographical Society*,1V 1932.

Glover, DG, '"Lord Dynevor's smart and efficient little corps": an historical account of the Carmarthenshire Yeomanry 1794–1815', *The Bulletin of the Military Historical Society* 44/176 May 1994.

Green, Francis, 'The Barlows of Slebech' *West Wales Historical Records* III (1912–13).

Hagen, G, 'Women and Poverty in South-West Wales 1834–1914' *Llafur* Vol 7, Nos. 3 & 4, (1998–9).

Harris, John, '"Neighbours": Caradoc Evans, Lloyd George and the London Welsh', in *Llafur* Vol. 5 No.4 (1991).

Howells, BE, 'Pembrokeshire Farming circa 1580–1620', in *The National Library of Wales Journal* vol. ix (1955–6).

Howell, David W, 'The agricultural labourer in nineteenth century Wales' *Welsh History Review* 6 (1972–3).

Howell, David W, 'The economy of the landed estates of Pembrokeshire c1680-1830', *Welsh History Review* 3 (1966–7).

Howell, David W, 'Landed Society in Pembrokeshire Circa 1680–1830', *The Pembrokeshire Historian* 3 1971.

Howell, RL, 'The Pembroke Yeomanry', *The Pembrokeshire Historian* 2 1966.

Jenkins, J P, 'Jacobites and Freemasons in eighteenth century Wales', *Welsh History Review* 9 (1978–9).

Johnston W Ross, 'The Welsh diaspora', *Llafur* Vol. 6, No. 2 (1993).

Jones, DJV, 'The corn riots in Wales 1793-1801', *Welsh History Review* 2 (1964–5).

Jones, DJV, 'The Carmarthen Riots of 1831', *Welsh History Review* 4 (1968–9).

Jones, David JV, 'More light on "Rhyfel y Sais Bach"', in *Ceredigion* v/i 1964. See also articles by David Jenkins, in which he publishes a petition, in *Ceredigion* 1951, and 'Rhyfel y Sais bach: an enclosure riot on Mynydd Bach' by David Williams in *Ceredigion* ii/i 1952.

Jones, DJV, 'Distress and discontent in Cardiganshire 1814-1819', *Ceredigion* V.3 (1966).

Jones, DJV, 'The Carmarthen Riots of 1831', *Welsh History Review* 4 (1968–9).

Jones, Francis, 'Disaffection and discontent in Pembrokeshire', *Transactions of The Honourable Society of Cymmrodorion 1946–7 Sessions 1946–7*. No Volume Number.

Jones, Francis, 'Owen of Orielton' *The Pembrokeshire Historian* 5 1974.

Jones, Francis, 'The Vaughans of Golden Grove: I The Earls of Carbery', *Transactions of The Honourable Society of Cymmrodorion*, Part 1 (1963).

Jones, Francis, 'The Vaughans of Golden Grove: II Anne, Duchess of Bolton 1690–1751' *Transactions of the Honourable Society of Cymmrodorion* II (1964).

Jones, Francis, 'The Vaughans of Golden Grove III Torycoed-Shenfield-Golden Grove', *Transactions of the Honourable Society of Cymmrodorion* II 1964.

Jones, Francis, 'The Vaughans of Golden Grove IV, Tory Coed-Shenfield-Golden Grove', *Transactions of the Honourable Society of Cymmrodorion*. 1966, p159.

Jones, Francis, 'Golden Grove', *Ceredigion* 4 (1960–3).

Jones, Francis, 'The Society of Sea Serjeants', *Transactions of the Honourable Society of Cymmrodorion* part 1 (1967).

Lewis, WJ, 'The Cwmsymlog lead mine', *Ceredigion* iii (1952–5).

Lewis, WJ, 'The condition of labour in mid Cardiganshire in the early nineteenth century', *Ceredigion* iv (1963).

Moore-Colyer, RJ, 'Thomas Johnes of Hafod (1748–1816): Translator and Bibliophile' *Welsh History Review* 15/3 (June 1991).

Peate, Mary Rose, 'The Blue Books and after: William Williams and his legacy', *The Welsh Journal of Education* 5/2 (1996).

Rees, Eiluned, 'Developments in the book trade in eighteenth century Wales', *The Library* xxiv (1969).

Roberts, Dafydd, 'Nhw dedd y chwarelwyr-arwyr y fro: The Pembrokeshire slate quarrymen', *Llafur* Vol. 5, No. 1(n.d. 1988?).

Salmon, David. *The French invasion of Fishguard in 1797. Official documents, contemporary letters, and early narratives* published in West Wales Historical Records vol. xiv 1929 Carmarthen Printed by W Spurrell and Son.

Skeel, Caroline, 'The cattle trade between Wales and England from the fifteenth to the nineteenth centuries', *Transactions of the Royal Historical Society* Fourth Series vol. ix (1926).

Stead, P, 'The Welsh working class', *Llafur* Vol. 1, No. 2 (1972–5).

Sutherland, G, 'Elementary Education in the nineteenth century', *Historical Association* London (1971).

Thomas, Colin, 'Agricultural employment in nineteenth century Wales : a new approach', in *Welsh History Review* 6 (1972–3).

Thomas, Peter DG, 'Jacobitism in Wales', *Welsh History Review 1* (1960–3).

Thompson, EP, 'The moral economy of the English crowd in the eighteenth century', *Past and Present*, Volume 50, February 1971.

Vaughan, HM, 'A synopsis of two tours made in Wales in 1775 and in 1811, *Y Cymmrodor* xxxviii 1927.

Wager, DA, 'Welsh Politics and Parliamentary Reform 1780–1832', *Welsh History Review* 7 No. 4 (December 1975).

Western, JR, 'The Volunteer Movement as an Anti-Revolutionary force, 1793–1801', The English Historical Review' 71 (1956).

Williams, Chris, 'Wales's "Unionist Nationalist" Sir Thomas Phillips (1801–67)', *Llafur* Vol. 8, No. 4 (2003).

Williams, David, 'Some figures relating to emigration from Wales', *Bulletin of The Board of Celtic Studies* vol. vii 1935.

Williams, David, 'The missions of David Williams and James Tilley Matthews to England 1793', *The English Historical Review* vol 1, LIII 1938. See also Williams, David, 'The Pembrokeshire elections of 1831', *Welsh History Review* vol 1 (1960–3).

Williams, G, 'The reformation in Pembrokeshire down to 1553', *The Pembrokeshire Historian* 1 (1959).

Williams, Gwyn A, 'Morgan John Rhees and his Beulah', *Welsh History Review* 3 (1967).

Williams, Gwyn A, 'Morgan John Rhys and Volney's *Ruins of Empires*', *The Bulletin of the Board of Celtic Studies* Vol. XX (November 1962).

Unpublished doctoral dissertations

Hugh, RL, *The theological background of nonconformist social influence in Wales 1800–1850*. University of London 1951.

Isaac, DG, *A study of popular disturbances in Britain 1714–1795*. University of Edinburgh 1953.

Morgan, DDJ, *The development of the Baptist movement in Wales between 1714 and 1815 with particular reference to the Evangelical Revival*. University of Oxford 1986.

INDEX